GUN FOR HIRE

GUN FOR HIRE

STEVE DEVEREUX

BLAKE

ALSO BY STEVE DEVEREUX

Terminal Velocity

No Fear

Published by Blake Publishing Ltd,
3 Bramber Court, 2 Bramber Road,
London W14 9PB, England

First published in 2000

ISBN 1 85782 367 2

British Library Cataloguing-in-Publication Data:

A catalogue record for this book is
available from the British Library.

Typeset by t2

Printed in Great Britain by
Creative Print and Design (Wales),
Ebbw Vale, Gwent.

1 3 5 7 9 10 8 6 4 2

TO FALLEN FRIENDS WHO NEVER
MADE IT BACK INTO CIVVY STREET

For operational reasons, the names of certain
individuals have been changed, and two incident
locations have been appropriately disguised.

With thanks to everyone at Blake Publishing.

ABOUT THE AUTHOR

Steve Devereux joined the Parachute Regiment in 1977. After successfully completing parachute training, he was posted to a rifle company in the 2nd Battalion, stationed in Berlin.

He first experienced the horrors of war in Northern Ireland. He was at Warrenpoint where he got a rude awakening as to the life he had chosen — during his first tour, 1979-81, 20 close friends and comrades were killed in action. In 1981, 2 Para reformed the famous 'C' Bruneval Company and successfully passed the selection into 'C' Company's Pathfinder Platoon.

1982 saw him on the first landing craft to hit the beach on the shores of the Falkland Islands. Shortly after, he was ordered to go 'point man' for the battle of Goose Green — a battle which has been described as one of the biggest, bloodiest battles the British Army has fought since the Second World War. He came through that unscathed, only to find himself in the thick of the fighting again, for the main assault on the mountains overlooking the islands' capital, Port Stanley. Following that battle, he was one of the first troops into Port Stanley, even before the official Argentine surrender.

After the Falklands War he applied to join the Special Air Service Regiment, and in late 1982 he was 'badged' in to 'D' Squadron 22 SAS, where he served with great distinction in theatres of war all over the world for another six years. He then left the SAS to work for Sir David Stirling — the founder member of this élite Regiment — as a security specialist.

Steve is the bestselling author of *Terminal Velocity* and *No Fear*, both books are about his worldwide combat experiences during the past 22 years. His writing has been described as 'bloody raw and in your face'.

Now, he has channelled his controlled aggression into writing. He has written for, and been quoted in, a wide range of national newspapers, including *The Times*, the *Sun*, the *Daily Mail*, and the *Sunday People*, and is now recognised as a consultant and commentator on military and security affairs. He was also a contributor to the TV documentary *Who Killed WPC Fletcher?*

More recently, Steve has written a screenplay, *Goose Green — The Battle*, and is now working on his first novel, *Menace*.

GLOSSARY

ARV	Armed Response Vehicle
ASAP	As Soon As Possible — asap
ASU	IRA Active Service Unit
BG	Bodyguard
Blue on Blue	Friendly fire contact — accidental
Box	Collective term for intelligence services
Comms	Communications
Crossgrain	Following the natural contours of the terrain
Det	Intelligence detachment in NI
Dicker	Hostile look-out or scout
DPMs	Disruptive Pattern Material — camouflage garments
DZ	Drop zone
End ex	End of exercise or job
ERVs	Emergency Rendezvous
(The) Firm	Collective term for intelligence services
First Parading	Checking the oil, tyres and general suitability of a vehicle
Int	Intelligence
LUP	Lying Up Position
MO	Modus Operandi
NI	Northern Ireland
OP	Observation Post
ops	Operations
PE	Plastic Explosives
Pickets	Sentries
Player	Hostile person
Recce	A reconnaissance
RTU	Return to Unit
Rupert	A slang term for an officer
SB	Special Branch — police
SOPs	Standard Operational Procedures
Stagging on	The act of being on guard or shift
Tabbing	Para term for a speed march with full kit (derived from TAB — Tactical Assault into Battle)

CONTENTS

'Shit happens.'

Unknown bodyguard

PREFACE

This book is based on my personal experience of a series of extraordinary and sometimes unbelievable events, including a combination of highly irregular practices of *this* country's Security Services. These incidents all occurred during a bodyguard operation I was working on.

The operation took place on the streets of London. It involved ex SAS, and ex Special Forces guys, some pretty switched-on front-of-house managers (the politically correct title for bouncers), and — more worryingly — members of M15, Special Branch and other agencies. As well as a particularly devious Principal — that's the term we use for the person being guarded.

I was prompted to write the story, not only by the members of the bodyguard team involved, but also by my own belief that you, the public, might like to know what can happen in the very complicated, often corrupt world of the private bodyguard. I hope this story gives you a greater understanding of my profession.

The very nature of the work requires me to tread that very thin legal line every bodyguard has to tread. Every day I have to make split-second decisions which affect my Principal's life, my life or those of my team, and of course, the safety of the public.

It's not a glamorous occupation, despite the way many people might like to portray it. Far from it: 75 per cent of the time it's painfully boring — waiting, waiting and more waiting, 20 per cent is bitching between ourselves, and 5 per cent is operating in anticipation of a possible physical, armed bomb attack.

Conversation invariably centres around huge amounts of back-stabbing. It ranges from questioning the ability of certain members of a team to do their job, to taking the mick out of the 'Batman Utility Belt' merchants who seem to stray into this business in ever-more-alarming numbers. They cut about with the misconception that *they* might just need the tools they carry around their waist, anticipating the slaying of some crazed attacking Ninja. As far as the webbing is concerned, it's probably a throwback to their army days, where the wearing of webbing (personal belt kit) was totally correct and essential for a soldier's well-being 'in the field'. You carried everything in your webbing, from bullets to burgers, bandages and personal survival kit. But it has no place in civvy street.

The other great talking points are the prospect of getting paid, the amount of the statutory 'bung', and the slippery characters who think that they can nick the job off the guy lucky enough to have been awarded it.

Being able to perform one's task efficiently, operating in this environment, is mentally hard enough, without that being interspersed with extreme surges of adrenalin, brought on by some sudden incident. It's not everyone's cup of tea. It could drive some people insane even before they get on the ground. Hence, only a very few men and women actually make good bodyguards. In short, you have to keep total control of all your senses, your mental and physical standing. You have to save that energy for when you actually need it, otherwise you will end up a complete bag of nerves on day one of any job.

This is a story of a team of professional men, some from a military background, some from civvy street. I still consider myself a professional soldier, and I look on being a bodyguard as another skill in my armoury. During my time I have been lucky to serve in not only one but two of the world's best fighting units: The Parachute Regiment and the 22nd Special Air Service Regiment. I am proficient in all the skills that are taught by these two regiments and have been operational in armed conflicts worldwide for the past 22 years, and I like to think I know what I'm talking about.

PART ONE

1.

SPOILS FROM ONE WAR

ARMY TRAINING AREA. SEGMENT 4. LONG VALLEY, ALDERSHOT. JULY 1982.

If it had been anyone else, the sight of a lone Para tabbing out of the Company Lines across the metal footbridge which spanned the ringroad of the garrison town of Aldershot might have caused the two duty Para pickets (sentries) who stood guard on the camp side of the bridge to question the soldier's sanity. After all, who the hell would go tabbing off on a ten-miler, just a day after getting back from the Falklands War?

I too wasn't particularly happy about the task I had to carry out over the next two hours either, but it was something I had to do, and do quickly, because to prolong it would mean certain compromise.

As I approached the two pickets I felt the all-too-familiar first few drops of rain starting to run down the side of my face. A look skywards told me that it was sure going to be 'well black over at Bill's mum's!'

'Shit, here comes a keen one, what a warrior!' one of the pickets said.

I recognised the voice and looked up. It was Mush, my old mate from Pathfinders, a real old sweat in the battalion. He'd spent the past few months on 2 Para rear party while the rest of us kicked arse down in the South Atlantic. There was no way Mush could have come to 'the party' with us, because he'd been medically down-graded, after getting the best part of a three-pound lump of granite embedded in his backside during the Warrenpoint blast in Northern Ireland, a couple of years before. But this still didn't stop him pleading with our colonel, Colonel 'H' Jones.

'Now, come on, Corporal, don't you think you've seen your fair share of action? Give the younger men a chance ...'

'But, sir,' Mush reluctantly had said. He'd have relished the fight, that's for sure.

I jerked a little and moved towards them. 'Oh, if it ain't old shaggin' slack arse,' I joked.

The other Para, much younger, stared at me in horror as I addressed his corporal in such a slack unmilitary fashion. He really was a fresh-faced kid, probably still only 17, and looked every part a crow. He moved nervously closer to Mush, like a young lad might do in the presence of his father. I didn't recognise him; he must have Passed Out of Depot Para when the Battalion was down south.

At the beginning, I hadn't taken much notice of these two fellow Paras, I was psyching myself up for the speed march. My head was constantly being forced down through my action of violently pulling on both bergen side-straps at the same time, in order to get the damn thing as high up on my back as possible, thus making it less of a burden to carry.

'Bollocks to it,' I said to myself out of frustration. I hadn't gone 20 paces, and already the horns of the metal 'H' frame were beginning to dig painfully into my old bergen burns. Against my better judgement, I'd strapped two field dressings to the lower part of my back, secured in place with a ton of black masking tape. But that didn't help, the bergen back-strap was rubbing even more.

The box of dead weight, which was the last piece of kit I'd packed, had somehow worked its way down past my light kit — the doss bag and poncho — and had slipped to the bottom. I couldn't stop now and repack it, I had to get out of sight of prying eyes first. Especially Mush — he would want to chew the fat with me and make a point of going through the contents of my bergen and showing the young kid what 'a soldier should carry into war', and 'not just the standard collection of heavy weights such as bricks and bags of sand they taught you down at the Depot'. I knew Mush all too well — yeah, I was *sure* he'd want to make a point out of our meeting by teaching his new boy some basic rules of soldiering.

'You're not still going on this summer's SAS selection, are ya, Devs?' he shouted.

I looked up, already aware of the beads of sweat trickling down the small of my back and being soaked up by the two large pieces of padding that acted as sponges. It really irritated me. 'Well, what the frig d'you think? You think I'm going out tabbing for the sheer hell of it, do ya? I'd rather be on the piss with the rest of the lads.' I didn't stop.

Mush laughed and slapped me hard on the back of the bergen as I passed him. The slap made my legs buckle slightly, which in turn threw me off balance.

'You got the rest of your life to go on the piss, man, get your arse up Flagstaff Hill and say hello to it from me, will ya, and let's hope this rain keeps pissing down,' Mush chuckled. The young kid stayed silent.

'Fuck, that'll be a first for ya. See ya at the front gate in two hours — and have a brew ready, will ya, Corporal?' I threw back at him.

'Fuckin' more like four hours, you fat twat. I'll have a medic standing by for ya!' Mush shouted out after me.

I didn't reply; without turning around I just gave him the finger instead. I was now totally focused on what I had to do, and on doing it without cutting corners. What I was up to was highly illegal. My pulse raced as I pumped with my legs to eat up the metres of tarmac ahead of me. I felt good, a sudden surge of apprehension burst through my body, brought on by the thought of what I was carrying and the consequences if I got caught. But I wasn't going to get caught. I was too switched-on, I felt there wasn't a man or machine around that could catch me out.

I'd been through some real shit over the past few months and every bit of my military training had been tested to the max, so there was no reason why I should fuck-up on a relatively easy operation like this.

As I tabbed, I kept an eye on both the road ahead and the road below my feet. Although the going was relatively flat, there was the odd pot-hole to avoid. I steadied my breathing, got into a rhythm with my stride, and cleared my head of any doubts about what I was up to. I had mentally covered all possible fuck-ups beforehand, and now that the plan was firmly ingrained in my head, I was going for it.

I know you can't plan for every shitty scenario — hell, the battle for Goose Green had taught me that — but this was a basic job; the only problem which might occur would be twisting a leg or getting hit by a vehicle (which sometimes happened to soldiers on the public roads around Long Valley). If that was to be the case, then it was just not going to be my day. Still, if you go through life like that, then you might as well have stayed in the womb. Risk-taking is all part of this shitty rollercoaster ride they call life.

During the battle for the Falklands I had experienced my own ultimate adrenalin rush, and that was the taking of another man's life — not once, not twice, but lots of times, and every Argy I had slotted or bayoneted had put me on a different hedonistic level. The feeling I was experiencing now was nowhere near that of being back down in the Falklands shooting at Argies, but it was as close as one could get in peace time, and I was enjoying every bit of it. As far as any onlooker was concerned, I was a Para out training on his own, which wasn't unusual. On the other hand, I'd given myself a timeframe of under two hours for this task, a slight deviation from the regular route, and I knew that was pushing it.

The first mile-and-a-half was easy. I was still tabbing on the stretch of tarmac road which took me past and around the Services Rushmore Arena. After that I would be tabbing across some of the shittiest ground the county of Hampshire had to offer — a vast expanse of undulating wooded and open land, mainly used by the MOD to field-test tanks.

Consequently, when it rained, the deep ruts (sometimes three and four feet deep) caused by tanks criss-crossing the whole of the training area, filled up with thick mire, like quicksand, and they became almost impossible to cross; during dry spells these same ruts would be baked so hard by the sun that once you were in one, it would be very difficult to get out to cross grain, especially if you were carrying the Full Fighting Order, upwards of 100 pounds, a mixture of webbing, weapons, ammunition and kit. Rain or shine, tabbing across Long Valley was always a physical nightmare.

The sky turned darker. It was really pissing down now.

My route would take me over ground on which hundreds of thousands of soldiers had trained for war over the past 150 years. I was fully aware that I was now following in the ghostly footprints of soldiers who had fought for this country in past wars and campaigns: the Crimean, the South African, First and Second World Wars, and now the Falklands War. Many died in the same sorts of shell scrapes and trenches as those in which they had practised 'digging in' in Long Valley. Many never ventured on to this hallowed training area again.

I crossed over the last of the tarmac, found a quiet spot in some dead ground amongst some low-lying bushes, and went about rearranging the contents of my bergen. This took less than a minute. I knew my way around this bergen all too well — I knew all of its idiosyncrasies, such as how the straps pulled down to tighten its contents or side pockets, and how smoothly the quick-release clips operated in haste.

Time and the serviceability of 'his' equipment are everything for a soldier, especially in combat, and the ability of my bergen to function now was no different. To put something in, or to get something out, in the quickest and quietest way possible, is paramount. Who knows what might be around the corner? When you're friggin' about in your bergen, you're in effect one man out of action, one less pair of eyes, one less holding a weapon, and one more making noise. During this time of fluffing about, you're a liability to the rest of your patrol, especially if you're working in an operational environment. So getting this shit sorted quickly and quietly is part of the 'field' soldier's SOPs (Standard Operational Procedures).

I headed up towards the first obvious high feature, a spot height on top of the western part of the ridge line, aptly named Hungry Hill. This was to be my first ball-buster. I knew that I was still about one k (kilometre) away, and past assaults on this hill had told my body exactly what pain to expect. I began to gasp, my lungs trying to draw in more and more air as I charged ahead. My nose was beginning to fill with rain and mucus as I breathed in, and I was conscious of having to open my mouth more to get more air. I clamped the side of my left nostril closed with my fingers, and drove out the shite. I did the same to the right. A large 'Green Gilbert' shot out and hit the toe of my combat boots. I took note that this had cleared my sinuses.

It usually took me at least three miles to get into my stride and the bottom of Hungry Hill was about the three-mile point. It was called Hungry Hill because it was the first major feature on the ten-miler and would usually eat up the strength of those 'whippets' who had forced the pace of a tab at the onset, for one reason or another. I reached the bottom in good time. I didn't stop.

It wasn't a particularly high feature — in fact, set against a backdrop of the Brecon Beacons, it would be a pimple. It probably rose no more than 300 feet, but its angle was a right twat. At first glance the ten-foot-wide dirt track looked almost sheer. Either side of the track was a three-foot-high bank covered in thick evergreen bushes, caused by years of soil erosion and troops scrambling up it. Consequently, on a platoon tab, if you weren't right up at the front when you arrived at the foot of this hill, then, by the time you got to the top (which was relatively flat), you would find yourself miles behind the leading bunch because there wasn't much space for passing fellow platoon mates, even if you had the strength.

Because it was still pissing down, the rain had begun to wash the mud away, exposing the rock below, and now had created a small gushing stream of water about a foot wide. That would be my route up: I'll go right up the centre of it, fuck the wet feet, I thought.

The rest of the track was covered with a thin layer of gooey mud, which when trodden on took on icelike characteristics. This would make my going ten times harder. It might have been all right if I had wanted to get my calf and thigh muscles burning, or if I was on some masochistic trip, but neither was the case. I had another objective.

I looked up for the first and last time to see if I could make out the top, but I couldn't. I knew that anyway, it was just habit, a personal thing. I never looked up again to see if I could see the top, once I started my ascent. This wasn't a tactical patrol, and I couldn't give a shit who was at the top looking down at me anyway.

All I knew was that I wasn't to stop for any reason, either to adjust my kit, or even to take a breather. If I did that, then I would break the mental barrier I had built up inside me for all these years, which helped me get through tabs like this. Once again it was a personal thing, it worked for me, and I wasn't about to chance fate and change my method of attack. If I had done, I would have deemed myself to have failed.

Once on top, I headed off to the right and tabbed in an easterly direction along the ridge line towards the main feature, Flagstaff Hill.

By now the wind was driving the rain straight into my face. Coming up Hungry Hill was pretty much easy going, as it had been sheltered from the wind, but now I was totally exposed to the elements. From the ridge line one could usually see for miles. You could see right across to the town of Aldershot and Farnborough Airfield. But today, the mist was down, hanging about like the aftermath of a gas attack.

Surprisingly I couldn't see anyone on the ridge. Usually, there would be at least one or two people out walking their dogs, but I guess the rain had kept them in. Without stopping I started to look around for some dead ground down off the ridge. It had to be well away from obvious tracks made by vehicles and men, but it had to be accessible as well as identifiable for future reference.

I put myself in the shoes of a bank robber who knew he was going away for a long stretch and was looking for a place where he could cache his stash of loot in order to pick it up when he got out.

The site I was looking for had to be in a spot where it was unlikely either for a structure to be built, or more importantly, for some future platoon commander to conduct a defence exercise and start ordering trenches to be dug everywhere.

I got to the small copse of evergreens which marked Flagstaff — the highest point, the most severe side of the ridge, and indeed of the entire training area. I was aware that if I could see for miles around, then I could also be seen. I used the elements to my advantage and blended into the mist.

I gave myself a couple of minutes while I scoured the ground in front of me. To my right, and slightly back, was the ridge and Hungry Hill; to my front were acres and acres of low-lying shrubs and tank-tracks crossed by the Aldershot to Church Crookham road. To my left was an area not so flat, a part of the Flagstaff spur which gradually tapered off. In the near ground were a few large trees and beyond them was this sort of 'space-age' domed roof affair, just sticking over the tops of the trees.

I had seen this many a time and had been told that it was some kind of water catchment processor. That was it, I had made my choice — it was my only tactical option. I'll look for something suitable over by the domed roof, I decided.

On the face of it, the ground I was looking across had all the text-book factors required for the placement of a long-term cache. I started to remind myself about all the problematic factors in selecting a cache site.

One, it had to be safe and secure and also accessible if and when I required its contents. I didn't think that Long Valley would ever be built on, not in my lifetime anyway, so I deemed the area safe and secure from that point of view. After all, this entire area was considered to be a bit of a beauty spot by the civilian population of the towns of Aldershot and Farnborough.

Two, pinpointing for future 'lifting' of it: I had to select suitable reference points. Well, there were many geographical features to choose from. That was okay.

Three, waterproofing the cache. I'd sorted that out back at the basha, and I didn't think even a half-starved crazed rat would be able to chew through my wrapping technique.

And finally, four, as important as the rest, there was making an exact record of where the cache was.

My senses were working overtime. I was excited that I had identified a suitable area in such a relatively short time. Another burst of adrenalin brought me back to life. I'd been stationary for less than a minute, but that was long enough for my body to cool down and for my brain to tell me that the driving wind and rain ripping through my bergen and DPMs wasn't doing my body any good at all. Without a second thought I started to make my way along and down the tapered feature. All the time my body's senses were working flat out, taking in all of my surroundings, looking and listening, assessing the possibility that I might be being watched.

This whole episode reminded me of an incident which had happened just a few weeks before. I was out on a clearing patrol with four others, the weather as shitty as it was now but a hell of a lot colder. We'd only been patrolling across this barren treeless island for about 20 minutes, and the visibility was horrendously grim. I could only see about ten feet in front of me, and the driving sleet and rain was attacking us head on and really impairing my sight; it made the patrol slow right down, almost to a pigeon step.

All of a sudden, I faintly caught the sound of a slight voice in the wind followed by a metallic 'clink' sound, then, almost immediately after, I saw a blurred figure come into view. Just for a split second I couldn't determine who it was. Our orders had told us that everything to our front was to be interpreted as hostile, but you can never take a chance, you always have to confirm your target before you engage it, and I didn't fancy being the instigator of a Blue on Blue (an armed contact between one or more friendly forces) incident. Then, more voices — Spanish!

Immediately I let rip with a couple of well-aimed double taps, then went to ground, all along keeping an eye on the target I'd fired at. The target dropped, it didn't move or make a sound — dead. There were no cries of pain or aggression, no long bursts of small arms fire, just the silence of the wind.

I caught sight of another shadowy figure, but before I could take it out, Dick, my oppo, fired across me, and that figure also fell. We lay there for a few moments, just seconds, taking it all in. No rounds came back at us. It was all so surreal. A brief encounter with the enemy, a few seconds of noise, death and then nothing, only the imminent mourning in some far-off pueblo. We quickly scurried off on the back-bearing we had come from, still very much aware that we might have inadvertently walked into an

Argy clearance patrol or defence position.

So it didn't matter if it was a nice sunny day or a right wet and windy one like now; I'd trained my senses always to work at their maximum in any given theatre of war, and today was no different.

Several minutes later I'd identified the exact place for my cache. I walked past it for about 100 metres or so, always aware of the possibility of prying eyes, then picked my way back carefully and found a fairly sheltered and concealed place to sit. Now I sat back and observed the route I'd just taken, waiting to see if I'd been followed. Doubling back on myself, or as I was taught to call it, 'breaking track', is a basic tactic normally used in the jungle to ambush the enemy if they happened to pick up on your trail. In a jungle environment you could be observing your 'route taken' for a few hours, but here, I decided to do it for just ten minutes; obviously the terrain and threat dictated that.

Ten minutes passed. No followers, no sign of being compromised. Quickly I took off my bergen and propped it up by a large oak tree, one of four in the close vicinity. I left it tied up for the time being, and set about taking three bearings with a prismatic compass off three features from my chosen location. First, the centre of the domed roof structure; second, a huge rock which protruded out from the side of Flagstaff Hill which lay embedded just slightly to the left and below the evergreen coppice; and the third — I moved ten paces towards it to get an exact bearing — the dog-leg bend in the Aldershot to Church Crookham road. I couldn't see the bend, but I knew it lay directly behind the centre of the old firing range butts. Those were clearly visible now, but might not be around in years to come.

All three features I considered to be long-term — well, as long-term as you can expect in this world of constant changes. Twenty years max I deemed for the life of the cache, and working on the worst case I still had two pretty solid bearings out of three. The rock had been there since the world had been formed, and was unlikely to be going anywhere in the next century. The bend had probably been there since it evolved from a cart track to a road 100 or so years ago. The dome might get pulled down sooner than I anticipated, but if I selected my cache as I had been taught, then I could still retrieve the contents with only two points of reference.

The last thing I did was march 15 paces back from my cache spot towards the large tree where I had placed my bergen, and take a back bearing. I stuffed the piece of paper containing the bearings into a plastic bag, and then into an inner lining pocket of my smock — a secret pocket which I had sewn in myself for just this reason. I clipped the lid of the prismatic compass shut, wound the length of para chord back around it (this was also attached to my smock), and then made sure it was well secured back in my top pocket.

My thoughts were now on timings. I checked my watch: good, twelve twenty. The bearings had taken me six minutes, longer than I'd planned, but I was still within my timeframe of 'in and out' in 20 minutes. Now I had left myself with 14 minutes to dig the hole, place the cache, back-fill, clean up and move off. Then another ten minutes to carry out a listening watch over the cache area, and, if that was all clear, start tabbing back to finish the ten-miler, though on this occasion I would take the short route back to camp to make up for lost time. Great, I thought, so far so good.

I then went over to where I'd put my bergen down and lifted it to where I was about to dig, always aware that any 'top' or 'bottom' sign I had disturbed — be it leaves, snapped twigs, fresh earth or footprints — had to be put right before I left the area. This was basic stuff, but was still very crucial.

After I'd spread out a poncho and gently placed the undergrowth to one side, I set about digging. The US Army trenching tool I'd brought along with me was a smaller piece of kit than the Brit one, and a lot easier to work with. The ground looked fairly root-free. The going, down to a depth of two feet, was — surprisingly — softer than I had hoped it would be. Every shovelful I lifted out I careful placed on the poncho. I made sure not to spill any of it and also made sure that it didn't get mixed up with the undergrowth.

At a depth of three feet I checked my watch: good, it was twenty-nine minutes past. A further three minutes of constant burrowing saw me looking into a hole about three feet by three feet by about four feet deep. By now I had hit a seam of hard rock. Good! That was deep enough. Quickly I put the trenching tool to one side, reached into the bergen and pulled out an old box wrapped up in a green waterproof weapons' sleeve which, in its day, used to contain 20 pounds of PE in eight-ounce sticks.

Next out, a bag of loose pebbles I'd liberated from around the barrack block. I tipped them into the bottom of the hole to act as a sump for drainage, then placed the PE box on top of the stones, and rammed earth around its sides until the box was firmly wedged in. At the top right-hand side, I placed a pre-decimal penny, dated 1963 with the Queen's head facing down. I covered the whole thing in a fine layer of twigs, then back-filled with earth to surface level. Lastly I replaced the undergrowth.

A quick check of the time told me I should get going. The extra dirt left over I rolled up in the poncho and put back into the bergen followed by the trenching tool. I pulled the top straps tight, lifted it up, and secured the bergen high up on to my back.

After a quick tidy-up of the leaves and dirt, I gave a last cursory look around the immediate area to see if I'd inadvertently left anything. No, I hadn't. I tried to spot where my cache was — I couldn't, leaves were acting as camouflage; good. I then cautiously headed off to a spot where I could view the cache site for the next ten minutes.

I covertly crawled into a position overlooking the 'ambush', made myself comfortable, and waited.

The rain was still coming down in buckets. It made a deafening sound as it hit and bounced off the canopies of the surrounding trees and bushes. I held out my hands, which by now were thick with mud, and rubbed them together in some attempt to clean them in the rain. It worked; it was like being in a shower, it was pissing down that much.

I should have been freezing my nuts off, what with the 'chill factor', but I wasn't. I felt warm, I felt contented, like I was meant to be here or something. I felt strangely very happy. I looked skywards, the clouds were dark grey and still moving about quickly. It seemed like God had the sky on 'fast forward'. The whole training area had taken on a very sinister feel.

My mind briefly started to drift. I began to picture the souls of those men who had been killed in battles past looking down on me, and knowing all about my future, and thinking that it would only be a matter of time before I too was to join them. But *how* was I to join them? They weren't going to let me into their secret.

Whether it was that or not I don't know, but a sudden surge of guilt mixed with remorse sliced through me. Were the souls of the Argy soldiers who I had slotted also looking down? How was this? Surely those friendly forces above didn't allow this transgression? If so, was I now the one to be judged? Was this going to be my judgement day?

I shook these ghostly thoughts out of my head and sat observing in silence. I purposely changed my point of focus and noticed that the rain had completely washed my hands free of the mud. For some reason I looked at them more closely than I had done for years. They were wrinkled, scarred, some of the knuckles were flat. They looked like the hands of an old man, for Christ's sake, but I was still only 21. Then I realised how un-tactical they appeared. I should have left the dirt on them — a natural camouflage.

The rain had now infiltrated down the back of my neck, and I felt my body heat warm it up as it continually penetrated between the natural gaps on my chest and back. The rain and the wind were trying to get me to give up my position, but they couldn't — I wouldn't allow it to happen. I began to enjoy the thought that over the past few weeks I'd gone through hell and back and, now, here I was in complete safety, still getting cold and wet through — to what end?

Was it my job as a professional soldier to endure this self-isolation; would it make me a better soldier? Would it make me less switched-on if I didn't do it? Of course not. I did it partly because I didn't have to, and also because I actually enjoyed it. (Remember that saying, 'You never feel more alive than when you're close to death.') But, much more importantly, today I had just got rid of a box of tricks that had been preying on my conscience — and it had only been due to chance that it had been pissing down with rain.

PART TWO

2.

GOING MOBILE

The traffic was beginning to move again. I was feeling warm, a stuffy sort of warmth. I reached for the air-conditioning control and turned it up a notch. Then, abruptly, my body was forced back into the grey leather seat. The smooth forward surge of three tons of black bullet-proof Bentley kicked into life again. We hit the Hyde Park Corner underpass dead on 30 miles an hour, heading out west.

The Bentley had been tailgating the silver Mercedes 600 since picking up its passenger some 20 minutes earlier from an address in the City.

Behind it followed a navy blue Mercedes 600. All three vehicles exited in the same formation as they had entered. Then they came to an abrupt halt some 30 metres later in the centre of three lanes of traffic trying to converge into two. It was eleven o'clock on a Friday morning in March, and the traffic was piling up. It was horrendous; traffic's always horrendous at this time of day anyway, but Fridays, especially, it was a right bitch.

'Prick!' Mick, the driver of the Bentley, whispered under his breath as a black cab tried to cut across his path.

A little bit of power applied on the accelerator caused the Bentley to lurch uncomfortably forward, leaving less than a metre gap between it and the silver Mercedes. I'd already 'clocked' the cabbie, from out of my left side, and the twin-axle Parcel Force truck now stationary on our right. A line of three double-decker buses hugged the inside lane.

The cab driver was shaking his fist and giving us a bit of verbal. I ignored him and purposely didn't make eye contact, I just made a mental note. 'Black cab driver to my left and slightly forward, acting in a very pissed-off manner, carrying no passengers, 30 plus, sporting a white football shirt, probably a Spurs supporter.'

At the same time I looked into my rear-view mirror, just to check that my Principal was still head down and thoroughly engrossed in his copy of the day's *Al-Watan*, the Kuwait version of *The Times*. Good — he was, indeed there was no reason why he shouldn't have been; London traffic is always stop go, stop go this time of day.

The cabbie was still holding his ground, he really wanted to get in between us and the leading Mercedes.

'Not a chance mate. No fuckin' way Jose,' Mike whispered under his breath again.

The chances were that all the cab wanted was to cross over lanes in front of us, to do a 'U' turn and head off back into the West End, but our team tactics would not allow it. Mike was sure as hell not going to allow it, working on the premise that if the vehicle was to break into our three-vehicle convoy, then the protection the convoy afforded would be greatly reduced.

As a professionally trained Defensive Driver of one of the bodyguard team's vehicles, it would also have been a reflection on his professional ability to let anyone get in between us and our lead. Since this was only a three-vehicle convoy, and he was the Principal's driver, he wasn't going to take no shit off no Indians — never. 'Poxy black cabbies, they've all got an attitude problem. They think they own the friggin' road,' Mike muttered. If he had let the cab in, he would have opened himself up to all sorts of verbal-ridicule references concerning his professionalism from the rest of the team.

Still, I looked across at him and raised an index finger to my lips. I sensed Mike was getting a real strop on and I didn't want the Principal complaining about the over-talkative nature of one of my team members. It was slightly unprofessional in my book.

Mike saw my gesture. 'Well, what do ya expect me to say?' He had one last moan. It was par for the course. I understood his frustration.

Mike was one of the best bodyguard drivers in London, his background being ten years in the Royal Marines, then four years with the Met Police and now six years doing this business.

There wasn't a lot you could tell Mike about London, driving in London or its people. Only sometimes did he let his temper get the better of him. Road rage is a phenomenon brought about by the pace of modern life. Latent road rage in bodyguard drivers goes with the job. Save it for when you're out on a Bank Holiday with the family, if you must. Letting it out has no place in this business.

There are two things that I've found out about the black cabbie in London. Firstly, if he gets involved in a smash, be it just a minor scrape, by law he has to stop working and get his cab repaired asap. Then, he's off the road and not earning, so he's always going to give way even though it doesn't seem like it at the time. Secondly, if you happen to be riding in one and the driver starts to piss you off for whatever reason, when you get to your destination, pay him from inside the cab, get out, preferably on the near side, and then leave the cab door open.

You can be sure to hear a few choice words from him, as he has to get out of the cab and walk around it to close the open door. I'm not really having a pop at London cabbies, but sometimes it appears that they are the only ones on the Public Highway trying to earn a living.

The traffic began to move forward again. The cabbie was still trying to cross over but as we passed him, still fuming, the rear vehicle held its ground. If the cabbie had got out of his cab then, I knew we would have been in for more than just a bit of road rage, since cabbies never get out of their cabs just to vent a bit of anger.

In that eventuality the team's SOPs would have been brought into action instantly.

Firstly, I would have radioed through to both vehicles to let them know the score, if they had not already sussed it out: a probable contact. The Advanced Party vehicle, call sign Black One — which was already at our destination and had it secured — would at the same time have been monitoring our radio transmissions, and would be ready to drive to the team's ERV (Emergency Rendezvous, a gathering point where the team should meet if the shit hit the fan), or if I thought it necessary to order it to come and act as back-up.

The object of the operation would be to get the Principal away from the threat as quickly as possible, the threat in this instance being the 'black cab' and whoever his or her accomplices turned out to be. In situations like this, every person and object is treated as HOSTILE. But that also had to be done as safely as possible, and hopefully with a driver of Mike's calibre behind the wheel to avoid smashing into or ramming any other vehicles — if that was humanly possible.

The job of the two back-up Mercs would be to act as blocking vehicles to assist our escape. The entire operation of 'bugging out' should only take a matter of seconds, especially if everyone on the team did as they'd been briefed, which was usually the case. Post-contact procedure would be to smooth-talk the police, should the cabbie turn out to be a real cabbie. This would usually be down to the Principal and his lawyers.

I fiddled with the covert radio's ear-piece which was beginning to agitate me slightly and then pressed the switch which ran internally down the left-hand side of my suit sleeve via a thin wire. The static radio-wave nearly blew my head off. I flinched as I tried to turn down the volume.

'Red One, Red One, Red Two, take the next left, Wilton Place, past the Berkeley, and cut across Sloane Street. We're gonna be here all day otherwise,' I said in a low voice to avoid distracting the man in the back.

The business end of the radio was concealed under the lapel of my jacket, so as I spoke I didn't need to look down and fiddle with anything, I could just keep on observing what was going on outside the vehicle and doing my job of constantly assessing the threat.

The silver Mercedes then started to veer off, only slightly, to the left. It was the job of the *rear* Mercedes, the navy-coloured one, to instigate the manoeuvre, since its role was to block anything or anyone — and that included the 'anoraks' wearing cycle clips on mountain-bikes — from coming up the inside.

I looked into the nearside overtaking mirror and saw the rear vehicle.

'Red One, yeah, Roger that. You got that Red Three?' John in the silver Mercedes acknowledged.

'Red Three, Roger, ready when you are. Over.' Red Three acknowledged my order.

'Go ... for ... it ... wait, wait ... now,' I heard John say.

'All stations, Black One, Roger that. Out.' The advance party acknowledged the change of route.

The rear Mercedes made its manoeuvre and pulled over to the left, blocking any other vehicles which might have been coming up along on the inside, and at the same time the silver Mercedes did the same. I didn't have to say anything to Mike, he had already pre-empted the movement and started to steer over to the left; at the same time we were being boxed in by our two back-ups. Mike was in exactly the right place, and we nudged forward another 20 metres. The line of red buses had now moved forward, allowing us to make our turn as one, and then we swung a left.

I called up the advance party. 'Black One, Black One. With you in figures five, over.' I heard through my ear-piece two short sharp presses of Black One's transmission switch. This told me that he'd heard my ETA. He would be expecting another ETA from me before we arrived.

Once through Wilton Place the traffic appeared less congested. We swung around Belgrave Square.

'Black One, Red Two, 30 seconds, three zero seconds,' I said.

Two more presses on the radio's pretzel switch told me he'd received my last message, and that the drop-off site was clear and secure.

We then cut across Sloane Street where the traffic was, as I feared, nose-to-tail. With a bit of brashness the convoy nudged its way across the path of two lanes of slow-moving traffic, then all three vehicles made the turn into Hans Place, a residential area just behind Harrods, and pulled up outside our destination where call sign Black was waiting. Within five seconds of our arrival, the Principal was secured in his place of residence.

For my part, and that of the rest of my bodyguard team, the job had finished as soon as the front door of the Principal's residence was closed, with the Principal secured behind it. His own Arab bodyguards would now take over the 'residence' security phase, and stag on. My team would not be required for another ten hours. From the Principal's operational point of view, we were now stood down.

There was one last job to do before I knocked the team off for the day and that was to secure all three vehicles in the Principal's underground garage just a short drive away.

As with the Principal's residence, his garage was covered 24 hours of the day, by Arab security. Having this sort of cover on our vehicles was essential. It is the best cover to have, as it prevents any outsider — would-be bomber, arsehole, whoever — from tampering with any of the cars for whatever reason.

You can never take things for granted in this business. You have to cover *all* the possibilities of the threat to the Principal, no matter how small and insignificant they may seem. A bomb, or some kind of tracking device, could easily be placed on the main vehicle, the Bentley, if it wasn't eyeballed 24 hours of the day.

It kept Mike and the other two drivers happy, because they didn't have to worry about keeping the vehicles clean if it were to rain overnight. It also meant that they only had to do cursory security checks of their vehicles when they came back on stag. No need to go to the great lengths of carrying out a full security check, which takes about an hour, as you have to if the vehicle was left outside, and unsecured.

Although all three vehicles had been fitted with the latest anti-tampering devices and alarms, there was nothing like a total visual check of the vehicle to confirm it being 'clean'.

One of the two security systems fitted was the 'ring' system. Basically, once the car was left unoccupied, the driver could be alerted as to the state of his vehicle at any time anywhere in the world, by means of a small computer he carried with him. An alarm would alert him if any objects had been placed by or under the vehicle, and if anyone had touched it, and where. The entire system worked by sending out a constant electronic signal that covered the vehicle like a glove.

The other device fitted was a bespoke highly advanced alarm system with a series of small cameras that could be viewed from a stand-off position. All very technical and all very expensive. But both systems work, and that's the main thing, especially if your own life is at risk all the time driving around in these special vehicles — which it is. Any assistance to avoid my getting imploded on the inside of the Bentley's roof is OK by me.

However, though I like the technical side of this job, I still understand the need for total vigilance; wariness is not a sense these computer alarms can detect and disseminate — well, not yet, at least.

The two men on the advance party and my four other bodyguards made their way to their relevant cars. Mike and the other two drivers had stayed in their vehicles, engines running. This was SOPs: never, *never*, if your job is being the driver, should you get out of the vehicle and leave it unattended.

I opened the door to the Bentley. 'OK guys, let's get to the obvious, then we can stand down,' I said, and without saying anything more we drove off. The movement was text-book stuff: it worked like clockwork, as it always should.

The 'Bentley' job, as I called it, is a regular of mine. My client comes over to the UK once a year, maybe twice if I'm lucky. He's never here longer than four weeks on any one visit, and he only stays in Knightsbridge, making the City journey three times a week. I don't know what business he's in, and I don't care. When you get to his level in business, where you can tuck a 200-grand motor car away for 11 months of the year in the basement of a ten-million-pound pad — well, who cares what he does. As long as he keeps using my team to look after him, I'm not really worried where his money comes from.

I might come across as a bit uncaring: 'What if he's into dodgy dealings in a big way?' you might ask.

Of course I'd like my clients' businesses to be legit. And, as far as I know, they all are. But at the end of the day, what business is really legit? What business doesn't have any scams or tax fiddles attached to it? One thing I was sure of, you don't get to have all this wealth without pissing off someone whilst climbing the ladder of success. I guess that's where my team and I come in.

In four years he's probably only said two phrases to me: 'Good morning,' and 'Wait here, please.' And he's never asked me for anything 'strange'. Also, he's never been rude to me or any member of my team; we just do our job and get paid for it — no great dramas. He's what you might call the ideal Principal. He doesn't ask me questions and I don't ask him. I suppose it's a bit like a high-class prostitute with one of her special punters. It's nice to have the repeat business and the professional understanding that goes with the job, but you wouldn't want to spend the rest of your life with them.

3.

AGENT CONTACT

ZERO HOUR, MIDDAY

A few days after the Bentley job finished, four of us met up in town — London — for a drink at one of our many West End safe houses.

'Now Mr Bentley's job's finished, anyone got anything to drop on to now?' Mick threw into the conversation.

'Shit, I know of a static job round going on in Cornwall Terrace. Jim, an ex Old Bill mate of mine, runs it. He's always looking for guys to work the night stag.'

'What's it paying, spunk money I bet!' John, the ex detective, chirped up.

'Naw, it's all right, honest. It's a oner. You do 12 on, 12 off, for a month, then you get a week off on full pay.'

'What's that, in your hand or what?' John was being pushy.

'Fuck, what do want, John, blood? It's a piss-easy job, and you want cash all the friggin' time. Fuck me, you get your own room, everything else is found, scoff and that ...'

'Well, I'll have some of that. Put me down, will ya, Mick? I don't mind what I do as long as I'm earning,' I said.

Mick turned to John. 'You've gotta keep earnin' too, mate, what with your friggin' family.'

John nodded. He had a wife and four kids, and another on the way. 'You're not fuckin' wrong. I'm just a fuckin' money-making machine to my kids.'

'No. A friggin' *slave* more like it,' Vic said, pushing a newspaper to one side.

'Fuck Mike, just because you're firing blanks, don't fuckin' get your arse out, will ya?' John snapped.

Vic cut the conversation dead. 'Shut the fuck up, will ya? Who wants another drink?' Vic and I could sense that a bit of tension was brewing up between Mike and John. If we were to carry this drink on — which we'd all planned to do — then 'handbags at ten paces' might be the order of the night for those two.

It was lunchtime and the pub was beginning to fill up with 'suits' from nearby offices. We were all dressed in suits too, but we didn't consider ourselves 'suits'. No way were we nine-till-fives.

Vic was struggling at the bar to pass the first two pints over. I could feel he was about to have a sense-of-humour failure. A group of 'suits' had surrounded him and were shouting loudly at each other. I could see they were totally oblivious to Vic's presence. I left Mike and John discussing future job prospects, and went over to give him a hand.

'Excuse me, mate,' I said to the nearest 'suit'. 'Here Vic, pass 'em over here, will ya?' Two of the 'suits' saw me and just turned their backs, blocking me from Vic, still in heavy conversation about their day.

'Excuse me, mate.' This time I said it more loudly. Another second — no response. 'Excuse me, mate.' I said it a *third* time. One of them moved. Only a bit though, a sort of token gesture. He just looked around with a supercilious grin stretching across his rather acne'd face.

As always, I did a quick mental assessment of the possible threat. It took three seconds: five guys, all early 20s, all with briefcases, all local office workers, probably surveyors or accountants, cheap black brogue shoes in need of a polish, silky suits covered by dark Crombie coats. All looked reasonably sober, and all were very much full of themselves. The biggest one was about six four and as thin as an Olympic high jumper. He seemed the quietest.

Vic also sensed that not one of this crowd was going to move or at least let him through with his first pints. I could see two more beers had been poured and were sitting on the bar behind him. The barmaid was waiting patiently for payment, and at the same time getting hassle from one of the 'suits' waiting to be served.

Now, these guys weren't being stroppy or acting provocatively or anything like that, they were just pig-ignorant. It was just the way they were, young executives who thought they were the horse's cock. You have to accept that, that's life, and every pub in the country has these patrons. Unfortunately, there seem to be more of these pricks around here than in any other part of London.

Still with arms outstretched and a pint in each hand, Vic towered over the 'suits'. He shook his head, I couldn't reach him without rudely manhandling one of the 'suits' — minimum force necessary, you understand — when all of a sudden Vic rolled his eyes and, not in an aggressive way, more just accidentally on purpose, tipped a good gobful of beer down the side of Mister Supercilious's mush. It hit him square on the side of his face, and strangely, one large glob rolled off his left cheek and exploded all down the front of his Crombie.

'Oh, fucking hell, mate, I'm really sorry,' Vic said.

The 'suit' looked up at Vic. 'Jesus Christ, man, what the ...'

'I've got 'em, Vic.' I took the beer from Vic and watched as Vic tried to brush off the spilt beer with his 'size-humungous' hands as he then pushed past the 'suits' with two more pints. Supercilious's mates just looked on in surprise to see their mate getting 'stroked' by this rather large Welsh man.

'Fucking Welsh twonk,' the 'suit' said under his breath. Without warning, Vic grabbed hold of him with one hand and almost lifted him off the ground — the Vulcan 'death grip'. The man's face was turning blue as he tried to struggle from Vic's grip. It didn't work. His gobsmacked mates just looked on in total amazement. Then Vic released him. The entire incident couldn't have taken more than ten seconds — but that's a long ten seconds when guys are puffing out their chests and debating whether to square up to the threat occurring right in their faces. Luckily, they didn't.

I saw what was about to kick off. 'You all right, Vic? Come on, mate, it's finished. Let's leave it.' I deliberately got between Vic and the 'suits' — it wasn't worth getting into a rumble over a bit of name calling. Vic had the last say. 'Don't call me a Welsh twonk, you cunt.' And with that Vic got the 'sorry' I guess he was after.

We went back to John and Mike who, by now, had commanded a corner of the pub. They hadn't seen the slight altercation up at the bar.

'Fuck, Devs, you took your friggin' time. Fuckin' dying of thirst here, we are!'

'Ah, Vic's up to his old tricks again. Some "suits" up at the bar wouldn't let him pass. You know the score.'

Vic nudged me on the back. 'Here, ya twat, grab hold of these.' He passed more beers around.

'Can't take you anywhere, can we, boyo?' John said, taking the piss out of Vic's accent. 'What's up, the bar's too crowded for you or somethin'? It ain't like the Valleys up here, mate. We're all ignorant pricks here in London. I thought you would've known that by now.'

'You know what the cheeky fucker called me?' Vic replied.

'No, what's that?' Mick said.

'He called me a Welsh twonk. He just looked at me dumb as he said it. He didn't even apologise. Twat should have bought me a pint for that,' Vic insisted. 'Anyway, what's a twonk?'

'It's a Rupert term for an idiot,' I said.

Vic looked around at me. 'Oh, well, that's not too bad, I guess. I thought it might have been a Cockney term for sheep-shagger or something like that.'

That seemed to have settled Vic. I looked across the bar to check what the 'suits' were up to, but the pub was pretty much full now. I couldn't see them, they'd disappeared into the masses.

What normally happens in these situations is that, if we were to stay for another couple of pints and the 'suits' did as well, then it wouldn't be long before something more serious happened. With blokes, it usually happens when two of the parties accidentally meet each other in the toilets and something is said. Not necessarily by my guys; we can all hold our own and, in general, try not to get into trouble. In fact, we try and avoid it.

There is nothing more off-putting or unprofessional in a bodyguard than ending up on a job the following morning carrying the scars of a previous night's battle. The Principals we work for don't take too kindly to this 'after-hours' activity. Sure, they want to know that the men they employ can handle themselves, but they don't want to be reminded of it should one of my team pitch up in the morning with a face like a bulldog chewing a wasp.

We finished our drinks and made a swift exit to a more local boozer just off the Edgware Road, where we could drink in a less punchy environment.

The Gloucester, an original Victorian pub and a regular safe house of mine, is just that little off the beaten track. It's ideally situated for not getting visited by all the tourists who seemed to flock to London's West End, month in and month out, in their thousands. Personally, I can't see the attraction of London in the winter months, I'd rather be sunning myself on a beach in the Med, but then again, it takes all sorts. The summers in London can be great — but winter, I don't think so.

Anyway, The Gloucester has always been a bit of a safe house with the guys I've worked with over the years. It serves good beer and wholesome scoff, and its local trade comes from those who are able to afford to live in this part of London. It's away from offices so you don't get the 'suit' syndrome.

Also, I've known David, the landlord, for years. He looks fairly distinguished with his grey hair, in a 'I'm sure I know that face, but I just can't seem to put a name to it' sort of way. A tall, very smart dresser, always wearing a collar and tie behind the bar, he's a laid-back, happy-go-lucky Londoner. I guess he's in his mid-60s. In a way he reminds me of some likeable rogue who used to cut around London in the 1960s.

Some years back, I was asked to do this little surveillance job for an Arab client — a small task, just a couple of hours' work. I had to follow a lady friend of his from an address in Hammersmith to a shop on the Edgware Road. I don't know what he or she was up to, but all I had to do was log down what she did *en route*: whether she went straight to the shop, or whether she stopped off, or met someone on the way. The usual operation a private eye might be asked to carry out.

She caught a black cab and I followed on a motor bike. It was an easy number, no drama, just a straight pick-up and drop-off for the cabbie. Once she was in the shop, that was the end of my task. I took note of the cabbie's number and his appearance and got it checked out through a mate of mine who had an 'in' with the black cabs. As it turned out, the cabbie really was a cabbie. Because the job was a bit of a doddle, I felt a slight twinge of guilt taking the cheque off the client. But it's nice to get an easy job once in a while, and it is even better when you get a result.

And I did get a result, by which I mean I didn't lose my target, and I didn't get compromised. It was the client who didn't get a result — or maybe he did; he didn't discuss it with me, clients usually don't. They always have their own reasons and hidden agendas to work to. Either way, I would find out if I had achieved his aim if he used me again on the same task — if he felt he wasn't throwing away good money on my service. After all, surveillance isn't like it appears on an episode of some police soap. To carry out a surveillance task properly requires time, skill, a hell of a lot of patience, and luck, and very rarely do you get the result the client expects on the first outing.

It's understandable that on TV you've only got a 30- or 60-minute timeframe in which to produce a result. In real life it could take days, if not weeks, to get the result the client is happy with, and at 300 pounds a day plus expenses, it isn't cheap.

At the end of the job my client wanted me to RV with him at a pub called The Gloucester, but when I arrived to give him the de-brief, he wasn't there. I called him from the pub's pay phone and he said he'd be down in five minutes. I was a bit dubious about leaving the bike outside — the traffic wardens are shit-hot around this part of town — so I just let him know that I was going to ditch the bike, so not to worry if I wasn't there when he arrived, I wouldn't be long. Hearing that he said, 'Leave the bike, ask David behind the bar if you can park it in his yard; it's all right, he's a friend, tell him it's a favour for Mr Abdullah.' It was no problem. David showed me where to stash the bike, and then proceeded to buy me a drink, which I thought was really nice of him, not ever having met me before.

Years later I still don't know what Mr Abdullah said to David, and I've never asked, but he lets me park my car in his yard every time I need a space for one of the bodyguard vehicles. It's a really handy contact which I don't take the piss out of, especially when the going rate for parking in the West End is 25 quid a day.

On this occasion, The Gloucester was quiet and David was out. All four of us pitched up at a table and started to discuss the nitty-gritty of our profession. Bit of a no-nonsense regular occurrence de-brief, in theory. More of a slagging match, in fact, I suppose, about who cocked-up this and who cocked-up that, and who was the biggest wanker, basically blokes' talk, which usually ended in the proverbial ego-stroking of praising each other's abilities to do the job.

'Hey, Devs, talking about work, you gonna phone that number you got earlier, or what?' Mick said.

'Yeah, go on, give it a call, Devs, it might be the bollocks of a job, you never know,' John added.

Shit! Because of the 'suit' business, I'd forgotten about the message I'd received some hours earlier. I had a fairly good idea of what it was about. It had come via the editor of a national newspaper who, along with the rest of the world's press, had featured me in a picture bodyguarding a honeymoon couple, Oasis-fame Liam Gallagher and his new wife Patsy Kensit. This editor had had a call from a businessman seeking my services and had passed this information on to me. It was nice of him to do that because I've learnt that, in general, nobody in the media business ever gets in contact with you to pass on info from which they are very unlikely to benefit. (The exception to this rule, of course, is if you're a class A film star or a topical politician.) For some reason, newspaper people and publishers always have a million things to keep their mind occupied during any one day — like the rest of us don't, of course — so I'd been pleasantly surprised when this call came through.

The newspaper hadn't vetted this contact, and indeed, there was no reason for them to do so, that was up to me. By vetting I mean checking the guy out to see if he was genuine, or just another Captain Bullshitter type with a dog's breath of an attitude.

Actually, I didn't know why I'd hesitated, after all it was only business. Maybe I was looking forward to a break. I had called him earlier only to get his voicemail. So I left a contact number.

'Fuck it, why not?' I gave in. 'Don't think for a minute I'll put you on the team, will ya, you prick. It'll be a pure SF [Special Forces] number this time. Know what I mean.' I was joking. John was a really good operator; he too was one of the best on the circuit. 'You're ex Old Bill, mate, I know you can't help that.'

'I suppose that counts me out as well, Englishman,' Vic chirped up.

'Hell no, mate, you're an honorary member of the Special Air Service, ain't that right, Devs?' Mick replied.

'Well, if he gets the beers in again, then who am I to disagree, Mick?' I downed my pint and handed Vic my empty glass, Mick and John followed suit. 'Cheers, pal. Get 'em in, Taffy boy. We'll have a bit of a conflab when you're up at the bar.' I laughed as I said it. Vic hated being called 'Taffy'. Only in select company like this could anyone get away with it. Anyone picking up on this familiar term who Vic didn't know, whoever they were, was sure to get both barrels from him.

Just as Vic told us all to fuck off and pointed out that it was *my* round, someone's phone started to ring.

'Hey, whose mobile's ringing?' All of us looked around and started to fumble in pockets.

'It's yours, Devs,' Vic said.

'I think you're right. He'll do anything to get out of a round,' agreed Mike.

I reached inside my suit jacket. Vic was right, it was mine. Panic over, the guys carried on talking. My mobile had somehow got stuck inside my suit. Damn thing! The aerial had found its way into a small hole in the pocket lining and was being a bit of a bitch to get out.

I had previously set a six-ring cut mode but had forgotten to change back to at least twelve rings. 'Fuck it,' I said as I just managed to free it and get the top cover down on the sixth ring. 'Hello, hello?'

I could hear a man's voice at the other end. The voice was faint and intermittent. I couldn't hear too much over the sound of the juke box, so I made my way outside the pub. Vic noticed me moving away, nodded to indicate that he would get my round in, and then carried on in deep conversation with the rest of the guys.

Once outside, I could hear more clearly. Then click, the line went dead. Not thinking the caller might just ring back, I quickly pressed 'last incoming call re-dial'. It rang only once, and it was answered as if the person at the other end of the phone was expecting it to ring.

'Yes, speak.' A rather sharp voice bellowed through the phone's ear-piece.

'Yeah, hello! You just called me ...'

'Oh! Right, yes, is that Steve Devereux? I'm sorry, are you ...?' The accent was of someone well groomed, who now came across as very apologetic.

'Who's that? I enquired, answering a question with a question.

'Are you the chap, well, the bodyguard, who was looking after Mr Oasis and his wife? I'm sorry, I've forgotten their names.'

I cut the voice short. 'Excuse me, who am I talking to?'

'Sure, I'm sorry, Stephen Roberts, I left you a message ...'

'Ah right, yes, sorry, Mr Roberts. You called the newspaper. What can I do for you, Mr Roberts?'

'Well, thank you for getting in touch. Are you in London?'

'Yes.'

'Oh good, that's great, so am I. I wasn't sure whether the editor would pass on my call. One knows all too well what the press can be like.' He paused and then carried on talking.

He was very friendly but not to the point. He kept talking as though he was trying to beat me in a verbal contest, or very much liked the sound of his own voice. I didn't have a chance to interject. I've always been a bit hesitant in dealing with someone through a third party, especially a source from the press, and over the phone too. You can never tell if they just want to chew the fat, are another hack searching for a follow-on story — in this case about the Gallaghers' honeymoon — or are actually serious about a job.

So I let him talk, that's always the best approach. That way you can at least get some sense of whether they're full of shite or not.

My first thoughts were: probably a Rupert; middle-aged; probably fat through years of a high intake of 'business lunches'; and used to strutting around shouting at people and making himself feel important — this came from the manner in which he answered the phone.

I also had a feeling that he was probably working for an Arab or some wealthy guy from the Far East — a banker. I don't know why, but I felt fairly sure about it. It was probably something to do with all the foreign business connections I'd met through a very good Kuwaiti friend of mine.

Most of these highly successful and extremely wealthy types had a middle-aged City type, ex public-school-boy, running around after them, acting as an adviser on financial deals, or educating them on the Brit way of life — whatever *that* was. But really they were just highly paid handbag accessories who enjoyed the prestige of their boss whilst, as far as I could see, not really giving much in return, other than introducing them to this country's 'old boy' network.

It transpired that Roberts's boss — not his word, I think he used a phrase like 'business associate' or something, typical of this type, always wanting to be in charge — had got himself into a spot of financial 'bother' with a bank and wanted to know if we could meet soonest and talk through a possible security scenario to look after his wife and daughter whilst the boss himself conducted business dealings with a series of banks in the City of London. It would require 24-hour cover, was I interested?

From his use of the term 'security scenario' and mentioning '24-hour cover' I could only surmise that he was ex forces, so then he was *definitely* a Rupert. That would explain his rather pompous officer-like manner when he was talking to me, in the way that an officer would address his men on the parade square. A less likely deduction was that he'd had dealings with other security companies in the past and had picked up on the lingo. No, I thought, probably the first option, because of that officer-to-soldier tone.

I might be critical of my prospective clients, but nonetheless, sometimes these sorts of introductions do pay off. So during the conversation I managed to force my choice of venue for our meeting, since he was coming across pretty much like the man about town. I said, 'Let's meet at a discreet table in the Library Bar at the Lanesborough Hotel,' — an elegant hotel filled with wood-panelled walls and furnished with Regency-period furniture to give it that 19th-century feel. I knew the place well and I would be a lot happier meeting this guy in familiar surroundings, on my patch.

'You know it?' I added.

'Yes, I know it well, let's say about six o'clock. Is that OK for you?'

I looked at my watch: it was only three thirty. I got the feeling from his tone that as I'd jumped in with the location before he did, he was now quickly suggesting a time; it was a sort of one-upmanship. It came across as arrogant, but these Rupert types always do! Anyway, I wanted to reduce the length of time before we met. From his tone I figured out that he'd never been to that hotel, and I didn't want him to have time to do a recce.

'I'm sorry, I can't make it for six. I've got something on then.' I tried to push his hand. 'How about four thirty?' After all, it was he who wanted me and I actually did have something planned for later that day, like going on the piss with the guys and getting slaughtered! He agreed.

All this might seem a bit too tactical and too much like thinking on your feet, but a lot of people — clients especially — expect it. It bores me to death but I still have to go through the routine of it all. It's par for the course in the security business — talking shite, pretending you're not available, thus giving the impression of being more in demand than you probably are.

The trouble is, sometimes I just can't help feeling very cynical about this entire profession. I've learnt so much on the bodyguard circuit, and it always seems that the business is full of people who appear to be living on another planet, in one way or another.

If it's not some member of a team who thinks he is some budding Jean Claude Van Damme, or Dark Destroyer who struts around like he's got a bore brush for a Challenger tank rammed up his arse, then it's some of the clients. Some never cease to amaze me with their inability to take advice from their personal bodyguard. Maybe they've seen too many action movies and live in that world where everything ends up perfect for the good guy.

'Yes, that's fine, Steve. I look forward to meeting you. The

Lanesborough at 16.30, see you there.'

'Yeah, half-four, great. I look forward to it, see you there.' I closed up the phone and went back into the pub. I could see four pints on the table.

'They want your money up at the bar, Devs. You can't slip out of this round.' Vic was pointing to the bar.

My mind was now not on drinking, but on the meeting I'd arranged for an hour's time. I told the guys that I had to go, and would meet up with them a bit later on, after the meet. I left them to it and headed off to my basha — the office — to get a change of shirt and a scrape of the teeth.

The Lanesborough Hotel is a grand old place, adjacent to the grounds of Buckingham Palace on Hyde Park Corner. I walked into the Library Bar early and Stephen Roberts followed soon after. He looked and spoke exactly as I had imagined. He was in his mid-60s, tall, about six two, slightly balding with greyish hair swept back to one side. The gel made it darker than it probably was. True to type, he was dressed in a well-cut, dark, two-piece pin-striped suit. Almost immediately he began to give a brief breakdown of his past military career. This was rather a bad move, as far as I was concerned. It always puts me on edge when someone tries to justify their past experiences. I think: Are you trying to hide something?

He said that he'd spent three years in the Guards and had come out as a captain. He had just missed conscription, of course; he was one of the 'old school'. I will say, though, we got on well. I actually quite liked him.

We spoke in general terms for about ten minutes about our past military experience, exchanging 'war' stories every now and then, before he got to the reason why he had called this meeting. It transpired that 'his' client, a Mr Suhail, of Asian extraction — whom I took to be his boss, or at least the man who paid him — was particularly concerned about the security arrangements on a forthcoming London visit.

It was good to listen to Roberts talking, not only to glean information from his polite conversation, but also to hear what he would expect from me, should I decide to take on the job. From what I deduced within the first 15 minutes of our meeting, he was looking for a bodyguard team to look after this Mr Suhail (whose main source of income, now confirmed, was from banking deals) during his stay in London, and as a secondary role, to look after his wife and kid.

At this stage of the meeting, what I wanted to ascertain from the man doing all the talking was: Are you the full shilling? And, are you really this Mr Suhail's main man? If so, is the boss the Full Monty? Is he a main player in the world of high finance, and can he afford the sort of 'security cover' I assume he requires, by the way you are talking? There were a lot of ifs, ands and buts to play around with. My initial instincts told me that Roberts was probably no more than an agent acting on behalf of this Mr Suhail, brought in merely to broker the deal.

'Mr Suhail will be arriving in two days' time from Germany, and I envisage he's going to require the best available cover immediately he checks into his hotel.'

'How long is his stay for?'

'Well, let's put it like this. His wife and daughter are flying in with him and it's hoped that the child will start schooling. She's only young, but she's already been accepted in a private school just around the corner from here. Length of job short term for the moment, but we *could* be looking at a long-term contract. *Very long-term.*' He pulled out a large Cohiba cigar from inside his suit and lit up. Instantly, a plume of thick smoke wafted my way. He didn't ask if I minded — I actually didn't, but in this politically correct world we all now inhabit, I might well have taken offence at being choked by this 100 dollars' worth of Cuban tobacco — a cigar rolled on the thigh of a young virgin, so the rumour goes.

He paused for a brief moment, as if contemplating life, then blew another puff over in my direction. 'He's been talking about buying a house on this trip,' he said quite nonchalantly. 'I cannot see him living in hotels, what with his daughter starting school.'

'How old's the daughter?'

'Suni? Oh, she's only seven.'

My instincts, as normal, were working overtime. I was doing a series of quick calculations in my head. I couldn't stop it, it was more of a subconscious thing than anything else. What I was hearing was possibly the best piece of news for a long time. Well, since the last client who'd wanted 'the best' long-term cover possible — and he had turned out to be an Egyptian full of shit.

There always appear to be a lot of people around who want the 'best' long-term security cover available. It seems to be a phrase they carry around with them. That might give the impression that there's a lot of work around, but the strange thing is that here in London, there isn't. It's a very closed-shop kind of business, with a lot of people using long knives stabbing each other in the back — jockeying for position.

Anyway, getting back to the plot, here I was, maybe, just *maybe*, being asked — provisionally — to carry out this short-term bodyguard contract, with a long-term view of running Mr Suhail's complete security requirements — in London initially, but perhaps leading to operations worldwide. You've gotta think big, haven't you? Otherwise there's no point in 'playing the game', is there?

Well, so far so good, I thought. But, as always, at this stage, I stayed on the side of caution. I take every day as it comes. My first thought was, Let's get basics out of the way first, just for starters: money, payment terms and all that stuff. Then, because I'm in the commercial world now and not in the SAS, the actual threat on this Mr Suhail came next.

After all, no one in their right mind is going to employ the services of me or my team — we don't come cheap — unless that person thinks he (or she) might be meeting his maker a bit earlier than he intends, if they don't have suitable security cover.

The entire meeting lasted for about 45 minutes, culminating in Roberts asking me to supply a couple of references; not that he really needed them, he knew what I was capable of, and at the end of the day it would be easy for him to check me out through his old school ties in the Guards. Even so, I think he'd got the message and understood what I was about. What was slightly worrying from *my* point of view, was that while I could check Roberts out superficially, there was no real way I could vet the Principal.

'Basically, Steve, I'm looking for you to provide me with some kind of flexible price for your men. Calculate it on a weekly basis, would you, please?'

I'm always cautious of people asking me to give them a costings of my services without even knowing the Bobby Moore. I mean, hell, I didn't even know the threat to this bloke, Mr Suhail. He could turn out to be Mr Devil Reincarnate for all I knew, with half of the Islamic Fundamentalists after him — I was thinking, Fatwah, fatwah.

'I can certainly do that, it's not a problem. What I have to take into consideration, though, is that — with all due respect — I know nothing about you or your client, and I'm rather going in blind here. I mean, we're not discussing supplying static guards, are we? I'm sure you would have thought it strange if I didn't touch on this point!'

'No, indeed we're not.'

'I take it you really do want the best?'

'Yes, of course, that's why I'm here.'

'Ex SAS guys, they don't come cheap.'

'My client is willing to pay. He specifically instructed me to find the best.'

'I don't want to put you off, I mean of course I want your business but .... payment?'

He knew what was coming next. 'Cash?'

My heart dropped a couple of beats. 'Cash is fine,' I replied.

He stood up to indicate the meeting was finally over and extended his right hand. I took it.

'I'll call you later to arrange a meeting for tomorrow morning.'

'I look forward to it.'

The waiter saw the movement at our table and quickly came over with the bill, enclosed in an arty-farty maroon wallet affair, the size and thickness of an average paperback book. Mr Roberts pulled out a fifty from a wad of notes out of one of those leather Filofax-type money wallets.

'Thank you very much. Please.' Roberts raised a hand. 'That's OK, Milo,' he added, looking at the waiter's name badge, and waved him away.

'Oh, thank you very much, sir. Thank you.' The waiter beamed with gratitude. He was a young, Italian-looking lad, dressed in a navy-blue two-piece uniform. (The type of lad some middle-aged women dream of running off into the sun with!) To me he looked effeminate, but that was just my opinion.

Hell, I thought, that's a bit steep for two coffees and a couple of Farley's Rusks type biscuits. Was he out to impress me or what! In my line of work I've met many a big tipper, and they always use fifties — why not a twenty or even a tenner? I swear to God, if there was ever such a thing as an English 100-pound note, then this would have been a 100-pound tip. 'A fool and his money are soon parted' ran through my head.

We arranged another meet for eleven the following morning, at the same place. He wanted me to bring along my costings plan, based on a four-week timeframe. Men and equipment, he said, and a brief resumé of the particular skills of the type of men I would employ on the team. 'Just something to hand to Mr Suhail, you understand.' I immediately knew that catching the guys up on the piss was no longer an option. I had masses of homework to do!

Roberts's guidelines — more like 'terms of employment' — were pretty loosely put together, but I'd already had a fair inkling of what he was looking for. Basically, a self-contained six-man bodyguard team (*he* came up with the figure of six. I was looking at a minimum of eight. I didn't tell him my initial thoughts on purpose. I would get on the ground first and see how it panned out), along with all the relevant vehicles, radios and associated equipment.

Once he'd gone I sat back down, pulled out my diary and started to take in the ambience of my surroundings. I flicked through it until I found a clean address page and began to make a few notes based on the meeting. At the same time I caught Milo's eye, and told him him I wanted more coffee, and to leave out the rusks this time. He cupped the used ashtray with a clean one, and then put the clean one back on the table. He found it a bit difficult, what with the large pile of ash and Roberts' half a stogie stubbed out in it.

It was just a longshot, but I thought I might as well try it. I struck up a conversation with him. 'Hey, Milo, tell me, why do you cover the ashtray like that?'

He looked at me slightly puzzled but said, 'It's because, sir, if I was to take ashtray from table, then ash might spread on you.' He indicated that the motion might create a draft. 'I put clean ashtray on top, so ...'

'Ah, OK, got it.' I nodded in comprehension, and then politely asked him if he had ever seen the man that just tipped him before.

'No, sir, no I haven't.'

'Ah well, he's a very good friend of mine,' I lied. 'We'll be back here tomorrow. What time will you be on?'

'I start at eleven.'

'That's good,' I said. 'I'll be back tomorrow, you look after us, OK!'

'Yes, of course, sir, of course.' Milo finished what he was doing and went to get my refill.

'Nice one,' I muttered to myself. I don't know whether he thought I was trying to chat him up or not. I just wanted to see his eyes as I popped the question. He might not have told me verbally but I could have got an indication from his eyes as to whether he was telling porkies or not. As I said, it was a longshot, and I was just trying to cover all the angles. Who knew, this Roberts guy might well have been one of these Walter Mittys who bullshit their way around London, full of their own weird egos, trying to pull off a scam for whatever their own reasons might be. I'm not kidding, my business is full of nutters cutting about town thinking they're something special in the way of high financiers or bodyguards. This time, however, my intuition was saying to me that Mr Roberts had not met Mr Milo before. Not much to go on, but it was something.

Thinking about the Walter Mitty angle reminded me of a funny episode which happened, not so much to me but to a friend, Danny D. Actually, it wasn't so funny as sad. I'd put Danny on one of my seasonal security operations looking after a Middle Eastern sheikh a few months before. The trouble is that in the bodyguard business, there are generally two or three main positions available. Two half-decent positions and one really naff.

Undoubtedly, the best job is the bodyguard. You get to go 'walk-about' with the client, visit all sorts of shops and nice restaurants, and you also get to do the job you're paid to do. Then there's the defensive driver's position — that is, if the Principal is switched-on enough to employ one, and not just a chauffeur. I can tell you that there's nothing more frustrating — and sometimes frightening — than getting into a vehicle on a job where the driver has spent his last 20/30 years ferrying the head of a multi-national around. Nice if you want to go sightseeing;

pretty crap if you get into a contact and have to ram your way out of a situation.

Last of all, there's the position of the 'corridor-man'. Generally, the job of the 'corridor-man' is to keep the Principal's hotel floor, room or residence sanitised from outside influences. If you're lucky, there might be two or three of you on at the same time, but Danny's position was only budgeted for one man. Basically, look at it this way: you're a well-paid static guard wandering up and down the corridors of five-star hotels, working out how many stitches per inch the deep-pile carpet you're walking over contains.

Now, I'm telling you, this is the most mind-blowing job in my business (apart from working on a long-term surveillance operation). I should know, I've done more than my fair share of 12-hour stags. And, if the job happens to run over the winter time, you never see daylight. You get up to be on stag, usually by seven or eight in the morning, then do a full twelve hours, most of the time eating your lunch in the corridor of the particular floor you're looking after.

A lot of the time there are no arrangements for ablutions. Then you have to use a bit of initiative! If the Principal's out, then you pop in and use his facilities, if not, you have to cut down on your eating and drinking habits and work around the Principal's routine, and 'go' when he's out on a visit. I'm a walking encyclopedia on Middle Eastern carpets and interior decor, trust me! Corinthian pillars, gilt-edged rococo-style mirrors, 17th-century French furniture — let's say I've got a good working knowledge of what the extremely rich favour.

Anyway, I had this little contract up at the Grosvenor House Hotel, Park Lane, and all that was required was for Danny to stand outside this Sheikh's room for 12 hours a day — for six weeks. He was the lucky one, he was on days; the night man I had to change every two weeks, to send them off down to the nut-house for a bit of a conversation refresher course! Understand that this job was for a straight 40-odd days with no time for remission, no days off. That's the norm in this business.

Danny was OK about the six-week job. He said he'd do it for the duration, as long as I relieved him once a day for an hour to get some fresh air. That, as far as I was concerned, was a deal. If I could stand in for him once a day, then it would save me the headache of getting someone to replace him, should Danny throw in the towel.

The night man wasn't too bad, because this particular Principal didn't go walk-about at night, unlike most other clients. All of his activities were during the day, and at night he never appeared after six, till he rose at about ten the following morning.

That wasn't too bad. But the 'day man' had to be right. Most Principals don't show that they care about their security, but they do, and possibly one of the worst things any bodyguard team-leader could do — apart from the obvious, and that's to disappear when the bullets start to fly — is to break the continuity of the faces within the team.

The Principal will notice that a certain face has changed and will probably ask his aide-de-camp to find out why, and in a lot of cases demand to have that face back, even though you might think that the guy you've just booted off the team is a right wanker.

Basically, it can cause all sorts of complications with the Principal — and upsetting the Principal is what you, as bodyguard, try to avoid. By doing that, you could lose the job, or at least the regular bung at the end of the job. Principals can be very, very fickle, and you would be surprised what goes through their heads when they address their security.

Sometimes I would wonder, Haven't they got better or more important things to worry about in their lives? But I suppose it takes all sorts. I'm not saying that every Principal I've worked for has this attitude, because they don't. It's just when you get one who thinks along those lines, the job becomes twice as difficult, when there's no reason for it to be.

Anyway, Danny stagged on and I relieved him every day for an hour to grab a bit of fresh air. As you can imagine, he wasn't getting too much exercise whilst in the corridor, so he asked if I could arrange for him to use the hotel's gym and swimming pool. A quick bit of smooth talking with the resident gym queen, who just happened to be ex Forces, and I'd cleared it for Danny to work out. He was really grateful.

So, at the end of his stag each evening he would wearily make his way down to the basement and spend 20 minutes in the pool or 30 or 40 working out on the weights. He said that it was a really hard struggle at the end of each stag, not just to get out of the lift as it stopped at ground level and bugger off home to bed. But he persevered and said that once he'd forced himself into the pool he felt better for it: 'It got easier as the days went on.'

It's not the norm for people to stay in hotels like the Grosvenor for more than a couple of weeks. At well over the average weekly wage for a room for one night, you can understand why. However, if you've got more money than you can shake a stick at, it doesn't matter how long your stay is. Most of the hotel's clients are obviously the very wealthy, on a two-week holiday, or are foreign businessmen cutting deals in the world's capitals.

Indeed, I've known of one who stayed and ran his business for over a year in one of these top hotels, living off the room-service menu (which must have grown a bit tiresome after about the second week), and using the hotel's business centre to do all his secretarial work, phone and fax calls and all that. Now, that's what I call rich — or being just plain stupid. It was pretty obvious that the hotel didn't mind — as long as they had access to this guy's business dealings, they would have been the first to know if he couldn't pay his account at the end of each week, month or whatever arrangement he had.

Anyway, after about the second week, Danny was becoming a bit of a regular at the pool side. He too was ex forces, ex 3 Para to be exact, and liked to keep up a level of fitness, so that if something happened he would be able to react to it.

Also it's a personal thing. A fit mind follows a fit body, so they say, and boy, he needed his brain cleansed out each day because of the sheer boredom, and the thoughts that pass through one's mind every minute of the day in the corridor.

One time when I came up to relieve him, he told me that he was working on a little project that had come about through one of his visits to the gym's treadmill. Danny had got to know this chap — I'll call him Mr Santos, but that of course wasn't his real name. He was a businessman from South America, Argentina in fact, heavily into the mining industry and lots of other things, as Danny told it.

I could see Danny sitting in the middle of the corridor reading. In a friendly way, I thought, I'll try and catch him out. It's a game,

just as it is to some hotel floor staff I've come across in the past —
they would make it their daily challenge to catch the security man
off guard. But Danny had quite clearly placed a wedge under one
of the fire doors which led into his corridor, so as I tried to open
it, it took that little bit more effort, thus causing it to make a noise
— a basic but effective early-warning system.

Danny heard me, and I acted normal, as if I wasn't testing him.

'Is he in?' I said in a low voice, pointing to the Principal's door,
at the same time kicking the door wedge back in place.

'Yeah, hasn't moved. Colonel Abdullah says he ain't going out
today, well not in the next couple of hours, anyway.'

'What's he like then?' I asked, trying to inject a bit of
inquisitiveness into my remark.

'Who? The Sheikh?'

'No, you prat, your Mr Santos.'

'Oh him. Here, pull up a chair and have a brew, it's a fresh one.'

There were only two chairs in the corridor, either side of a
small hall table. Underneath the table was a pot of tea and one
cup, and a stack of crumpled newspapers and magazines.

'Got another cup?' I said.

'No, just the one. Now, look at this.' He offered me the 'game
plan' he'd been working on. I read it. It had all the arrangements
for a 12-man bodyguard team to secure a large yacht moored
somewhere in the Mediterranean for a meet with Mr Santos's
'people'. Dates, times, places, costs. You name it, he'd covered the
whole lot — even, under a heading named Entertainment,
Women!

'I take it these women are ladies of the night?' I looked at him
with a big grin.

'Yeah, I thought we could touch your mate James for that one.'

James ran a very exclusive West End escort agency. Danny
didn't look up. He was still looking down at the paper rather
excitedly.

'Sure, I guess, but you know 80 per cent of those on his books
are chappies.' I sensed Danny's reaction.

'Small problem,' he sneered, as if I'd caught him out, 'but I bet
he knows a man that could help though.'

'I'm pretty sure he would.' I carried on reading. It was a good
plan; Danny had spent a lot of time working on it.

'I didn't mention anything earlier, because I wanted to suss this Santos chap out.'

'And that's what you've been up to after work, doing a bit on the side, eh?'

'Nah, it's nothing like that, you know. It's just that he's in the gym most evenings when I knock off and we got talking. You know how it is.' Danny suddenly turned sideways. There was a noise at the far end of the corridor. Someone, a guest, had opened one of the fire doors which secured the other part of the corridor. Evidently they'd taken the wrong turning out of the lift. Danny stood up and walked over to a little old lady. 'Sorry, madam, this floor's out of bounds.' Danny was very polite. I carried on reading but kept an ear open.

'Oh, I'm sorry, young man. Is it anyone famous?' the voice said in an American accent, as she took in two big men in dark suits. 'I met Fred Astaire once in this hotel, but he didn't have *any* security men.'

'No, madam, we're hotel maintenance, bit of a problem with the lighting, nothing to worry about though. Which room are you looking for, madam?'

'Oh.' She hesitated, not too sure. 'Three three five,' she said slowly.

'This is the *second* floor. You need to go up one more floor, madam.'

As Danny came back he got on to the radio and called up the hotel security, just to confirm that a little old American lady was indeed residing in room three three five.

'Any probs?' I said.

'Nah, she's OK, a bit lost, that's all.' Danny sat back down. 'Well, what d'ya think?'

'I like it, if it's legit.'

'Well, like I said, I've had a couple of meets with him after work. We meet in The Churchill just for a drink and to talk over things, nothing too serious. He has to leave early each evening. Always meeting friends about nine at the Palm Beach [a London casino]. He seems to be pukka, all right.' Danny clasped his hands behind his head and leant back on his chair. 'I mean, he dresses and looks the part, appears to always have a wad on him, and he says he has a place just off Belgrave Square.' He said all this with great excitement, as if he'd found the goose with the golden egg.

I'd known Danny for a few years and he was an OK guy, not one to get strung along by the overt wealth one is generally exposed to. He was streetwise in this business, so I went along with his game plan. There was no real reason for me not to. Mr Santos was Danny's contact, and it was Danny who was going to call the shots on this one. It isn't unheard of for 'clients' to befriend one of their bodyguards and take them on their multi-million-pound rollercoaster ride, then retire them with more than a few quid in their pockets. I secretly hoped that Danny had found such a 'client', and good luck to him if he had.

Sometimes you're a Chief in this game, and sometimes you're just an Indian. This didn't bother me, as long as I was picked for this team, which I was sure I would be. Generally, I don't give two hoots what position I'm asked to do. I'm just happy to get the chance to earn a few bob.

'What's the timeframe? When do you think it's gonna come off?'

'That's the good thing; shortly after this job finishes. It'll be good if it happens. We'll all be quids in.' Danny rubbed his hands, because he was the man who had priced the job up, and only he knew what the exact profit margin was going to be. From my past experience on similar jobs, the profit would be that of an average mortgage, which wasn't bad for a few weeks' work.

As an operator, Danny was just as well-informed as I was, as regards putting the right team together. There are certain channels one goes through, which you only get to know about if you have the right 'pedigree', or have spent time on the ground working with these guys. He was good at putting round pegs in round holes, and knew the way of the 'beast' very well.

I've always felt that there are in general two, or possibly three, bodyguard 'circuits' working in London. There is the SAS/SF one; then, ex police and their contacts; and finally, 'others' as I once heard them called. I generally draw my manpower from the first two 'circuits' — that's not to say the third is no good, it's just that I've never really had any dealings with them. As I see it, the third is made up of ex forces people and 'front-of-house managers' — nightclub bouncers.

By the end of the fifth week of this job, I felt that Danny's personality had changed somewhat; he appeared to have taken on the persona of the next 'Bodyguard King' or something. He was still stagging on every day, and every other day meeting with Mr Santos, 'just to round off the sharp bits', as he put it. I, in the meantime, had become Danny's Number Two on the contract and it was my role to identify the guys for the job. Danny would, of course, have the final say on who did what, who went where, and with whom.

The change was that he was becoming very dictatorial, and I think he'd forgotten that he was actually working for me at the time, so preoccupied was he with his forthcoming contract. He was beginning to use the corridor to hold court with various members of the hotel, rather like an office, and on one occasion, unbeknown to me, got a guy to stand in for him for a couple of hours so he could meet up with Mr Santos in the hotel's restaurant for a spot of lunch. I figured that the combination of the corridor job and this Mr Santos business was becoming all too much for him.

I'd certainly spent enough of *my* company's money on phone calls and the like to accommodate Danny and, as far as I could see, not a dollar had yet changed hands. All this running around was done on speculation at my expense. So on the day the corridor job finished and the Sheikh was in the air, confirmed as homeward bound, I suggested to Danny that it was about time he jacked up a meet with Mr Santos — for the both of us, since I was the one who was actually financing his project thus far.

You see, over the previous weeks I'd begun to get a bit concerned that Danny was getting me — and the guys I had 'stood to' for the job — involved with something more than just a bodyguard job somewhere out in the Mediterranean.

So I had to meet this Mr Santos. Danny was OK about that, so we arranged to meet with the Argentinian in the bar of the Four Seasons Hotel, Park Lane. But he didn't show — what a surprise! He phoned Danny while we were waiting for him, making some excuse that he had a problem 'of a personal nature' to take care of. I'm not saying 'I knew all along', but I had had my doubts, even though I had ear-marked some guys for the job, and because of that, I'd told Danny; but he wasn't having any of it. He'd convinced himself of Mr Santos's credibility.

'Have you checked this guy out, Danny?'

'Well, what's there to check out? He is what he is, everyone knows him at the Grosvenor.'

'Come on, let's go over to the Grosvenor and speak with Denzil at security.'

I hailed a cab and five minutes later we were having that conversation.

'Yeah, yeah, of course I know Santos,' Denzil said, rather puzzled.

'Who is he, then?' I asked. Danny just listened. I think perhaps he now knew what was coming next.

'Well, I thought *you* knew him.' Denzil turned to Danny.

'I do, but where do *you* know him from?' Danny was now looking worried.

'From The Knightsbridge Intercon. Santos says you're old mates.'

'Really? That's news to me,' Danny said. 'I only met him on this job.'

'What's he doing over at The Knightsbridge?' I enquired.

'Oh, he's the night concierge there, of course.' Denzil paused. 'Come on, guys, what's the joke?'

'Fucking *great*! So what's he doing over here every day then?' I queried.

Denzil was laughing by now. 'He only comes over here to use the gym, of course. It's a sort of inter-hotel thing!'

'He *what*?' Danny went bright red. 'Twat, son of a *bitch*!'

Deep down I already knew it. My instincts had told that Mr Santos wasn't who he said he was. But, I must admit he'd been a brilliant schemer, especially to dupe Danny. Understandably, Danny wanted to go over to Knightsbridge and bash him up there and then.

'That's why the arsehole had to be somewhere by nine every time we met. Fuckin' casino, my arse. He was going to fuckin' *work*! He was stagging on like you, mate.' Actually, I felt sorry for Danny. Then we both burst out laughing. Denzil hadn't a clue what was going on.

'I'll kill him, the twat, I'm gonna go over there and I'm gonna *kill* him,' Danny said, still laughing uneasily.

'No, you won't, just put it down to experience.'

Because of his job, Mr Santos had been in a position to observe just how these rich businessmen operate. In short, both Danny and I agreed that he'd taken on the personality and idiosyncrasies of one of his hotel's regular guests. After all, how else could he have managed to fool Danny — and to some extent me, even though I'd never met him — so convincingly? But something we both never really worked out was, *why* did he do it? What did he have to gain? He was probably 'losing the plot' a bit — well, more than just a bit — what with all that, 'yes-sir-no-sir-carry-your fucking-bags-sir' night job.

Unfortunately, Danny had also lost the plot. He and I fell out over his share of the phone bill this whole episode had cost me. He reckons he didn't have to pay the 260 quid, and I calculated he did. He still owes me, and he knows that one day he'll have to square me away. And with interest accruing each month, sooner rather than later for his sake.

The point is, then, that you can never be too wary in this game. But having decided that Roberts probably was half-genuine, and having considered the implications of such a job as the one he had outlined, there was something very important I had to do.

4.

CACHE EXTRACTION

DAY TWO, BEFORE FIRST LIGHT
ARMY TRAINING AREA. SEGMENT 4. LONG VALLEY,
ALDERSHOT.

I pulled off the metalled road and on to a dry scar of brown earth and cut the engine and lights straightaway. I looked at my watch. I'd deliberately taken it easy; even so, the journey had taken me less than an hour: central London, M3, Aldershot. I hadn't given much thought to anything else since making the decision to lift my cache after all these years. It was on the walk back from the Roberts meeting that my instincts told me that if this job kicked off big style, then I at least wanted to have a fighting chance, and in order to give myself that chance, I had to have the option of being armed. I knew that the prospects of being paid a huge sum of money to carry out the operation didn't come without risk. Nothing in life ever does.

Looking up at the sky I reckoned I still had about ten minutes before dawn broke. I took off my helmet and refocused my eyes to the new surroundings. The area looked the same as it had done all those years ago, and after the exhaust fumes from the Kawasaki drifted away, it smelt the same too. That freshness of a new day, that earthy smell you only ever get just after a downpour on pine, as the rays of the sun attack the wetness.

That smell, and just being here, instantly brought back nightmare memories of my very first defence exercise as a raw recruit. The whole platoon spent an entire day and night digging a series of interlinking trenches and acting out getting attacked by an enemy, and then being ordered to bug out. It was my first introduction to what a soldier's job actually entailed and was probably, in mental terms, the hardest thing I had to endure during the first six weeks.

But that was chicken feed compared to what I had to go through on a phase called Advanced Wales — a week of defence exercises out in the snowdrifts of the Brecon Beacons, being made to carry out the task of digging in on the aptly named Concrete Hill. It was an impossible task, digging through rock with only picks and trenching tools. We knew it, and the staff knew it, too. Just as the Guards have their drill to instil discipline, the Parachute Regiment has a series of ball-breaking tasks to instil its kind of discipline, and this had been one of them. Memories — bad memories.

I took off the Dayglo yellow waistcoat which had 'CCC Couriers' written on its back in a greasy black, stuffed it and the helmet into the back pannier, then made sure that was locked and that the bike alarm was on. That done, I crossed the metalled road and headed up in the direction of Flagstaff Hill. I was dressed in DPMs, army boots and a woollen Norwegian Commando hat. Along with a bergen, this made me every bit a soldier.

It had been many years since I had trodden this route, and I'd had a vision of change for some reason, I didn't know what exactly, maybe a housing estate or something. As it happened, the only thing that had changed during the years was that the Parachute Regiment Training Depot had moved to the garrison town of Catterick in Yorkshire; in fact I'd heard of a rumour that the entire Parachute Regiment was to be moved up to Crap-Hat-land. I could just imagine how that would really piss off the old sweats of the Regiment. In my experience, nobody in the army likes change, especially if it involves fucking around with a Regiment's place of birth.

Within ten minutes I was at the base of Flagstaff. There was going to be no breaking track and doubling back for me today. My MO (modus operandi) was going to be: in and out and no friggin' around. A part of me wanted to go up it for old times' sake but another part, the sane part, denied myself this indulgence. I had to be as covert as possible. OK, I'd arrived on two wheels and might have been seen, but I doubted it this time of the morning, and after all, it was still relatively dark. Going for a trip down memory lane would be like sticking my neck out big time. I didn't need the extra exposure. I was sure there would still be the early-morning dog-walkers making regular use of the training area.

I could quite easily see the group of oak trees to my right. Good, I was on the right track. I'd lost the map a long time ago, but I'd known there was every chance that that would happen, so my chosen reference points were obvious ones, picked for that very reason.

Five minutes later, I'd positioned myself in the rough spot I thought was the place to start digging. The ground around me was covered in plentiful vegetation, more than I recalled. I had no prismatic compass either, so I had to line myself up with all three reference points as accurately as possible. I double-checked my position.

Again I lined myself up with the domed roof, then looked around until I could eye the rock. Soil erosion over the years had made the rock look a lot bigger than I remembered, but if I looked at its middle I wouldn't be too far out. To my left, I was in sight of the bend in the road. I kicked the dead leaves away to mark that spot.

By now it was light, so I had to work fast. I was aware of a bit of light traffic travelling along the Aldershot to Church Crookham road — soldiers and camp civvies going into work. Once I'd walked the 15 paces back from the oak tree I found I was a couple of metres away from my mark; a shrub had subsequently grown over this new spot, so I ripped it out and started to dig with the aid of a collapsible spade.

The only thing that had altered was that at some point a drainage ditch had been dug around the base of Flagstaff. It was about a metre deep and half that wide. It didn't affect my hole, the now-hardened spoils from the ditch were some two metres away, but it did bring home to me just how careful one has to be in cache selection. There was no geological reason I could see for the workmen not to have dug the ditch straight through my cache. That was a bit of luck.

I worked furiously, shifting mounds of earth, only occasionally stopping for a brief second to listen for human or animal noises, working on the assumption that a dog would probably precede its owner and act as some form of early-warning system. The going was good and it took me no time to dig a hole two metres wide and half a metre deep. For a while I thought that maybe I was right off target — after all, however carefully you plan, it's not easy trying to pinpoint a point on the ground after so many years.

My first indication that I was indeed on target was when I hit the side of the PE box, coming in from the right-hand side. My heart dropped a beat as I knew I'd struck 'gold'; the green plastic weapon sleeve looked as new as it had done when I'd cached it.

There was no way I could tell if the box had been disturbed, but certainly the earth around it didn't look as if it had. I worked fast to pull the PE box from the weapon sleeve. The box looked in surprisingly good nick, but as I pulled it out, it broke apart — rotten — revealing what I knew to be its contents: three Browning semi-automatic pistols, and one Walther PPK, individually wrapped but in one package; another package of a box of 50 rounds for the Browning, and a box of 20 rounds for the Walther; and a third package containing the magazines for all four pistols. I hurriedly stashed them in the bergen.

I made good the site, back-filling earth, and threw the bits of the PE box into the bushes. I then went over to the drainage ditch. It was full of clear water so I cleaned up the best I could, and then made my way back over to the bergen. As I did so, I saw a small lump of earth, a greeny-blue colour. I bent down to pick it up; some form of oxidisation had occurred. I crushed the sod and out popped the old penny — I'd totally forgotten about it! I slipped it into my pocket, since I was going to keep it for good luck.

By the time I'd got back to the bike there was only one other vehicle in the unofficial car park, a white 740 Volvo estate. No sign of anyone around, though. I stripped off my DPMs and changed into clean gear I'd brought in one of the side panniers, put on the Dayglo yellow waistcoat and headed off back up to the West End — just in time to hit the rush hour in full force.

5.

CLOSING THE DEAL

All the time during the ride back to London I kept thinking about what to do with the hardware. I only wanted the Walther, so I had to struggle with my conscience over the Brownings. I knew that a 'clean' weapon would fetch a lot on the black market, and I was carrying about a couple of grands' worth of them. I also knew one or two close colleagues who would take them off me for about the same price.

But quite honestly, it was just a thought. It had never been my intention to make use of these weapons, other than for my own personal protection. Why I'd brought them back in the first place was a mystery to me now. Probably I did it because it was something a lot of young soldiers did after their first war.

By the time I had got to the Hammersmith Flyover, I'd already decided how I was going to dispose of all but one of them. And like hundreds, probably thousands, of soldiers before me, who'd wanted to get shot of their 'spoils of war', I broke the three Brownings down — barrels, top slides, and magazines — drove into the West End and threw them into the deep silt beds of the River Thames, which luckily was at high tide, under Hungerford Bridge at Charing Cross. I remembered what a river-police friend of mine had said: 'If you ever want to get rid of something, chuck it in between Hungerford and Waterloo Bridges at high tide. You'll never find it in a thousand years.'

Back at my office I tried to rest up a bit on my old Chesterfield leather sofa. It looked nice but was really uncomfortable to sit on, let alone sleep on. The office was ideally situated, bang-smack in the middle of Mayfair. It looked like an old private eye's office, something from a film set.

Although it was small, five by five metres, all its walls were covered in Edwardian oak panelling, with a fireplace on one side which hadn't been used, as far as I was aware, for years. Two large windows let in more than enough light. The only thing missing to give it that real 'Mickey Spillane' feel, was the opaque-glass-panelled door with 'Devereux' acid-etched into it. Instead, the door was solid with a double Chubb lock set-up.

It was on the third floor of the building. I hadn't picked it for any particular reason, it just happened to be in the rent bracket I could afford when looking for an office, some years back. It was all I needed to operate from: small, clean, unassuming, and *relatively* cheap to rent.

During the previous evening I'd tried several times to call Vic and the rest of the lads, just to let them know I might be requiring their services in the morning, but couldn't get through to any of them. Stacks of beer and rowdy company, you can hear everyone's mobile but your own. I guessed they'd left The Gloucester and gone on to a club somewhere. John had a few good contacts in the club scene and they'd probably had a great time dancing the night away.

I looked at my watch: eight thirty, still too early to call Vic if he'd been on the piss the night before. I felt like having a kip but I couldn't, my senses wouldn't allow me to rest. I was beginning to feel the first signs of stress brought on by the forthcoming operation. I decided to go for a run.

Before I knew it, I was hoofing it up Curzon Street heading towards Hyde Park. An hour later, after a shower and a quick scrape of the teeth, I made my way around to a little safe café I often used as a second office, just behind Berkeley Square in Lansdowne Row.

Even now it was really still too early to give the guys a call but nonetheless I thought, Sod it, I'll call Vic on the mobile anyway. I let it ring and ring until his answer-phone cut in. I didn't leave a message. I'll try again later, I thought. Ten minutes later my mobile rang. It was Vic.

'Good night, was it, mate?' I said in an insistently chirpy sort of way.

'What the fuck are you callin' me this time of the morning for, you wanker?' He wasn't impressed. 'Fuck off and leave me to die.'

I ignored him. 'Game on, mate. The job's on,' I said, fingers crossed. I was anticipating the day ahead.

'I don't care. You can still fuck off. I'm not playing.'

I still ignored him. 'What the frig happened to you guys last night? I tried calling you —'

'What part of "fuck off" don't you understand?' Vic paused, obviously trying to get his brain into gear. 'Oh bollocks. We got waylaid at one of John's drinking holes, you didn't miss much. Spent a friggin' shedload though.' He sounded knackered but I could tell he was coming around. 'I've got a head on me that'd kill a squadron of SAS.'

'Yeah, sure you have.'

'What's the score then?'

'Can you get down here soon after ten?' I knew they could. They were all sharing an apartment off Eastbourne Terrace, Paddington.

'You're havin' a shaggin' laugh, aren't you?'

'Get down here! I'll have a bit more info when I see you. I reckon we've got a couple of weeks' bodyguard work. I'll fill you in when you get here.' The line went quiet. 'Hey Vic.'

'What?'

'Bring the rest of the guys, will you, suited and booted?'

'I'll try.' He was now fully awake. 'Where's the RV?'

'The Lansdowne safe house. See you at quarter past ten at the latest.' I closed the phone.

Good, I thought, so far very good. I gulped down a large cup of espresso, ordered another and headed back to the office to sort out the proposal.

Commuters were pouring out of Green Park tube and filling up the streets. Lansdowne Row, a cut-through to Curzon Street, is particularly busy that time of morning, what with 'suits' and secretaries walking about carrying polystyrene cups of tea and coffee on their way to work. I remember thinking at the time that working in this part of London was really good for the 'attitude'. I certainly had the feeling it was going to be the start of a good day; even the sun was up and shining.

The guys arrived at about twenty past ten, all looking as rough as a Serb paramilitary policeman in a suit. By half past the hour I'd briefed them up on what I wanted them to do, and by ten forty-five I walked into the Library Bar of the Lanesborough Hotel once more. It was quiet, just two businessmen occupying a small glassed-top table, both on the edge of their seats perusing a thick, plastic-bound document. I found myself a discreet table in an isolated corner at the furthest point from the bar, then I pulled my document out of my briefcase, and flicked through it. A waiter — not the Milo I had met at the first meeting — came over. I ordered a coffee.

I'd only been there five minutes when three stocky men dressed in dark suits strolled in, looking like rugby league players. Only two were carrying briefcases, the other was on hands free. They sat a few metres away — two table spaces.

The waiter returned with my coffee, and then went to receive his three new guests. One was looking at the small menu which every table had. Don't you friggin' dare; don't you *dare*! I thought.

'What can I get you, gentlemen?' the waiter murmured.

'I think we'll have three club sandwiches and three teas, please,' one of them said in a louder manner than necessary. I didn't make eye contact. I'd just spilt my coffee.

'No. I think we'll just have three teas, please. It's a bit early in the morning for lunch,' he corrected.

'As you wish, sir,' the waiter replied in a somewhat monotone manner, then turned and left. Mick looked over and covertly winked at me. Twat, I thought. I could run to buying the guys a cup of tea each, but a club sandwich at 20 quid a throw was a bit out of my league.

I sat in silence waiting for Roberts; the guys meanwhile were just making small-talk. I'd briefed them up to give me a call on the mobile if any of them recognised Roberts: 'Let it ring twice if one of you susses him out. Either way, get up and leave after about ten minutes and I'll meet you in Shepherds Market later,' I'd said.

Roberts was on time. I watched him looking round, then he saw me and came over. I stood up and handed him the proposal. My mobile didn't ring. Soon the guys got up and left, right on cue.

'I see, I see,' Roberts kept saying to himself, not giving anything away to suggest whether my price was favourable or not. I took that to mean that I was spot on with his line of thought — or that I had gone in lower than he had anticipated. That was a surprise, since the sums involved were very large!

I'm not a greedy man but one has to pay for a service. And the service I was providing was the best you could find in London — I was confident of that. The trouble is that if you want the best, then you have to pay for it, just like most things in this life.

The waiter brought over another coffee. After a few minutes Roberts looked up. He was reading through a pair of those half-lens glasses — the type you might expect a nutty professor to wear — and occasionally peering through them up at me. I felt like I was back at school and about to have my essay critiqued by the teacher.

'Good.' There was a moment's silence. 'Good.' He finished without much vocal emotion.

'I've had to price on a day-rate, as you can see, for two weeks minimum, and not the weekly rate you first suggested,' I said.

'Why?'

'Well, I thought it better, given the immediate circumstances. We don't know how long the contract is going to run for. If it runs over two weeks, then it might be prudent to draw up a longer-term contract.' I tried to justify the higher daily rate. It was a lot of money by anyone's standards. Roberts didn't reply but just nodded in agreement.

'This time of year, most of the guys would be working on the big static Arab jobs. You know the Saudis and ...' I carried on.

'Yes, I understand.' He paused. 'When could you start? There's been a change of plan — he's coming earlier than I indicated yesterday; in fact he's due in this afternoon. His flight's due to land at two.'

'This sort of thing happens all the time. I've aimed off for it — no problem,' I replied.

'I've booked him into the Marriott up at Regent's Park. Do you know it?' he carried on.

'Yes, been there a couple of times,' I replied. That was my first white lie. I knew its location, but I hadn't actually been *inside*. This was turning out to be a bit of a fast ball, as if I hadn't already predicted this would happen!

'Assuming the money's in place, I could have four guys on the job within a couple of hours. Two to carry out a recce of the hotel, myself, and one up at the airport.' (Actually, of course, the guys were already on standby, but I wasn't going to tell him that.)

'Good. But the airport isn't necessary, I've already arranged that.'

This threw me off track a bit. This Roberts chap said he wanted the best service, yet our not being at the airport to pick up the Principal would undermine the security operation from the very beginning.

The summer before I'd had a bit of a run–in with a Colonel who runs the security operation for a certain Princess from the Gulf. He too said that there was no need to meet the arriving Princess and her entourage up at the VIP gate at Heathrow. But she went ballistic with him when my team wasn't there — not because of the 'threat', more to do with her kudos as a visiting Princess. Her British BG team not being there to meet her was like a slap in the face to her rank and standing. Her Arab security people were more than adequate to cover the task, but that wasn't the point — she wanted the prestige, and why not? The Colonel was left with large amounts of egg on his face and, consequently, the job didn't kick off in the way it was meant to.

As a result, there were the usual puffed-chest problems during her three-week stay between us and the Colonel. He'd lost a lot of face, and this wasn't conducive to cementing good Anglo/Arab relations. I took it on the nose, kept my gob shut this time and shouldered the blame for his cock-up — well, I had no choice, he blamed me. Nonetheless, my team and I just did the job, and once again took the money. But it had been a needlessly bad experience.

It was vital for everything to kick off on a professional level, and not being up at the airport could leave the team open to all sorts of problems, apart from fairly superficial issues of personal prestige. If the team was not there, it could not, from the out-set, guarantee the Principal's safety. Who could know if someone had been following him? That's not unheard of in this game.

Had that been the case, the anti-surveillance techniques my men could have put in play would have sorted out anybody tailing. But that wouldn't be feasible if the team wasn't going to be represented at the airport. The last thing any of us wanted was for the Principal's place of residence to be compromised even before we'd had a chance to see him. It wasn't a sound foundation to kick off from, I was definitely sure about that.

A part of me wanted to ask Roberts why, and then another part said, Well, sod it. I'll just have to work around it. I knew that the guys wouldn't be happy about the situation, but what could I do? Should I say, 'No, I can't do the job, Mr Roberts, because your understanding of my profession is coming across as totally slack, by not meeting the Principal airport side.' And, 'It puts my men at risk.'? No, of course I shouldn't. He would just have said, 'Well, I'll get someone else to do it, if you have a problem with my arrangements.'

I pressed the issue of the airport a bit more, but Roberts clearly wasn't going to give way. So I thought I'd have a go at another area which I hadn't really explored in any great depth. As the boss of the operation, I felt it was about time I asked, but I waited to pick my moment.

'Well, everything seems to be in order. I'll have the initial funds transferred into your company account within two hours.'

'That's fine. I'll call my bank later on.'

With the nib of his pen, he pointed to my advance payment figure. Ready to leave, he closed the proposal, took a last sip of coffee and stood up. He began to open his briefcase. 'I'll keep this if I may. You have a copy?'

'Sure, of course. Just a small point, Mr Roberts.' I was aware
that he was keen to leave and that I'd stopped him. Perhaps this
wasn't the right time to bring up such a point, after all it was a bit
late in the day for what I was about to ask. 'Can you tell me what
sort of threat there might be against Mr Suhail?'

Roberts looked rather alarmed. 'What do you mean, threat?'

'Well, what I could really do with is some kind of CV for him.'
I tried to play down my question, and instantly thought CV was
probably the wrong word. 'You know the sort of thing, I'm sure,
possible enemies, family problems, you know. Any death threats,
things like that.'

'Death threats?' He looked around cautiously as he said that
and I got the feeling that I'd definitely dropped the big one. 'No, I
don't think so,' he added calmly.

Did he think I was taking the piss? I was only putting to him a
salient point which my team members were definitely going to
ask me about, that's for sure.

'Steve, I understand where you are coming from.'

Of course he did. He'd done his homework and I was probably
not the first person in this business he'd approached. 'The answer
to all those questions is this: I really don't know.' He was lying, for
sure. 'What I *should* say is that, as far as I'm aware, there is nothing
outstanding ... How should I put this? It would be news to me if
there were.' Now, I knew he was playing with a snide deck. 'OK,
that's fine, only —'

'There are, of course, the usual problems which go with
looking after a man with money,' he interjected. 'But it's not for
me to tell you your job, is it?' The 'old-boy' tone was beginning
to come across more pronouncedly.

'No, sure, I understand.' I didn't really, but I had a bloody good
idea about what he was insinuating: This Mr Suhail is no saint.

'I'll call you on your mobile when I've sorted the money, and
then I'll see you and your men in the Marriott, at four.' These
were his parting words.

This time he only left a twenty spot to pay and tip.

I looked at my watch. It was pushing twelve o'clock now.
Again, I decided to take in the ambience of the hotel, just a little
bit longer this time.

I caught the eye of Milo the waiter, he came straight over. 'Another coffee, please, Milo ... Just started, eh?'

'Yes, sir.'

'Put it on the same bill, will you? Oh, and have you got today's paper, *The Times*?'

'I'll bring it over right away, sir.'

Once in a while there's nothing wrong with indulging oneself with a bit of high living. I could really get used to this way of life. A part of me saw me living out of one of these hotels, being pampered and waited on every minute of the day. Then another part said, 'What a total waste of money. Yeah, great, live it up for a week or two, but that's about it.' I knew, in reality, that I'd get really bored in no time.

Vic, rocking back on his chair outside one of those cafés in Shepherds Market, didn't see me approach. I came up behind him and yanked hard down on the back of it.

'Ahh, you *twat!*' he shouted, having a sudden sense-of-humour failure.

'Switch on, pal. Gotta stay alert. Know what I mean.'

'You prick, Devs.' He stood up to straighten his tie. There was a couple of American tourists sitting across the way who gave a short burst of laughter, but they turned away shyly once they saw Vic wasn't amused.

'Where's Mike and John?'

'Gone to get a paper. Be back in a minute.' Vic shrugged. 'What's the Bobby Moore then, are we on or what?'

'Don't try to blend in with us Londoners. You're Welsh, remember,' I remarked. Vic said nothing, just rolled his eyes. 'Yeah, we're hot to trot for sure,' I confirmed. 'How about we're on wages now?'

'So he's changed his plans, coming in early, is it?'

'Got it in one.'

When the others came back I quickly got down to the nitty-gritty of a briefing, and told them how I saw the whole operation panning out. There wasn't really a lot I could tell them beyond what I'd said a few hours earlier.

They didn't have a problem with the fast ball, but they did ask the obvious question: 'Do we know what this guy's all about?' I had to tell them that I didn't. We would have to take every day as it came. As far as ascertaining what Mr Suhail was all about, we had to do that 'on the hoof'. It wasn't the best start to a bodyguard operation, but, at the end of the day, all of us knew we had two choices. We could jack it in right away, or we could go through with it. I put it to the floor. I'm as democratic as the next man. But I knew what their answer would be anyway — an unequivocal 'Yes, let's go for it.'

There was that uncertain feeling all of us had about the precise nature of this job, but none of us wanted to end up stagging on on the Cornwall Terrace job — that option, the most boring aspect of BG work, was thrown right out of the window.

We had one more round of coffees and I wound up the informal brief. I told the guys to RV at the Marriott asap. There wasn't a lot any of us knew about the place. I'd never worked in it before, and it wasn't one of the usual hotels worked on the 'circuit'. I had to carry out a recce of the place, that was a must, so Vic and I decided to make the necessary introductions to the management. I sent Mike and John up to a communications dealer in north London to pick up the team radios and covert earpieces and mikes which I'd put on stand-by earlier.

The first impression of the Marriott was that it looked a smart hotel. Although in no way could you compare it with something like the Dorchester, it was still a top-of-the-range hotel, a four starrer, pretty much full of Americans as far as I could see. I made myself known to the manager and his in-house security team. They were really forthcoming in accommodating us — it wasn't every day they had a bodyguard team working there.

Some hotels don't really like the idea of suited lumps hanging around the corridors and foyers of their hotel; it can sometimes put the other guests on edge. I could certainly see their point of view, and was always aware of that when operating on new ground. However, one very famous West End hotel — which I'd better not name — actually tolerates BGs rather well, probably because the revenue received from the stay of only two Royal families from the Gulf region in effect supports its entire operation for the year.

Frequently the client supplies an operations room on the same floor as his. But if he hasn't, and if I'm working on a big team —

and by big I mean over eight BGs — then I try to get the guys to hang about outside the hotel, in a nearby café or sitting in their vehicles. On more than one occasion I've entered a hotel and have seen other BG teams in operation. Slack drills, their radios blaring out transmissions, making themselves look and sound important. Hanging around the reception, chatting up the staff with a 'Hey, look at me, everybody, I'm a real-life bodyguard' attitude. Seriously, they're a total embarrassment to the profession.

Unfortunately, this small band of Chinese knifefighters sporting their metal-tipped shoes is growing in strength. This is probably to do with unqualified people cashing in on an ever-expanding market, by running these weekend or six-day BG (or, as some people call it, Close Protection) courses. But, as we all know, you can't teach very much about any subject in a week — and a little knowledge is really dangerous.

The trouble with this job is that there are far too many unskilled people doing it. Too many ego-seekers who think that the best way of operating is to cut about the place in the highest-profile manner possible, looking menacing.

Yes, it does happen, and it happens all too frequently. These are the blokes who give this industry a bad name. The ones who turn up on jobs wearing a Batman Utility Belt — basically a belt full of useless showy ancillaries: a hip-hung mobile phone; a torch; a thing for getting stones out of horses' hoofs; all neatly wrapped in their own individual leather or Velcro pouches, like someone out of the Village People might wear. Looking more like hotel maintenance in suits as opposed to professional bodyguards. The funny thing is, they know who they are — don't do it, it ain't big and it ain't clever. It's just very sad.

All too often many budding bodyguards, with hardly an ounce of experience, find themselves being a member of a bodyguard team. Don't ask me how this happens, because I find it hard to comprehend at the best of times. 'How can some guy without any obvious experience get on a bodyguard team?' It's a question I always ask myself as I bump into other bodyguard teams working in and around the London area. Some of these operators are barely just out of school, or so it seems. What do they know about the game; who the hell employs them and how did they get the contract?

I hope I'm not coming across as revelling in my own self-gratification, but in my opinion there's no substitute for a military, police or a security background for this job. That'll have conditioned you to stagging on for weeks on end, in extreme situations and often in real-life environments such as live theatres of war.

During my time in the business, I've worked with an array of men from various backgrounds, all related of course in security in one way or another. Army, navy, police, even the occasional front-of-house manager, all very switched-on guys who are street-wise, and know the score.

Indeed, I will say that when it is up to me to select a particular team, I frequently prefer to choose guys other than from my SAS background. That's not to say I don't have confidence in SAS guys, of course I do, it would be ridiculous to think otherwise; but it's a lot to do with the old saying: 'Horses for courses.' Because you have spent time in the SAS, it doesn't automatically mean that you're an all-singing, all-dancing bodyguard.

When I can, I generally use a mixed bunch to make up teams — this formula works and works well. On an admin point, it tends to cut down the inter-Regiment slagging on the job, because a lot of the banter goes straight over the head of the non-military guys, thus avoiding offence. If you could imagine the amount of bitchiness — yes, *bitchiness* — that can go on amongst the guys, then you would understand and agree with my formula.

Getting back to the layout of the hotel, it was quite posh; nothing like as elegant as the Lanesborough, but it was all right for me. It was set back from the heavy traffic which constantly engulfs the Regent's Park area. In a typical American style there was a large driveway, in-and-out type, covered in thousands of those brindle-coloured block pavers and surrounded by a mixture of conifers and tropical-type shrubs and plants set in their own raised beds.

The entrance was serviced by a large glazed revolving door with a separate door either side, and the foyer beyond was filled with potted plants standing in large terracotta urns, while mirrors on every wall gave a feeling of openness. Several low two-seater modern-style leather sofas were scattered around this area. It struck me that the hotel catered more for the tourist than the business trade, which probably liked to be more centrally located in and around the Mayfair area.

The place was busy with staff and guests, all going about their business. The reception, a large light-oak oval bar, was on the left; behind it were numerous pigeon-holes for guests' mail and messages. Immediately across the marbled foyer floor stood a bank of three stainless-steel fronted lifts.

The majority of the guests — mostly Americans, but there were a few Japanese too — were sporting casual dress. An odd combination I thought, since being ex military I immediately thought of Pearl Harbour — not in any sinister way, I just made the connection. (Just as I do when I hear an Irish, Argentine or Iraqi accent.) Apart from the staff, it seemed my team were the only people in suits.

Once our courtesy tour of the entire hotel had been conducted by the manager and the in-house security man, we were left to get on with setting up our security procedures. We were really quite lucky, the hotel had been very busy that morning — the staff had just had a large party of guests check out, and were not expecting anyone else to book in until the following evening. Then, the hotel would be back up to running at almost 95 per cent capacity. This gave us a lot of scope to select the ideal rooms for the Principal, his family, and us. As I'd thought, most of the pre-bookings were tourists, so the hotel had very few rooms held specifically on a client-request basis.

During my tour of the hotel I was purposely looking for one two-bedroom suite with a lounge, and two twins next to each other. Ideally, I was looking for them to be away from the floor's main corridor, and any other rooms as far as possible. I found all this on the fourth floor.

The corridor set-up was perfect, three rooms with their own fire escape, at the end of the corridor, but not too far away from the lifts. Between our rooms and the next one was a large open area with a couple of comfy sofas where people could sit, relax, read a newspaper and perhaps smoke a cigarette. I was happy with what I'd found. This area would act as a buffer zone, and there would be no reason why someone should enter our particular part of the corridor.

My next problem was, did the change in rooms pre-booked by

Roberts affect the client's budget? I called Roberts on his mobile — by then he was *en route* to the hotel with Mr Suhail and family.

'No, it's no problem. Go ahead and make the change.'

'Everything is fine this end too — no problems,' I confirmed.

'Will be with you in just over an hour.' Then the phone went dead. Their ETA would be around three, which was fine.

There was still much setting up to do. I gave John the job of sorting out the radios, getting all the spare batteries on charge and going around the whole of the hotel carrying out a comms check. Basically, he was making sure that if there were any dead spots (an area where the radios would not receive or transmit), then we would know where they were.

I asked Mike to carry out a spot of 'hearts and minds' on the in-house managers and our floor staff. Nothing too heavy, just a quick introduction. I also asked him to check out room service routine, laundry and things like that, and told him to get the numbers of all managers' telephone extensions and mobiles. Vic went with me, to really get to know the lay-out of the building. The in-house security had given us a detailed floor plan of the entire hotel, so we set off on our exploration. Once that was done, I took Mike and John on their familiarisation tour.

All in all, this took us about an hour, during which time my bank had phoned to say the initial payment had been made. We all RV'ed back in the Principal's room, and did a quick map study of the local outside area. This wasn't a great problem because all of us knew the West End really well; what's more, we were at the northern part of Regent's Park, a park all of us had run around whilst out training on previous jobs.

I wasn't too concerned about sanitising the area of the rooms until I knew for sure the Principal was actually coming to this hotel. It has been known in the past for a Principal to pull up outside a hotel, take one look at it and say 'No, take me elsewhere.' I was ready for that one, having made a couple of calls to similar hotels in the area to confirm availability. It didn't look too good, however. London hotels, even this early in the year, were running at over 90 per cent booked.

Sorting out the telephone numbers was another major consideration. Since the four of us knew the score on local ERVs pretty well, there was no need for us to cross-check hospital and police locations. I knew the Park Police, and Mike knew the guys at the local nick. We planned to touch base with them as soon as the job allowed — maybe meet them for a beer somewhere, to do some more hearts and minds.

This was all par for the course. You never know when you're going to need 'the Cavalry'; furthermore, you never know when you're going to need a free 'get-out-of-jail' card. I took nothing for granted. All I knew was that I had recently been paid a very large sum of money to look after a man, his wife and child whom I've never met and about whom I knew nothing. Still, I was duty-bound to give him the best security cover I and my team could — that's always my professional attitude. Until he lets us down.

At this point, some readers might just think, What's this Devereux bloke on about? Isn't he being paid to do a job? Just get on with it. Fair enough, but the sum of money involved was, how shall I say this, a bit on the large side. Sure, I wasn't complaining, but what price is your price?

This isn't Hollywood. It's not sitting in front of the fire with your feet up, a can of beer in one hand, and bag of cheesy Wotsits in the other, reviewing the tactical pros and cons of Kevin Costner in *The Bodyguard*. No, I operate in the real world and I value my life and try and cover all the options possible.

What was preying heavily on my mind at this moment was this: in most things in my life, I've always paid before I've played. Now, as far as we were concerned, Mr Suhail had paid, and was about to play — *but*, in someone else's view, had he recently played without having paid? This was the big question. After all, why was he employing one of the best bodyguard teams available? To look good and impressive when attending his meetings? I think not. He was doing it because he had a problem — a big problem.

PART THREE

6.

CLIENT CONTACT

DAY TWO, AFTERNOON

Mike was loitering outside the hotel, chewing the fat with the concierge in anticipation of the party's arrival. He was acting as the team's early warning — a 'trigger'.

My phone rang — Mike. 'Looks like our people. They've just pulled up in a black Merc complete with chauffeur. Our man Roberts is with them.'

I told him thanks and reiterated to him to 'blend in' and not make an approach. Basically, his job now was to act as a covert eye, to see if Roberts and co. were being followed — looking out for any suspicious vehicles, cars, motor bikes, that sort of thing, which might be carrying a 'tail'. I couldn't ignore the possibility that if Mr Suhail was really a man with a problem, the 'chasers' might already have had advance warning of his departure and eventual arrival at the Marriott, and so already have got this place under *their* surveillance. This, of course, was one of my main concerns when first carrying out my recce of the hotel. Who knows, Roberts might even have been a spy for the other side.

Since the pick-up and choice of venue had been out of my direct control, my team was basically going into what we would call, in the SAS, a 'hot' DZ. But once I'd had a chance to feel Suhail out, then I would push for a move to another, more secure hotel, one which had been totally recce'd and sanitised by my team. This had to happen before he and his family had time to 'bed in' in this one. I would have to pick my moment of switching locations very tactically indeed.

It was a little after four in the afternoon when Mr Roberts walked into the lobby of the Marriott. With him was a rather short, dumpy-looking man in his late 50s, with a just about visually tolerable pockmarked skin. He sported a rather larger-than-normal black mole on his left cheek. Another visual feature. Other than that, he looked the typical stereotyped foreign businessman from somewhere in Central Asia. Not, I must say, oozing an abundance of wealth — remembering first impressions and all that — and complete with a dark but shiny-looking three-piecer, tailored to his unusual body shape — small but with a vast girth. On his feet were tatty-looking black brogues.

Behind him came an attractive-looking woman, also of Asian appearance, late 30s, wearing a two-piece grey designer tracksuit and trainers. No jewellery apart from a pair of tiny gold studs and a wedding ring. The daughter was the most smartly turned out: a red and white floral dress, white ankle socks and a pair of black patent size twos.

'Come on, we're on,' I said. I had to kick-start Vic into gear.

He gave a sigh. He'd been sitting in a comfy chair and had his head well engrossed in a glossy magazine he'd bummed off the girl on reception. Of course, Vic had seen the party walk in at the same time as I had. He'd caught their reflection in a mirror he kept looking into, in a perfectly natural manner.

All four of us had been trained in the 'blending-in' techniques that are taught by the SAS, and by other lesser-known government agencies that run surveillance-training courses as part of their activities. But there's nothing like on-the-job experience, and lots of it. It's an art, a state of mind, apart from being a skill. In my opinion, you either have it or you don't.

I've known guys who are great bodyguards, but put them in a situation like this, and they would unfortunately compromise a job by their unnatural reactions. Giving away small body signs to every bit of movement around is, of course, a no-no. Some guys get so wound up waiting for that bag-carrying bomber to come through the door that they wouldn't show any of the quite natural reactions one would expect to, for example, 'the innocent tray-carrying waiter slipping up on the shiny floor' routine — a dead giveaway.

Vic prised his 240-pounds-plus frame out of his chair. He didn't look out of place though; after all, just because you're a 'big mother', it doesn't mean that you're a thug in a suit. There are big-bodied businessmen all over the place, and some, I'm sure, couldn't throw a punch to save their life. Vic can look quite threatening, but today he blended in with the rest of us.

He and I talked quite normally as we made our way towards the entrance. I caught a glimpse of Mike through the glass entrance doors chatting on his mobile. He was probably briefing up John, who was secured in the Principal's room.

I saw the black Mercedes with its boot still open. Mike would get a good description of the chauffeur and the Merc's registration number to 'P' check (vehicle registration number check) later, through his contact. I saw the baggage for the party being wheeled in on two of those posh-looking brass trolley affairs, balancing on four swivel wheels, with space for luggage below, and a suit rail on top. It was piled high with their kit, all the way up to the suit rail.

I registered the expensive-looking leather-bound designer cases and carriers. That was a good pointer in this environment for proof of their owner's wealth, one I hadn't seen in the party's order of dress. Meanwhile, Roberts and co. had stopped just short of the reception.

Vic and I stood off to a flank about four metres away. The reception wasn't really busy now, just a few guests mingling about. A big bouquet of fresh flowers, which had just been placed in a terracotta pot, stood proud in the centre of the foyer. I caught a whiff of their aroma and at the same time made eye contact with Roberts. He waved me over.

As is usual in these cases, there was no formal introduction.

It was obvious Roberts had briefed Suhail and co. I just wished he hadn't waved me over in the manner in which he did — a bit like some Arabs do when addressing their servants: '*Impshee. Impshee.*' — 'Come Come!' Anyone observing his entrance would now have 'clocked' me and Vic. Hell, I couldn't have it all my own way, could I?

'Hello, Steve,' Roberts said quite casually. He turned to his client. 'This is Steve, he's arranged the entire programme for your stay.' Oh, had I? I digested the presumptive tone of his remark. I'd done nothing of the sort.

'He'll show you to your suite,' Roberts finished off. The two men shook hands. Roberts said goodbye to Mrs Suhail and the daughter and went towards reception, presumably to book the party in, with what looked like three passports in one hand. I couldn't quite make out the colour of them, blue I think. His other hand was gripped tightly around a heavy-looking briefcase.

It was one of those neat, aluminium ribbed types; inside it had a removable but lockable Gucci-type file compartment, a bit of an extra. Really expensive, but also really out of character with what one might expect a mature 'billionaire' to use — far too trendy. It was a piece of kit a 20-something advertising executive would be seen carrying, as he or she cut about Soho. I'll have to have words with him about ditching the case and getting something more covert, I mused. If he was carrying large sums of cash around in it, as I assumed, it was an obvious 'attractive item' to a would-be bag-snatcher. Why attract attention? I made a mental note for one of us to buy a less overt one next time we drove down Oxford Street.

'Hello, sir.' Suhail looked at me and bowed his head. Not in a Japanese sort of way, but in a way that suggested a condescending 'Lead on Macduff' attitude. At the same time I looked across at Mrs Suhail and their daughter. The smell of rich, heavy, musky perfume surrounded them both as they wafted my way.

They greeted me with a single, subservient-sounding 'Hello'. I got the feeling they had succumbed reluctantly to Mr Suhail's plans and were here out of loyalty rather than anything else — he definitely wore the trousers in the outfit.

You might think it wrong of me to presume so much about these people so rapidly. But it was only natural for me to start building up a mental picture of the Principal from the first second we met. The long and short of it was that my team and I were walking into this little operation in total darkness, and I was very much on my guard.

But you can do that too much, so mentally I had to keep it in check. I've known of some inexperienced guys on bodyguarding ops (operations) who would fill their heads up with all sorts of crap about what if, and why, and when. So much so that they would build themselves up into a right old panic, and end up walking around in a state of paranoia. Thus they became a complete waste of space and totally surplus to the task at hand — a liability, in other words.

In my case, my instincts were naturally working overtime. They always do, it's part of my make-up, walking around in a certain level of stress, it's what makes me tick.

After eyeballing the party of three and hearing Roberts's quick conversation, Vic moved to secure one of the lifts, and the Principal and party followed. It was a casual walk. I felt we'd blended the 'meet' into the background of the foyer's activities really well. No call on my mobile meant no problems from Mike or John. Jesus, five seconds into the contract and I was beginning to get the trickle of sweat and fear I usually got when I was just about to throw myself out of a very serviceable aircraft at 25,000 feet! But I felt alive. Living this life was a drug, a self-induced one, and my instincts were reacting to it as they had done many times before. I laughed to myself, once again thinking, So far, so good.

Once in the lift, it became quiet. We were shut off from the noise of the foyer. No one spoke. This wasn't so unusual: 'Only speak when you're spoken to' is the name of the game. I always brief the guys up on the 'no-talking' rule. In my experience, if the Principal wants to say anything, he or she will; if they do, then the score is to keep the conversation short — one sentence and leave it at that. I would say, remember you have a job to do, and it doesn't include making small-talk with the Principal in some vain attempt to get on their good side; brown nosing — I think that's what they call it.

More often than not the guys I've worked with have been

pretty good on the no-talking rule and on keeping a low profile. There is, of course, always the Principal who wants to have a chat, so you have to work around that without coming across as discourteous. After all, conversation like that is harmless — as long as it's very short.

On one particular job I was working for a businessman from Pakistan. It was a small short-term contract, two weeks. And it was a small team, only three of us: one guy, Malcolm T, acted as the bodyguard driver, whilst Johnny P and I carried out the bodyguarding. Easy job — pick-up West End mid-morning, drop off in the City; pick up City, late afternoon, drop off West End. One or two daily meetings, sometimes held at a bank, other times in a restaurant — dead easy.

It was the client's wish that I and the other bodyguard followed in a back-up car — he probably didn't want us to hear what he was up to. I guess he thought that the driver didn't matter. That was OK by me, he was paying the wages, but I did, however, gently brief him up that it might be a good idea if I rode with him; at least one bodyguard should ride with the Principal, that's the sensible tactic to employ. But no, he wasn't having any of it. I felt confident that I'd covered myself in a professional manner by tentatively pointing out the obvious possibilities of not being able to react as quickly to an 'incident' whilst in another vehicle. Still, he was happy with that, and like I said, he was the boss, so I wasn't about to stand up and argue the toss.

The job ran like clockwork, and we had no incidents, well, none to talk about. The only thing was, because I had delegated Malcolm (a newcomer to me, but one who had come highly recommended from a good mate) as the driver, since he'd said he knew London very well, Malcolm alone had the 'ears' of the Principal for a lot of the operation. He knew most of what was going on from day to day by overhearing many of the Principal's phone conversations. Now, this Principal was always on the mobile, in fact he had two of them on the go, regularly ringing simultaneously. (I wouldn't have liked to have paid his monthly bill, that was for sure!)

Now, because of Malcolm's position, so close to the Principal and all that, it appeared that he had struck up a sort of working friendship with him, to the point where, after work every day, Malcolm would give us a de-brief on the 'life and times' of my Principal — as he saw it. By the middle of the second week, Johnny and I were under the impression that Malcolm was going to join my Principal's worldwide business operation to act as his sort of bag-carrier, or something like that.

'Well, lads, I'm really getting on well with the boss,' Malcolm had said confidently. 'It's looking like he wants me to drive him around Europe when he finishes his business here.'

I think I said something like, 'Oh, nice one, Malcolm, any room for me and Johnny?'

'Naw, I thing he uses bodyguards "in country". ' Meaning that, every country he visited, he employed local bodyguards. This is quite common in countries not using English as their first language.

'Oh well, just a thought. When are you off?' I tried not to sound too sarcastic. I've seen so many blokes, thinking they are the new 'kiddy' on the block, come a cropper by trying to circumvent the pecking order of the day.

Some jobs have a habit of turning a once really good soldier and bloke into a complete dick. Maybe it's because most of us bodyguards come from less-than-wealthy backgrounds, and when we see the pound signs as we encounter someone who has a lifestyle fit for a king and the dosh to go with it, and who talks to 'us' in a very genial and friendly sort of way, then we lose it. We think we are special because this Principal likes us. Common sense just flies out of the window. I've seen it many a time, guys falling for the old trick of being promised the world by some Principal they have no idea about, because they're dazzled by the sweet talk and pound signs.

There's nothing wrong with trying to better oneself, but *not* with my clients. The point is that an individual should only network with a Principal if it's going to benefit the team as a whole. Work on the bodyguard circuit is, in general, short-term, and the majority of the work comes about through referrals. Referrals from team members on your last job. As I've said, one day you're a Chief, and the next you're an Indian.

Unfortunately, Malcolm was seriously displaying the 'fuck you lot, I'm off on a cushy little number with a rich dude' load of bollocks. I knew little about him apart from he was an ex Royal Marine, and had a diving certificate for every day of the week; still, he appeared to carry out the physical side of his job with no great problems.

'You know, he owns a shit-load of land in Pakistan and an *island* in the Indian Ocean! I told him that I was an ex Booty and that diving was my skill.' That was how Malcolm had sounded off.

Johnny and I were not so much getting bored by Malcolm's apparent misinterpretation of the old 'Buddy Buddy' system (a procedure all service personnel are trained in — basically, look after your mates), as by his mental approach to this job. His selfish line of thought was an eye-opener to me. Didn't he realise that he was fucking with my client? And after all, I *did* give him a job.

But no, he was on a high. He would carry on: 'Yeah, he says he has a couple of boats that will need a security survey on them, and so have his friends. He says the island's a great place, he says it's idyllic. Dolphins and everything.'

Malcolm had fallen into the old BG pit-of-vipers school of thought: *Never* overestimate your own individual importance on any job. You are there to do your job, a *team* job, and not to network for your own ends, to the detriment of that team.

By the end of the contract Johnny and I just did our job. We had none of Malcolm's aspirations of cutting about internationally with a Principal that was apparently promising him the world. Malcolm hadn't offered to invite either me or Johnny on board, but that wasn't my gripe. We'd both been around too long not to get worked up, or to do flying cock-stands about what some Principals might say to their security people about future 'golden opportunities'. I just do my job and take the money.

Anyway, the final day saw us dropping the Principal off at Heathrow Airport. I told Malcolm to wait in his Mercedes outside the terminal, whilst Johnny and I escorted him inside. Malcolm wasn't too pleased with this arrangement. I got the feeling that he was just itching to shake hands, exchange goodbyes and all that old bollocks, and to see his new boss off in the 'proper' fashion. But it didn't happen. When the Principal got out of the Mercedes, he said nothing at all; he didn't even give a parting glance to Driver Malcolm. Just as I'd thought.

Malcolm was also pissed off because I'd told him to wait at the drop-off point. He was bound to keep getting moved on by the airport police. It's a right pain in the arse, having to drive around the block every five minutes, but I had no qualms about Malcolm's standing. He was the driver on this job, and as he knew all too well, the driver never leaves his vehicle.

Once inside the airport, my job was to run around sorting out the Principal's paperwork, do a bit of hearts and minds with the duty police sergeant, and look up my old mate DI Doc Staples, who was in charge of Special Projects Heathrow.

I'd met Doc a few years back and had stayed in touch ever since. He'd been working for the drugs squad out of the West End when I first ran into him. I was taking a beer along with Sammy, a girlfriend of mine at the time, in The Café Royal, Regent Street. It was the usual score, I was trying to impress the arse off her, when I saw this face I hadn't seen for over ten years. It was Topper Tomlinson, an old mate from 2 Para. The last time I'd seen Topper was a couple of hours before he got hit by a burst of 7.62 which ripped through his body during the battle for Goose Green. I couldn't miss him. Who could? — those ears! They stuck out like the bomb-bay doors on a Stealth Bomber.

He was sitting at a table with another guy reading through a document. They looked like normal businessmen, haggling the finer points of a contract over a bottle of wine. I told Sammy I thought I'd recognised an old friend, so we went over. The other guy looked up at me as I made my approach.

'Hey, it's Topper, yeah!'

He looked around in total surprise at the mention of that name. There was a couple of seconds' silence whilst two old friends weighed each other up.

'Fuck me, if it ain't old Devs!' A bit thin on top — but he recognised me.

He had joined the police after leaving the Paras and was now on a surveillance with his boss Doc Staples — the other guy at the table. To any onlooker, the introduction looked as natural as it actually was, a chance encounter. I didn't know that they were actually on the job, following a top London smack-head. Topper said, 'The target's just left for a piss and is probably sticking it up his nose in the gents as we speak.' They were keeping an eye on a table of young champagne-suppers who were acting a bit louder than the norm, as you might expect for that time of evening. 'They're big fuck-off dealers,' Doc said.

Anyway, back to the job under discussion. I had a last-minute shopping list from the Principal. Firstly, I had to square away his reservation, First Class (naturally), whilst Johnny sat in silence with the Principal. When it came to check-in time, the Principal said his 'thank yous' and added that he looked forward to seeing us on his next trip. Then he handed me three envelopes from the inside of his suit jacket. One for me, one for Johnny and one for Malcolm.

We were off-duty as soon as we saw the back of our Principal's head disappear through passport control. I had mentioned to a couple of Doc's men to keep an eye on my Principal, it was a bit of good PR, both for me and the police. It's always good to let the Principal know you have good contacts in the Establishment, it's a sort of 'Brownie-point' scoring thing.

Meanwhile, Malcolm was parked back in the same spot as the drop-off. We'd been gone less than an hour. Both Johnny and I got in the back of the Mercedes for a laugh — Malcolm was to be our chauffeur for the trip back into the West End. He didn't like it, and sounded pissed off that the Principal hadn't said a proper goodbye to him.

Speeding off down the M4, I cheered Malcolm up and handed him his envelope. There was a 50-pound note in his, which was better than a poke in the eye with a sharp stick. But in mine and Johnny's were six crisp nifties apiece. Malcolm was well pissed off. 'Why have I only got a fuckin' 50, and you pair of twats have 300?' he demanded. He was insulted — *that* was pretty clear.

'Well, mate, you're only the driver; *we're* the bodyguards, you see,' I said. And Johnny threw in, just to add insult to injury: 'And, because you're goin' swimming with dolphins, too — aren't you, bollocks?'

The point of the story is that I don't know why some Principals do this sort of thing, but they just do. They say things, especially to the drivers, that get the drivers' tastebuds going. Whether it's out of boredom or what, I don't know. Maybe it goes back to a few hundred years ago when the landed gentry had the serfs doing all sorts of insane things for money — gambling on their workers crossing an icy lake and paying the winner a farthing just for a bit of light entertainment, and laughing at the rest who had fallen through the ice, for example.

That's why the only time I ever get close to a Principal is when my job tells me to — when the shit hits the fan. The moral of the story? Keep your big fat gob shut, and your business cards in your pocket. Better still, don't tempt fate and leave the cards at home.

7.

LOCATING THE ENEMY

Had we stopped? The lift felt like it hadn't moved. Only the green illuminated figure of the number 4 indicated we had moved floors. There was just a muted hum as the lift-motor gears changed upwards and then changed downwards, controlling the speed of the ascent. A slight jolt told us we had reached our destination — we'd come to a halt. The lift was filled with the opulent smell of perfume as we all stood to rigid attention, waiting for the doors to open.

I was standing at the back of the lift, Vic was towering by its doors, his head almost level with the top of them. He would be the first out, ready to secure the corridor. On my left was Mr Suhail staring straight ahead. I glimpsed his reflection in the lift's mirrored walls. He looked uninterested in anything. His wife and child also stood in total silence. I could see that Mrs Suhail had a half-decent body beneath that baggy track suit. But though I sensed she knew I was looking her up and down, I didn't give a reaction. I just stood there, expressionless. Looking down at the daughter suddenly reminded me of another incident involving a BG and his Principal.

I knew of one BG — actually he was a bit of twat — who would not leave the hotel this particular job was running out of, until he'd said good night to his Principal, an eight-year-old Sheikh. I could hardly believe it. Having spent the best part of 12 hours running around half-a-dozen toy shops and parks holding and eating copious amounts of ice creams, the last thing on my mind would have been hanging about the place just to say good night to a kid who probably didn't give a shit anyway. I think I'd have had enough of him by then. Grabbing a couple of beers before I recharged my batteries ready for the next stag would have been number one on my list of priorities.

The end came for this joker when I heard that he'd waited for about an hour after his time. Ten minutes was about the cut-off time I'd have given him.

'Sheikh Khalid, Sheikh Khalid, good night, Sheikh Khalid,' he said as the Sheikh's nanny brought him out in the corridor. The Sheikh just ran past him without even an acknowledgement. He was off and running through the door of his older brother's room. He obviously didn't give a flying fig about anything — and why should he? He was only a kid.

'Why do you hang about waiting to see the Sheikh? You don't get any Brownie points on this job, or overtime,' I said. He got my sarcastic tone and turned away, embarrassed. The rest of the team knew what his game was.

'Listen, we *all* know what you're up to. You're just a brown-nosing twat who's making a complete ass of himself. He's a kid, for Christ's sake. He don't give a shite about you. Can't you see that?' I said.

He went redder. He knew he'd fucked up. His scheme was to try and get close enough to the Sheikh to bond with him, perhaps in some vain attempt to secure a job for life. What a complete prick! Needless to say, he was gone the next day and I got someone more reliable to hold the ice creams and push the swing.

As the lift doors slid open they revealed a long low-level corridor, lit by a series of evenly spaced low-voltage down lights and covered in a top-quality navy-blue-and-gold, pattern-edged carpet. Vic took a couple of steps forward and secured this part of the corridor. 'Clear,' he said, just audible enough for me to hear but not so commanding as to arouse our party. He moved forward with the rest of us in tow.

There were no other guests or staff around, only John at the far end of the corridor. I could see he had the swipe card ready for Suhail and family to make a swift entry into their suite. A few small glass-framed prints of 'Old London' hung from the pastel-coloured walls, but apart from that there were no other fixtures. The doors to each room were panelled and surrounded in light oak. The door furniture was a lustreless silver colour. Each had a spy hole, a bell to the left and the box of electronic tricks to work the swipe-card system. Very clinical but obviously functional.

We reached the suite; I made eye contact with John.

There was no need to exchange verbal niceties; we knew our jobs and exchanging pleasantries wasn't part of it. He already had the door open, so we filed into the room like a squad of Guardsmen doing a left-wheel.

The view from the suite looked across and down the main northern route into London — not the nicest of views. The room was done out in the same modern style as the corridor, but this time a lighter-coloured carpet covered the floor. Two small light-oak sidetables with brass lamps and green shades stood either side of a low-level leather sofa, similar to those downstairs in the foyer.

I'd arranged through the floor manager for flowers to be placed in the main room of the suite. They sat behind a large gilt-framed mirror on top of a low refectory-style table. They appeared to have gone down well because Mrs Principal commented on how nice they looked and smelt. As well they should, since they'd cost £200.

Trying to open even a short conversation with Mr Suhail to feel him out proved a bit difficult. There seemed to be a hell of a lot of tension, family tension, buzzing about the place. The type that stems from just after, or just *before,* a row breaks out. I'd had next to no conversation with Mr Suhail; indeed, at first it appeared that he didn't want to discuss *anything.* Maybe it was jet lag, maybe it was the pending row, I didn't quite know. But I had to discuss the most basic of security measures. My main concern was that since the room had been kept sanitised by John's presence, I didn't want anything arriving in the suite — or our rooms for that matter — *especially* the luggage, without one of the team giving it the once-over, a quick sweep with the box of tricks, one of a couple of bits of kit I'd brought along with me — a handheld explosive detector, a device aptly named the BL-X6, for reasons I'll explain later.

It's a neat piece of kit; when I say neat, I mean it was small (about just under half a metre in length), light, and did the business. Forty centimetres in circumference, battery-powered and encased in black plastic, it could be easily concealed on the body by the operator without causing too much discomfort.

Its manufacturers had designed it with two aims in mind. Obviously, one, to do the job of sniffing out explosives; and two, to be used quickly and effectively by someone who might be more challenged in the brain department than the rest of us.

It had two dials. One was the on/off volume knob, the other was for tuning. When switched on, it would emit a high-pitched squeal.

In order to tune the device in, you had to hold it up in the air, and away from the person, package or object you wanted to check out — something to do with static electricity — and turn the tuning dial down until the high-pitched sound became almost silent. Then you'd turn it up a bit until the constant noise became a series of clicks; optimum tuning was about two clicks a second. The sound and rate of 'clicks' to achieve wasn't dissimilar to that of a Geiger-counter — the device used to suss out radioactive material.

Once the piece of kit was tuned in, then all the operator had to do was, without touching the object, pass ('sweep' is the technical term) it over the object he wanted to check out. For the untechnical amongst us, the detector had a snout at one end, shaped a bit like a flash-idler at the end of the barrel of a rifle (the part that breaks up the 'flash' of the bullet as it leaves the barrel), to let you know what end of the device to hold.

If the clicks were constant, that meant that the object was free of explosive material, but if the clicks sped up and became a constant high-pitched scream, then you knew that that particular day was going to be a bit more stressed than the previous one. Funny, on the device's instruction guide, it said that, 'If the BL-X6 detects traces of explosive material, carry out a complete re-sweep; if positive, inform an Officer immediately. DO NOT PANIC. DO NOT RUN. WALK.'

That was an amusing instruction: 'Inform an Officer.' I mean, what the hell could *he* do? The instructions were clearly written for the military, and their authenticator was no doubt an ex Rupert himself, and probably regarded anyone who didn't have a commission as not possessing a brain either.

The last part about not panicking reminded me of that character out of *Dad's Army*, Corporal Jones, who always screamed about the place when he was under the slightest bit of pressure, 'Don't panic, don't panic!'

At least someone down at the manufacturers had a sense of humour — well, I *think* they did — in calling the device a BL-X6. We naturally referred to it as 'the bollocks'; but maybe some professor-type didn't see the connection; maybe B, L, X and 6 were technical references to the materials used in the make-up of the device. Still, I liked to call it 'the bollocks', because it really did do the bollocks of a job.

Getting back to Mr Suhail, however important it was, I felt that this probably wasn't the best of times to talk about the basics of security — bombs, bugs and that sort of thing. I knew I had to work up to it. I certainly had to resolve some of my immediate concerns, but decided rather than to put them directly to him, to wait until Roberts showed up. He could then slip in my tactical observations and recommendations in a style more congenial to Mr Suhail and his family, something which I wasn't yet close enough to them to work out.

Vic was waiting outside the suite, and I could make out through the radio transmissions that Mike had joined him. I made eye contact with John who was hanging around looking like a stranger, which of course he and I were. I made a motion for him to leave, then spoke to Mr Suhail. We were alone now — his wife and daughter had immediately made their way into one of the bedrooms as soon we entered the suite. 'Excuse me, sir, if you're OK here, I'll go and have a word with Mr Roberts and sort a few admin things out.'

His first words to me were not exactly what I'd anticipated. 'That will not be possible. Mr Roberts will not be joining us. He has made other arrangements.' He said it in a very matter-of-fact sort of way that didn't warrant a reply, so I didn't want to ask him, Why? That would make me look a bit dumb. I'd just assumed that Roberts would be around for the duration of the contract — but clearly he wasn't. This was unusual (though not unknown) but there was nothing I could do about it.

Then Mr Suhail said curtly, 'I want a car for tonight, at seven.' He paused before he gave the time, as if his mind was elsewhere. We were to take him to a rather mysterious merchant bank — I'd certainly never heard of it — in the City. (The City being, of course, the financial district of London, and not the West End area most famous for its shops, as many people outside the Home Counties might imagine.)

'I've some urgent business to attend to,' he added. Unusual, I thought. Do banks open this late? I wondered. Possibly, if his custom is that important! Banking has never been one of my strong points.

Just before I left on the team's first mission of hiring a car, he said he needed his briefcase brought up from reception. Strange, that was one piece of attire missing from his entrance. I dealt with his request immediately.

Back in the corridor I told Vic to take charge of the stag list and to put me on it as well. Depending on how the job was to pan out, I would most likely have to stag on with the rest of the team, to lighten the load.

Leaving John outside in the corridor, Vic and Mike double-checked our two rooms. We'd left them locked, but nonetheless unattended, so we set about carrying out another bug sweep of both team rooms. A little thing, more of a habit than anything else but still a good security pointer, was to put a marker somewhere on the door as you leave the room, as a sign to tell you if someone has entered it whilst it was unoccupied. Something like a small piece of paper that could be wedged between the door and its frame, something small enough not to be spotted by the intruder. The one for Vic and me was still in place, but that for Mike and John's room had been moved, indicating that door had been opened.

'Probably a maid changing towels or something, but give it the once over just the same,' I said, not showing much concern about it. I knew these guys; they didn't have egos that needed to be stroked, and didn't need to be told how to suck eggs. They were the bollocks of a team, and I was lucky to have them working with me. I left them to get on with the sweep whilst I went down to the reception to pick up the briefcase.

'The safe deposit details are in the briefcase. The manager has seen to it all. It's all there, sir,' the receptionist said. The case was light; it was also locked.

Back upstairs I paired us off for work. Vic and me; Mike and John. Then I got a call from Mr Suhail stating he wanted to have a talk in my room. I hoped Mr Suhail would now begin to open up a bit. Neither Vic nor I really had a clue what was going on. I'd assumed Mr Roberts would have been available to brief the team up on what was what. I hadn't figured I wouldn't see Mr Roberts again.

After I introduced Vic, Mr Suhail set about giving me a rundown on his foreseeable agenda for the next two days. Not once did he offer any intelligence as to why he required such heavy-duty cover. Nonetheless, I was keen to make some headway on that front as soon as possible; but I had to wait until he'd finished his piece, and then pop the question. Vic stayed silent throughout.

'I've been thinking. What I require is four vehicles. You know, Mercedes 600 S-class type?' Suhail was saying.

'Yes, of course,' I responded in a slightly subservient manner — taking down notes.

'One for my wife, one for my daughter. The other two will come with me. All to have air-conditioning; the one I ride in is to have a fridge.'

'Yes.' Not such an unusual request. I made some more notes as he talked through his list of requirements. Four Mercs, all with air-conditioning, one fridge. Was this guy getting his priorities in the right order? It was a bit like taking down a set of 'snap orders' back in the Regiment. Only the barest of details given, leaving the imagination to fill in the rest.

'I want you to arrange all this for this evening,' he went on. I looked at my watch; the time was rapidly ticking away. I'd have to move fast to secure the vehicles, but fortunately I knew of two very good contacts in the vehicle-leasing business — so delegate! I took in that Mr Suhail was wearing a pair of glasses not dissimilar to those of Mr Roberts. He didn't look up as he spoke, he was looking into his briefcase which he had opened and placed on a bed.

I noted the heavy-looking gold pen — another surplus sign of wealth, along with his gold Omega Constellation hanging off his right wrist. Funny, when my parents bought me my first watch, Dad said, 'Wear it on your left wrist, son, girls wear them on the right.' I don't know if that's true today, but I logged that in the back of the subconscious anyway.

Suhail certainly appeared to be on top of what he wanted as far as the team went. He made a note of our names and mobile numbers. He never questioned our ability to do the job. Nonetheless, I did confirm to him that I was ex SAS and the rest of the team were from similar backgrounds. 'We're well up to the job,' I remarked, still not really knowing what the job actually entailed.

The meeting took about ten minutes. Then he closed his briefcase, the cue I'd been waiting for. I started with the relevant operational questions as I saw them at that particular moment. I had a string of them to put to him, such things as, 'What do you see as the immediate threat to you and your family?' 'Who knows you are here — family, friends, business associates?' 'Do they know you have security?' And 'How do you see the next few days working out?'

Minutes later, I was a lot more enlightened than I'd been a couple of hours earlier. Vic and I began to make sense of the information we had just been given: Suhail told us a hell of a lot, but concluded by insisting that he saw no immediate threat to him, his wife or his child, and only his brother and nephew knew of his whereabouts. (I made a mental note: That *really* means that he's under a serious threat of having his head ripped off, or worse still getting slotted, and all of his family know where he is. Another point: who and where are this brother and nephew, and where do they fit into the picture?)

He said, 'Of course, my business associates and the banks know I am in London, but not where,' and, 'Yes, my brother and nephew know that a security team is looking after me, but the banks do not.' Again, I had my doubts.

It's essential to get such clarifications from a Principal — even if they may be telling half truths — if only to keep the team one step ahead of the game. Most of the time a Principal's security requirements are quite straightforward and there's no need to go in to such a seemingly in-depth questions-and-answers session. But already, this job was full of potential complications. I sat back and pondered the possibilities of the next few days. One thing was instantly apparent: this was no regular Principal. I had to up the team's manpower. Things were going to look pretty shitty if I couldn't get the men I wanted on board. A bodyguard's work rate, the physical and mental capacity to do the job 100 per cent, is about eight hours max, although it's not unusual for BGs to work 12-hour shifts. Unfortunately, stagging on for 12 hours is still very much standard practice. Anyone who says they can do the job effectively beyond this eight-hour period is either not doing the job properly, or they're walking around with the old Walter Mitty head on — or the task they're doing is not true bodyguarding.

On the surface, Mr Suhail wasn't backwards in coming forwards. But I figured he had only told us as much as he dared at this early stage: 30 per cent truth, 70 per cent bullshit. As soon as I met him I sensed he was of a nervous disposition. This could have two possible causes — a hereditary thing, or something more immediate, brought about by the situation he'd got himself and his family into. Already my opinion was: This is a bit of a dodgy job, to say the least — in fact, *well* dodgy.

Despite what I'd just been told, I believed my Principal's situation was a lot more 'heavy' than he was letting on. I was sure as hell confident that he wasn't telling the truth, the whole truth, and nothing but the truth. If he was, then more fool him — and better for me and the team, we could easily work around what he'd told us. But, in general, people who've got themselves in the shite for whatever reason, especially in this business, don't spill the beans at the first sitting. They tend to let it dribble out over a period of time, probably because their subconscious won't allow them to blurt it out all at once. Sort of like a built-in safety valve. Still, I couldn't be certain; I was only presuming; I'd never been in a situation like that which Mr Suhail had apparently got himself into.

By late afternoon, I'd addressed the manpower situation, and brought in two guys just to cover the corridor. I put them on a 12-hour stag each, and arranged for one to relieve the other. A corridor man is not a BG, he's more like a static guard in a suit. There's a big difference and the brief I gave reflected that.

Anyone and everything that went into the Principal's suite had to have the once-over with the BL-X6, and anyone and everything entering our part of the corridor had to be cleared by me beforehand or, if I wasn't available, then by Vic. *Not* by Suhail or his family. Common sense and discretion was the order of the day for the corridor men.

Once the corridor men got to know the faces on the floor, the hotel's staff and the Principal's family, then their task would settle down to a routine of constant boredom, sprinkled with rare heart-wrenching moments when an unknown face came strolling up the corridor.

Actually, it was a stroke of luck to get two guys willing to do the corridor at such short notice. I was paying slightly over the odds, £15 an hour per 12-hour shift, to get this task covered, but it was worth it. It released me and the others to concentrate on the more immediate operational concerns.

I initially intended to give the team a bit of a formal brief, but decided against that approach. I didn't want to sound too military, after all I wasn't speaking to a bunch of soldiers just about to go on a search-and-destroy mission in Kosovo. I was about to address my BG team — Vic, John and Mike — who were all self-employed, all friends and all with an opinion worth listening to. The last thing I wanted was to come across as dictatorial, especially at this early stage of the game.

I gathered them in my room and kicked off.

'Well, this is long and short of it.' I heard a slight huff from Vic as if he knew what was coming. I ignored it and carried on. 'From what I can dig out from Mr Suhail's brief, he's over here to collect monies already raised through certain City banks in order to continue with a real-estate deal which has been set up in Russia, Azerbaijan to be precise, if you can believe Suhail.' This time Mike gave out a sigh. Just because I'd been told Azerbaijan, I didn't necessarily believe it. As far as I was concerned, it might as well have been Timbuktu. Where large sums of money are involved, it doesn't matter what colour or creed of people you're up against. The only thing you can be sure of is that they would be extremely pissed off if they felt they were being ripped off.

'Roger so far.' I tried to inject some humour, by using a bit of radio transmission jargon. I didn't think it worked. No one said a word after the mention of the Russians and money; the guys now had their serious heads on.

'Anyway, it looks like something or someone on the Russian side has gone a bit pear-shaped over the availability of certain funds — or, *non*-availability of funds, I should say. It seems that the Russians, in their wisdom, and based on our Suhail's sweet patter and sales pitch, have kicked off this project without actually seeing a penny of the so-called funds.'

'Nice one,' Vic said, as he clasped his hands around the back of his head and leaned back on two legs of his chair. 'Fuckin' great.'

Mike put his thoughts to the floor. 'I bet it's all to do with something called bonds and certificates of insurance, letters of intent and all that old bollocks.' He was trying to show us his so-called knowledge of the world of banking. 'Probably guaranteed by some big-name banks, or written on their letter-headed paper without their knowledge.' (Mike didn't know it at the time, but he might have hit the nail right on the head.)

'I'm only relaying to you what Suhail has told me, isn't that right, Vic?' I said.

'Yes, mate, you're spot on,' Vic agreed.

Mike carried on. 'Are you trying to tell me that Boris and co. started digging before they saw dollar? I fuckin' don't think so, Steve.' He was now in full flow and was going to tell us about a job he'd been on, a job he's told everyone of us about, a hundred times before. 'Remember that job I did in that shit-hole of a place last year for that US oil company, also in Azerbaijan? You couldn't cross the friggin' road or go for a shit without paying in dollars.'

'Yeah, yeah, Mike. Is it all right if I carry on or what? It might not be Azerbaijan, it might be Georgia or Armenia. All three are in that south-eastern corner of Russia bordering Turkey.'

'I was only going to say for the benefit of Vic and John that these fuckers don't mess about. It's as manic as West Africa. Some

of those cunts over there will cut your balls off just for the hell of
it —'

'Well, let me finish what I've got to say then we can all toss the
options around, all right?' I interrupted. Mike nodded in
agreement. I could sense that he was chomping at the bit to pre-
empt the outcome of my briefing.

I pushed on. 'Right then, undoubtedly the line Suhail spun to
the Russians worked; or perhaps there was a mix-up in the
translation of how the deal was to pan out financially.' I moved to
sit on the bed and glanced at my notes.

'You wanna eat that fucker after the brief,' Vic said, pointing to
my briefing sheet. I saw a smirk cut across his face. 'If the Old Bill
get a sniff of this fucker, we'll all be out of a job.'

Ignoring Vic's sarcasm, I carried on. 'I haven't quite worked the
scam out yet, but the mention of "guaranteed funds available"
might have put the Russians into overdrive, spurred on by the
greed factor, so they then employed a substantial Turkish labour
force to clear the site to prep it for development.' I turned over
my briefing sheet and read from the back, my eyes picking out the
key phrases.

'They're probably gonna build a Russian-style Disneyland or
something,' John suggested.

'Don't ask me!' I replied. 'You're probably not far off. But why
or how this deal was done without the money in the bank, *fuck*
knows. I've already put this to Suhail, but all I got was a blank
stare. Anyway, the Turks want a stage payment, something like
three million dollars for their efforts. Why the Turks, and not the
indigenous peasantry to do the donkey work, I haven't a clue.'

'Probably someone cutting a deal somewhere along the chain,'
Mike said. 'What do the Russians want?'

'Good point, Mike. Probably their commission, or the three
million. Whatever,' I said. I wanted to push on again. 'All I can
get from Suhail is that the money is in place and ready to be
transferred, that's why he's over here; and the reason why *we're*
here is that the Russkies and the Turks think he's done a runner.
Suhail assures me that he *isn't* on the run, but merely here to
oversee the bank transaction.' I could read the guys' minds. High
finance, Russians, Turks and double-dealing. This job was going
to be a first for all of us! Though it was quiet, the tension was as

great as anything I'd experienced before. In the military, you always have the might and the technical support of the British Government to fall back on. But here in this hotel room, as civilians, we had fuck all.

'That's all I've got, so far anyway, but this is what I think. The Russians and the Turks are feeling a bit pissed-off because they think they've been had over by some prick. But Suhail insists that he hasn't double-crossed anyone, and to prove it, he's meeting with the banks immediately. Basically, it's all about ... well, you've already guessed it — money.'

I went on to say that although we needed to know a bit of the background in order to formulate a tactical game plan, we didn't need to get into the personalities of individuals whom we might meet in the course of this job. That would just be filling our minds with needless rubbish, and draining brain cells, brain cells that would be required in large amounts to deal with the immediate physical threat. And as far as the immediate threat went, I couldn't overlook the worst-case scenario — a successful Russian or Turkish hit-team kidnapping Suhail, or worse still, killing him (even though it's a known fact that dead men don't pay their bills, so they wouldn't get weighed in).

John had stayed relatively silent throughout all this. He didn't let too many things get to him, he just did his job and took the money. He didn't like getting into the nitty-gritty of the politics of jobs; he had enough of that back home with his wife and kids.

I'd said all I had to say, there wasn't too much to debate because we all had immediate jobs to do, but the obvious question had still not been asked. Vic knew it and I guess John didn't care one way or the other, but Mike was almost off his seat wanting to have the final say. I finished off with the standard 'Any questions?' routine, followed by an offer of a brew.

'Yeah, I've got one,' Mike said. 'Basically these Russians or Turks or whoever, they want their money back, do they?'

I nodded in agreement. 'Yes, that's about it.'

'Typical,' Mike said, then asked the obvious. 'How much money is he in for?'

I looked over at him. 'A lot, a fuckin' lot. What do you want, tea or coffee?' I turned to flick on the kettle. 'Tea, mate, cheers,' came a chorus of three.

I thought I'd killed the brief with the offer of a brew, but now I knew their questions would come thick and fast, once the phrase 'How much?' was uttered. I also knew that I wouldn't be able to answer them.

John interjected for the first time. 'But they can't find the person who's done a runner with the dosh, I bet?'

'Get with the programme, John, for fuck's sake,' Vic ordered. John's thinking clock was clearly running on slow-time mode.

'Yes, it's about money, what fuckin' else?' I got up off the bed and wandered over to the window. 'And like I've said, they apparently want their money back; and I would suggest that they can't find the person at the moment. But they will, they ain't stupid. No — Suhail's the stupid one. You can bet he hasn't covered his tracks. That's one thing we can be sure of. It won't be long before they're hot on his tail — correction, *our* tail.'

'Who, the Russians? Whose tail?' John asked, now looking a bit excited.

'No, the fuckin' IRA, you twat,' Vic said. 'What is it with you, John?' John stayed silent.

'Looks like it,' I said.

'Probably the fuckin' Russian mafia knowing our fuckin' luck,' Vic finished off with one of his terse opinions.

The brief had now turned into a debate about the threat to our Principal. It was just beginning to heat up. Opinions were being thrown around thick and fast. I let them voice their views.

My thoughts drifted to the time I had spent a couple of months in Ankara, Turkey's capital. I was hosted by the Turkish Police Department and commissioned to carry out a weapons and equipment upgrade. This allowed me to go out on patrol with these guys. Violence has never really been an acceptable method to settle street disputes but I can say that it worked on the streets of Ankara. 'It keeps down the paperwork,' one policeman told me, 'and anyway, we've got more bullets than we have sheets of A4 in this department.'

Because of the breakdown of the old Soviet bloc, Turkey was receiving an influx of migrating immigrants, mainly from Russia, and they all seemed to end up on the streets of Ankara. This overspill sometimes caused outrage amongst the locals, and then there were the frequent shoot-outs and armed fights. Foreign drug-lords running prostitution rackets (new girls, incredibly good-looking ones at that — ex ballet dancers now turned table-top girls were the main trade) muscling in proved the main cause of this crime explosion. One thing I learnt about Turkey was that you didn't mess with their police, who were always armed and always ready for trouble. Take that psyche and times it by ten, then you have the mentality of the crime gangs they were up against. One hundred per cent pure nutters.

Having got myself out of that brief trip down memory lane, I now considered the more immediate problem of jacking up the team's vehicles. The pending trip into the City wasn't far off, and getting a quick brew down my neck was a good idea before I left the cosy confines of the hotel room and experienced the realities of looking after arguably the most wanted man in Great Britain, if not the world. After all, who would be stupid enough to turn the Russians over? Who would be stupid enough to turn *anyone* over on a deal like this?

For some reason I began to think about the Knightsbridge job Mike and I had carried out a few years back. We had to go down to a famous jewellery shop there to pick up a couple of suitcases stashed with a small fortune. The job was to drop them off to a client the following day. Since the contents of the two suitcases were estimated to be worth in excess of 40 million pounds sterling, there was no way we could afford to pay the insurance premium, even for one night, so the two of us stagged on in my office until we dropped the stuff off the following morning.

The reader may think, Why only two of them, and not an armoured truck and an army of guards? Well, sometimes the client doesn't want to draw attention to him or herself. A covert pick-up was what the client had wanted, and from my point of view, that was the right option — it was the best approach. Of course, I had employed 'sleepers' (a surveillance term used to describe undercover members of an operation) very close in. I'm not *that* stupid!

Now I butted in as Mike was reliving the Azerbaijan experience, with John and Vic looking bored with having to hear the same old bullshit one more time.

'You know that jewellery job we did a couple of years ago, Mike? You know, the big one, 40 million in two bags?'

'Oh, fuck no, not another big moral thing, where I've to decide if I want to live life on the run?' Mike sighed sarcastically. 'Yeah, I remember it. How the fuck could I forget it? I should've taken the jewels and run!' (Mike was joking.)

'No, mate, you don't have any moral issues to address this time,' I said.

(Mike and I had spent that night in the office talking through all the scenarios that might come about if we did a runner with 20 million apiece. Even the 'fence' price might have tempted lesser mortals to do a runner. Anyway, it passed the night hours away as we daydreamed about the ifs and buts, and how we would spend the money.)

I carried on. 'The overall value of the entire complicated deal is just a little bit bigger.'

'How much bigger?' Mike's voice rose a couple of octaves.

'Almost 20 times bigger. At least 700 million,' I said coolly.

Mike threw a few expletives around before coming to his senses.

'Right. So I take it we're still all up for it?' I asked.

'Count me in,' Vic said.

'Fuck it, why not,' John added.

'Mike, you in or out, dude?' Vic turned and looked at him.

'What the fuck do you think? In, of course. I'm in, I've never been out, you bunch of twats.' Mike paused. 'You don't suppose he's done a runner with the lot — do ya?'

'Don't be a tosser all your life, will ya? He's probably just taken out his expenses, and a little drink,' Vic said. 'What the hell do you think?' He was in sarcastic mode. 'Greed is good, money is power, with it you can build your castle walls high and fight off regiments. Of course, he's taken as much as he could. Expenses and a little drink, my arse.' I gave a bit of a nervous laugh about Vic's last comment.

We spent the next few minutes talking around key issues of what needed to be done in the immediate future, and addressing the possibilities of what could happen; and if anything *did*, what we could do to counteract it.

In short, the problem I had was that, because I didn't know if this Principal was for real, I didn't know that if the story he'd told me was real — and if it *was*, whether it was part of a bigger deal involving other 'parties'. At that precise moment, there was no way I, or any of us, could get the answers to the questions we'd all been throwing around the place.

Basically, this job was a high-risk operation, all four of us were sure about that. What we had to do over the next few days was to gain as much information on the Principal as was physically possible. If that meant going in to his briefcase, making note of his passport details and other bits of information, then we would have to do that. (In particular, Mike and John were past masters of sifting out information. If there was a degree course in reading upside down and back-to-front, both of them would have passed it with First Class Honours.) After all, we weren't only looking after him and his family, we were looking after our own backs, too. And if he wasn't going to play the 'White Man', then it left us no option.

Just let me point out that building up such an in-depth intelligence profile on my clients isn't the way I normally work. In fact, I'd never done it before, and I've never done this sort of thing since. I've never had cause to, basically, because I've never allowed myself to be put in a situation like this since.

8.

UPPING THE MUSCLE

DAY TWO, EARLY EVENING

During this first 24-hour period, then, I had to address a number of problems. The two pressing ones were vehicles and manning. I had to hire these four Mercs the Principal was on about, and to make it more complicated, I had my doubts about his choice of vehicles. I made a couple of command decisions.

First, a quick change in the vehicle set-up. I opted for two top-of-the-range Range Rovers to act as the main team vehicles. Mercs are great motors, but there's nothing like a heavy four-wheel drive like the Range Rover for bulldozing your way out of trouble. They are high off the ground, powerful enough to accelerate away at speed, and four lumps, tooled up, can get in and out of them a lot quicker than they can a Mercedes. It wasn't only the first choice of vehicle I used when on the SAS Anti Terrorist Team, it was also my choice of vehicle if I was out in Africa — assuming I could get hold of one over there.

Usually the aid organisations and NGOs (non-governmental organisations) I'm sometimes commissioned to carry out work for opt to drive the more refined and up-market Toyota Land Cruiser. All very pretty looking, and they are generally purchased fully loaded with extras at no additional cost; but I will always put the ramming and cross-country abilities of the Range Rover above that of a vehicle aimed at the supermarket set.

The second command decision was to go firm on what type of guys I was going to beef up the team with.

I sent Mike and John off to a car-hire company where he could get hold of two Range Rovers, and the two 600 S-class Mercs. I told Mike to make sure all the vehicles were dark in colour. I didn't want to cruise about town in citrus-lemon or anything like that. We were going to play 'the grey man' (acting in a low-key casual manner, but being 100 per cent switched-on, ready to react with full force), as much as this operation would allow us to do. I also told him to make sure his Range Rovers had a fridge on board — if that was possible. Personally, I wasn't aware that Rover offered such an option.

Then I addressed the manning. I sat down with Vic and upped the team from four bodyguards and two corridor men to eight bodyguards and three men in the corridor working in shift rotation.

The extra cost didn't seem a problem to the Principal. He rather welcomed it.

'I do understand that your price will go up. This isn't a problem. You will be paid as before,' Suhail said.

'Yes, of course.' I tried to reply without sounding too worried about the extra sums involved. I just had to be sure that he was completely aware of how much extra this operation was now going to cost. 'As you will understand, I do need 50 per cent of this extra cost, just in —'

'Come with me,' he interrupted in a no-nonsense manner. In his bedroom he pulled five bank-vacuum-packed two-grand bundles, made up of fifties, out of a brown envelope.

'That should cover it?' he said, without further ado.

The contract price had now almost doubled. My charges were £450 per man per day for the BGs and £350 for the corridor men, plus vehicles, radio kits, technical equipment, hotels and expenses, so the weekly cost of the entire team to the client was now running at over £50,000. Maybe it wasn't his money he was playing with, or maybe it was. I didn't care, as long as my payment was forthcoming. I had no reason to suspect it wasn't, so I didn't give it any further thought. As for the team, we were all in it together, not only for the money but for the 'crack' as well. It's these types of jobs which make you feel alive; it's the closest feeling you can get to combat in peace time.

I made a phone call to an old mate of mine, Dai the Hammer. It was a pity he was working on another job at the time, he would have been a great operator to have on board, a no-nonsense bloke who gets on with the job and says very little, a bit like John. However, he managed to give me half-a-dozen names of guys who he thought would be useful.

What I was looking for was a few more heavies, but bigger ones. This wasn't because the other guys couldn't handle themselves, far from it. It was because, in life, size does matter, and if we were to have a bit of rumble with a bunch of foreigners, or at the very least, have a verbal head-to-head with them, then the physical presence of some 'lumps', plus Vic, might go a long way to making the 'enemy' see sense and not have a go. This was working on the principle that prevention was always better than cure. After several phone calls, I'd sourced three guys.

Two of them, Tom the Box and Ken the Nose, were both highly experienced in the art of street fighting, the modern way. Tom the Box was an ex Para who'd been out for years and had worked a lot of the clubs since leaving the mob. He had the look, and the credentials to back them up. A little over six two, late 30s with collar-length jet-black hair, he had that lived-in gypsy look. His cheeks were covered in thin red veins. One might mistakenly imagine that he had a drink problem but he didn't, although he did come across as a bit punch-drunk.

We had a quick rerun of our past service in the Paras — a ritual which all ex servicemen do on their first meeting, especially ex Paras. It's a sort of vetting process, this exchanging names, places and operations either of us had served in, just to find if our paths had crossed, but more importantly, to check out if each was who he was making out to be. Tom was pukka, he'd served nine years in 3 Para, round about the same time as I had.

'... well, the money's good and everything's found. But I can't emphasise enough that this job's *hot*. We've got some right slags sniffing up our arses,' I said.

'Take your point. I ain't got a problem with it,' he replied. He dropped his voice a bit and motioned to me out of earshot of the others. 'If you need any pieces [he was referring to weapons] I can get my hands on a couple of untraced Brownings if you want.'

'Fuck off, Tom, what sort of job do you think I'm running here?' I joked.

'Well, the option's there if you want it. Just give me a day's notice to sort 'em out.'

Since the publication of SAS and similarly themed books (my last two, *Terminal Velocity* and *No Fear*, will have to be included in this list), there's been an influx of Walter Mittys into the BG business, all believing that they've been bayonet-fighting in the Falklands War through to scud-busting behind enemy lines in the Gulf conflict — as I've said, a little knowledge can be dangerous. These types of guys tend to pick up on the salient points of such books and then try and convince the less knowledgeable members of the public that they are the 'real deal'.

Ken the Nose, on the other hand, wasn't ex services — he'd learnt his trade on the rugby fields of South Wales and in particular nightclubs all over Europe. A loud joker of a Welshman, he was six three with a number three crop. He was a lot fatter in the face than 'the Box', with a pale complexion that came from being a red-head. His nose was a feature he was strangely proud of. It had obviously been battered over many years; it didn't protrude much, and its width was almost as long as its length.

'Well, what happened to it then?' I said, referring to his nose and trying to force a reply.

'It's my nose you're on about, isn't it?' he said, sounding a bit dull.

I threw a glancing look over at Vic, who had come down to meet a fellow countryman.

'Don't look at me, you Anglo-Saxon faggot,' Vic joked. 'That's a fine Celtic nose, isn't it, Ken?'

'Fuckin' right, and if any of you English bastards have a problem with it —' he was now pointing to his nose '— then come and tell me and I'll give you one just like it.'

Ken obviously had a sense of humour, but I got the feeling that he could 'turn' quite quickly if he couldn't get a grip of the constant military-style slagging off which the rest of the team used as humour. Still, Ken could back up Vic's constant sniping at the English — devolution and all that. This could only add to the light-hearted debates about the two different cultures in the quiet hours that this job was likely to produce. Hours of hanging around and waiting.

Although Ken, at least, was rather a different breed from the rest of us, I immediately warmed to both of them, and got the feeling that I could put my trust in them. It's a sort of instinct one learns to pick up on in this business. Not only that, I felt confident that my contact wouldn't have put their names forward merely to show me that he could deliver.

This wasn't a numbers game, I didn't want men who would be 'too busy looking good'. I wanted men who could not only tell a good story, but could also blend in with the other members of the team, acting polite and unintimidating when situations required, while being capable of springing into controlled 'nutter' mode, doing the business if push came to shove.

They were certainly what I'd had in mind, really humble-looking with a touch of menace. That's the look of a good BG. It was going to be interesting to see how they fitted in.

Third was Little Al; he came recommended through Ken the Nose. Little Al's skill was a blend of traditional contact karate mixed with several years on the 'circuit'. I'd heard about Little Al over the years — showing again that it's quite a small world we BGs operate in — but this was to be my first meeting with him.

So far, I'd got seven guys for bodyguards, and that was including myself. In order to put two bodyguards with the wife, and two bodyguards with the daughter, I had to source another bodyguard. I needed three men with me, that was the bare minimum I wanted to set foot out of this hotel with; and as things stood, I only had two. I ran the problem past Mike. He said he'd got a mate who was still serving 'across the water', but was currently on a month's leave. 'I'll give him a call now if you like,' he said. And before I could give any thought to his question, Mike started to push buttons on his mobile. That was his style, and I had no reason to doubt his judgement, so I let him make his call.

'What's he in?' I asked as he waited for a connection.

'Oh, 14 Int [14 Intelligence Company, the specialist undercover unit which works over in NI, also known as the Det], he's on a two-year tour.' Mike moved away as he began to speak to someone at the other end of the line. I heard him mention the daily rate and then mentioned London. Mike finished his call. 'Well?' I said, not actually trying to anticipate his answer.

'Yeah, he's up for it, but he can't get here until tomorrow morning.'

'You *sure* about him? I mean, the bloke's still serving and this isn't the usual run-of-the-mill job. It's a bit near the mark, a bit in-your-face.'

'Yeah, *course* he's up for it. He'd be just the bollocks on the job. He's current, he knows his way around London, and he looks the part.'

'Problem solved then,' said Vic.

'What's his name, then?' I said cautiously, hoping that I hadn't heard it before.

'Pete, Pete Litman.'

'Unit?'

'SBS [Special Boat Squadron].'

'Fuck no, not another fuckin' bootneck. I might have guessed!' I was being funny. Most of the lads I've met from the SBS have turned out to be good operators.

But I still wasn't too sure about having a serving bloke on the team. I'd had a previous experience — a bad experience. The year before, Ray W, one of my mates back in the Regiment, phoned me up, he was working in London at the time on a small official task. This task only required him to work a couple of hours a day, so he had a lot of time on his hands. He asked me for a bit of short-term work, and against my better judgement I decided to give him two weeks of bodyguarding.

The trouble was that Ray got sussed out only a few days into the job, and was then unceremoniously RTU'd back to Hereford, and got a 'Gypsy's Warning' for his efforts. I felt bad about the entire incident, and didn't want the same thing to happen to Mike's mate.

Of course, it wasn't my fault Ray got sussed out. He told me later that someone 'inside' had bubbled him up to the hierarchy, but it wasn't a problem because he was going to take care of it. Ray didn't know at the time whether it was another regiment guy who'd bubbled him, or one of the many attached personnel. Whoever it was, he was likely to get a good kicking eventually. The tactics the Regiment uses in war do spill over into peace time: hit and run, or shoot and scoot — revenge is always a dish best served cold.

So the incident with Ray made me think a lot about using Pete Litman. Yes, he would undoubtedly be current in all the skills required: bodyguard, surveillance and anti surveillance (apart from lacking the art of being streetwise, a skill which, surprisingly, is not taught in the SAS or other Special Forces), and apparently he did know his way around London — and if he didn't, he sure knew how to read a map. And I was being pushed for time. So I came to the conclusion that he was a big boy and could look after himself. Anyway, learning on the job would not be new to him; it's par for the course in the Special Forces.

The only niggling doubt I had was, What if the job kicked off big style, how would he react? Would this serving guy have the same commitment about mixing it with the 'enemy' as the rest of us, or would he think about his career, and so take a back seat? After all, it wasn't like he was a normal squaddie home on leave and doing a bit of moonlighting on the door of his local 'sticky carpets'. Pete was a live 'operator' across the water, jumping in and out of fast-moving cars, and doing all that sneaky-beaky stuff, if you know what I mean. So that could be a problem. The last thing I wanted was to be one short when the action started. I was already working on minimum manpower levels as it was. But at the end of the day, the advantages of having him on board now outweighed the disadvantages. After all, he was meant to be one of the best trained operators around.

Within a couple of hours of the job kicking off, I'd managed to write up some set of orders, some kind of security plan, and put it into operation, and with a bit of charm, and an injection of urgency, managed to get the Principal and his family to take it all quite seriously. It was a bit awkward for the daughter, though. She was young and was having trouble coming to terms with all these lumps hanging about the place. If the wife and daughter wanted to go for a local wander around the hotel, take tea in the lounge or go to the restaurant, then one of my guys would have to be with them.

For example, this is how it worked. It was agreed that they would inform the corridor man of any pending movements; he in turn would tell me. I would then send one of the team downstairs (if they were going to the restaurant), then two of the team would carry out a recce and secure two tables. After that, two team members would escort the family down in the lift. Once they were secured in the restaurant, one team member would drop off and make his way back upstairs.

When any members of the family were cutting about the hotel, then those team members who were resting up in the ops room (Operations Room: my and Vic's basha) were to act as a QRF (Quick Reaction Force). Well, that was the basic game-plan to kick off with. The family seemed to accept it. I also asked them not to go outside of the hotel for any reason until the following day, saying that it was just a precaution. As it happened, they didn't move from the room all evening.

In the meantime, Mike had done an excellent job of jacking up the vehicles, just in time for the trip to the City. At £800 a week for the Range Rovers and £550 for the Mercs, it was a deal, considering the timeframe which I'd been given. Parking them up wasn't a problem, as the hotel had a secure underground parking facility.

Adjusting the game-plan on the hoof, I had to get one more man in to carry out a 24-hour cover on the vehicles. This worked well, because I alternated him with the corridor men, just to break up the monotony of their duties. In between dealing with all the party's luggage and running about the place picking up faxes that were already arriving, and sorting the vehicles, manning, and everything else, I eventually gained enough time to allocate men to their specific jobs. I now had seven BGs, and two corridor men.

Mike was to be the Principal's driver in Range Rover One, radio call sign Red One. I designated Ken the Nose as his bodyguard. I would ride in the back-up vehicle, Range Rover Two, radio call sign Red Two, with Vic as my driver, and when I wasn't riding back-up, John would take my place. I paired Tom up with Little Al and told them Pete would join them when he turned up, and also to rotate the wife/daughter duties.

I purposely put Little Al with the daughter because he *was* small, size being uppermost in my head when making my decision. Al was five seven and she was less than four foot. At least she wouldn't feel too overshadowed. I also decided that Al would be her sole BG. I wanted Al to strike up a good rapport with her so she settled into the running of things with the least hassle possible. She was under enough personal pressure as it was — a change of environment and human lumps hanging about all over the place couldn't have been much fun for her — and at the end of the day, it wasn't her fault that her dad had pissed off some heavy foreigners. Al had a daughter of his own, so he had some idea of handling the situation — kid gloves were called for. If Al happened to be unavailable for some reason, then Pete would take over his duties.

I had toyed with the idea of using a female BG. I don't want to come across as sexist, but she would have had to have been quite a large woman to handle the possible punchy scenarios which this operation might throw at us, and that would undermine my line of thought about size. Also, I couldn't rule out the possibility of one of the guys mixing business with pleasure. It does happen on mixed jobs, and I didn't want the extra admin problem of that risk floating around the place.

Women BGs are a fairly new development, and it's about time. However, not every client sees their value. They do have a point, and like I've said previously, in this business — particularly in London — size does matter, and generally a bloke BG can come across as more of a prevention than a woman might. That's just a fact of life and not just a dig at women. In addition, a lot of the older princes from the Gulf tend to prefer a male BG. There are exceptions to the rule, and the good news for women BGs is that their use is now being recognised more and more, in particular with children. It's not unusual to have not only a male BG on a Principal's children, but also a woman too. The trouble is that there are very few women BGs about who don't have the build of Soviet female shot putters. And they have to be of that build to be able to take on an assailant.

Like war, nothing on these jobs ever goes according to the plan, but if you all have a shared basic working knowledge of how things are *supposed* to go, then at least when it does run smoothly, as it does from time to time, then you have something to work to. Bearing that in mind, in normal circumstances the only people who would not change their jobs would be Mike and Ken. I had assigned them 100 per cent to the Principal. Keeping continuity with him was paramount, and I thought that this strategy would also work in our favour, as a solid point of contact through which to gather more intelligence on him. Naturally, I understood that I had to slip that rule if it became necessary to put more emphasis on the daughter's safety.

In fact, at the end of the day, I was more concerned with the daughter's safety than the Principal's. Having her snatched by 'these people' would be a catastrophe, so it wasn't going to happen, I would make sure of that.

It may be clear by now that during this early stage, I was just as concerned about how quickly I could suss out the Principal's personality, as I was about the threat to him and to my team. Initial thoughts were: Would there be enough time for me to paint a true picture of the Principal? Would I be able to get enough intelligence on him to pass to my contacts in the police and other agencies, before the people who were after him eventually found us?

Found us was the right phrase. I had no control over who the Principal was phoning, I had no hard intelligence as to who he really was, and more importantly, I had very limited knowledge as to who the hell he had pissed off so much. Lastly, I had no idea why Mr Roberts had made himself so scarce. Why had he done a vanishing act? It was my bet that he had got 'weighed in' with his commission and had decided to bug out for a short holiday overseas, to lie low and wait for the outcome of his client's affairs.

Still, his disappearance didn't really bother me. I had enough on my plate controlling this operation without worrying about Roberts. All in all, I concluded that Roberts being out of the way gave me a direct line to Suhail — and that meant it might be easier to control him on a day-to-day basis. That in turn would make my life a little bit easier.

9.

GOING MOBILE

DAY TWO, EVENING

We hit the ramp at speed, the roof of the Range Rover just clearing the top of the security roller gantry. I hit the central-locking button. It clunked shut reassuringly, and Vic and I were now entombed. We shot up the slope, looking all around. Vic stopped at the point where the car-park ramp blended into the street.

It was much darker outside than I'd thought. The heavily lit interior of the hotel had given me a false impression of what it was actually like on the outside.

'Clear left,' I said. Vic pulled out in a goose-neck style to the right, to block off any oncoming traffic from his left, whilst my eyes were covertly scanning all the parked vehicles on both sides of the road for any suspect vehicles and their occupants, lying up in wait.

Small specks of rain immediately fell on the windscreen. Wipers on delay. It was going to be a damp and windy evening, compounding the problems of making a clear tactical appreciation: the validity of pedestrians, and the locally parked-up vehicles. I couldn't hang about. A shot of apprehension warmed my insides, letting me know that we were now 'active' — game on. I fumbled with the wires of my covert radio set. 'Red One, route clear, route clear, over.'

'Roger out.' The reply was crisp and professional. Only two transmissions were expected from me. 'Route clear,' or 'Contact'. 'Contact' covered a multitude of sins, all bad, but the drill on hearing this would be that Red One would not leave the hotel.

No need for small talk, just unambiguous transmissions requiring no further comments. All of us focusing 100 per cent on the task ahead — just as it should be.

This was a two-car operation. I could just make out Red One in my rear-view mirror as it manoeuvred around the dog-leg which indicated the exit of the underground car-park. It too bounced as it hit the ramp. Within a couple of seconds it was level with us, and then in front. Checked: it was three-up, Mike and Ken up front and the Principal in a half-cowering position in the back. Vic quickly pulled in behind it. Fifty metres then a junction. Mike turned left and found a gap in the traffic. Vic followed suit and neatly tucked in behind Red One.

Hundreds of red tail-lights flickering on and off, their glare blending in with the rain, cut my visibility in half.

No headlights came on from any of the parked vehicles and no suspect motorbikes or pedestrians were seen. Luckily Vic had removed the glass cleaner from the windscreen (hire companies routinely smear it on to their vehicles to make them look nice) with an old copy of the *Evening Standard* which led with a headline 'Yardies In Shoot Out'. I couldn't help thinking, Who with? The Russians?

Also, I had previously set the offside wing mirror to suit my line of vision before we took off. With this I could see who was coming up the inside, as well as keep an eye on what was happening behind us, without physically looking behind and giving the game away. As a matter of fact, defensive drivers learn to drive without the use of this mirror. They rely on the passenger to feed them any necessary information.

Every driver and cyclist was jockeying for position, even the pedestrians were cutting across the lines of traffic, hurrying to catch a bus or tube. Mike and Vic settled into a bumper-to-bumper pace following the line of traffic. The absence of any internal stereo system on, and the heater blower on low, only heightened the sense of tension Vic and I had.

At this time of evening it didn't matter in what direction we were headed, the traffic is *always* bumper to bumper. Both Mike and Vic had to drive for each other, but Vic, being in the back-up vehicle, had the worse job. It would be stop-start, stop-start all the way into the City.

Our radios faded as we got to the other side of Regent's Park, along the Marylebone Road well before Madame Tussaud's. We would now rely on mobile phones as our primary means of communication. Using the larger Motorola radios in the vehicle might just draw unnecessary attention to ourselves. Also, as soon as we were out of comms with the hotel, I called John up on the mobile. First time out with Suhail, I wanted to know if anyone had made a move on the hotel. No. Everything was OK. Wifey and kid were squared away watching TV.

Good, no problems at that end and no suspicious vehicles following us either; the only threat came from those company car drivers who would try and weave in and out of the traffic as they pushed in, to gain that extra metre, or race to clear that amber-to-red traffic light. The odd hooting of the horn in our direction fell on deaf ears. We ignored it; Vic didn't give way. You could feel the glares of these drivers as they tried to make eye contact with one or both of the occupants of the two Range Rovers. But it didn't happen, and the gestures weren't reciprocated.

Before we left I had briefed up Suhail not to worry about any of the tactics the team were going to implement. I gave him a couple of fairly light situations which we might find ourselves in: suspect followers and the RTA (road traffic accident). I didn't want to put him more on edge than he appeared to be already. The chances were that he would react in a totally different manner if given a 'hard' briefing. By 'hard', I mean in your face, no holds barred, about the possible incidents of such an operation. Whatever happened, the team would look after him, and if it seemed as though he was going to do something unnatural, then one of the guys — if needs be — would punch him out; just to become less of a liability, you understand.

I also pointed out to him that, apart from not worrying, it was best not to get involved with the driver's, or any of the team's, tactics. I told him what I would like him to do when in the vehicle, which was basically not make eye contact with other drivers. 'Just keep your head down in all that paperwork you carry around. You're in good hands.'

His response was one of total agreement. I'd done a good number on him, he was now 'our baby' and we would look after him in the style for which he was paying us. For the moment Suhail was completely under my control, a remarkable contrast to his earlier attitude. But God alone knew how long it would last. The team was now in full gear. One short in numbers, true, but that would change in the morning when Pete came on board.

Our journey would take us straight into the London rush hour. I'd decided to take a rather longer route to the City than perhaps a black cab might have done to take us to the bank at Cheapside in the City, avoiding the obvious Euston Road.

With a bit of aggressive driving through the park and down to Marylebone Road, and then along the Georgian-façaded Harley and Wigmore Streets, we cut across Portman Square, past the much-later Churchill Hotel, and down to Marble Arch. Both vehicles accidentally jumped the lights at the bottom of Edgware Road — Mike had mistimed them, consequently Vic had to drive through as well. Luckily the traffic came to a sudden halt ten metres past the lights so it didn't look too obvious.

'Fuckin' twat,' Vic mumbled to himself, as he had openly broken the law. I ignored his comment; it would be the first of many expletives he would unleash before the journey's end. It's normal talk from a back-up driver. Vic and Mike would have their own debrief when we got back so they could sort out their own driving skills then, I was sure of that.

Once around Marble Arch we headed down along Park Lane, with its old but multi-million-pound apartments overlooking Hyde Park, past the Dorchester and Hilton Hotels, and then swung a half right around Hyde Park Corner and down towards the 'big house' at Green Park — Buckingham Palace. The traffic around here was moving surprisingly quickly, so we made good time.

It wasn't long before we went around Nelson's Column and up past Charing Cross Station, towards Covent Garden and The Strand. Thereafter, the buildings became less glamorous, more grey and monolithic. We were now heading straight towards the City, and soon buildings began to grow: grand old structures made way for huge impersonal blocks of concrete. The traffic was less heavy. Pedestrians scurrying for the sanctuary of the tube commanded more of the road than vehicles.

Then the roads narrowed as we entered the City's heart. I was aware of large concrete blocks painted red and white standing along most of our City route. The pavements were now bare of anything other than lampposts. No rubbish bins or unnecessary advertising boards — the City of London Police had been operating a 'clag'-free zone since the IRA had bombed the shit out of the City a number of years before.

The concrete blocks were intended to slow and divert the heavy traffic away from the City, and the lack of pavement clutter prevented the covert placement of bombs. Along with the CCTVs now in place along every street, the police have got the City sewn up. This was uppermost in my head as we approached Cheapside. Without doubt, we had now been caught on camera from Regent's Park all the way through to Cheapside, and if we had been subversives and up to no good, we would have required a quick change of vehicles and a disguise to get away with anything dodgy.

In all, it took us about 40 minutes to reach the bank. I'd planned that Ken and I would go in with Suhail, whilst Mike and Vic drove off and parked up out of sight. I wasn't sure if we would be allowed into the meeting. If we were, then all very good; if we weren't, then that would be our first headache — letting the Principal enter 'solo' into a possibly 'hostile' environment.

It was still raining as we approached the bank, a 20-storey mirrored block of glass, set well back off Cheapside. I noted that all the lights were on apart from those of the top floor. It was one of those modern structures with glass sheets where bricks should be, complete with a piece of 'modern' bronze set on a huge marble plinth to mark the bank's main entrance. Thrown up in the 1980s during the Thatcher boom, the time of Yuppies and New Romantics, it was really in your face. A 20th-century architect's dream some might say, an eyesore I called it. I've always been a bit of a traditionalist, Georgian façades and Queen Anne windows, you can't beat them. By contrast, glass gives the image of being cold and unwelcoming. A building in glass is far too sanitised-looking for my palate. No warmth.

In contrast to my private thoughts, Vic commented, 'Nice-looking building.' He didn't look directly at the bank, not wanting to draw any attention. We were just two guys heading off home to Kent.

'Still, wouldn't want to pay the rent on it. Must be a mortgage a week.'

'Yeah, right.' I wasn't particularly interested in Vic's observations, I was too concerned with checking out the local surroundings.

'Do a drive past, that's it, Mike. Good,' I said to myself. 'Keep going.' We followed him as he drove past as briefed, for another 500 metres, then made a left down a predetermined street to avoid carrying out a 'U' turn on Cheapside. The traffic was still light.

As Vic turned into the street he parked up a few metres behind Mike — this was tactics. We waited for a few minutes to see if we'd been followed. We hadn't, so we made our way back to the bank.

'Red One, Red Two, all clear from me, over.'

'Roger that. Did you see the small BMW opposite the obvious on the initial drive past, one up?'

'Yeah Roger, I did, keep an eye on it as we approach again, I don't think it's anything,' I said.

'Roger out.'

'Famous last words,' Vic mused.

'Hell, Vic, if they're on to us that quickly, then we should have got tooled up before we left the hotel.'

'I did.' Vic was still looking ahead. 'Look what I've found.' He'd taken the wheel brace from the vehicle's tool box and hidden it under his seat.

'Nice one, what did you find for me? Frig all, I bet.'

'Nothing, Englishman. Only a rolled-up newspaper. I hear you guys use them, eh?' Vic struggled with trying to be funny while at the same time driving in Mike's wake. I didn't rise to the bait.

Once again Vic just made it across a set of traffic lights on the turn. 'Mike, you cunt,' he said to himself, but less annoyed than last time.

Think — look for the police car out on a nightly lurk patrol; left, right, left, right — this went through my mind as we shot across the junction. Nothing. I gave a deep sigh: 'All clear.'

'Thank fuck for that, don't fancy getting pulled tonight. I've gotta have a word with that twat,' said Vic, referring to Mike's driving.

'Don't fancy getting pulled any time,' I replied.

You've always got to have a cover story on this job. Not that you're doing anything illegal, it's just that getting pulled is a bit of a pain in the neck for the rest of the team — and, of course, the client. I always make sure we have the correct documents on board and always have a bit of a cover story, and if one of us does get pulled then it's SOPs for all of my team to send the pre-recorded message from the mobile to the other vehicle commander. Something like, 'Got pulled, call me on mobile.' That way, you get an immediate call and you can brief the caller right away if the 'pull' is going to be routine, a warning, or the Full Monty.

It lets the rest of the team get on with what they've got to do. If they have a Principal onboard it gives them time to make up a cover plan should the Principal start asking awkward questions such as, 'Where's the other vehicle?' Thinking on your feet has to be done all the time.

With regards to the police, *never* say that you're on a BG job, even if you're rigged out with HF radios all over the place. I don't know why, but the police tend to go a bit over-the-top then, pulling out the stop-and-search laws and all that. It happened to me in the past. I was on this solo job, in Milton Keynes of all places, following a 'suspect' who'd done a runner with my client's money — the usual story. My task was just to follow his movements. He was driving at the time, and he wasn't hanging around, when all of a sudden a police patrol car appeared behind me from out of nowhere and pulled me over.

'For fuck's sake!' I said, though not directly to the officer as he asked for my details. It was just an expression of frustration about having lost the target I'd been following for the past two days.

'So where are you going at such a great speed?' he asked.

'Does it fucking matter, you're going to nick me anyway, so can we just get on with it?' I replied. 'I'm on a surveillance job.'

Unfortunately, the policeman took my comments rather personally. He held me up long enough to give me a lecture about how speed can kill and to issue me a speeding ticket for doing 40-odd in a 30-mile-an-hour zone. End result — three points on my then-clean licence, and a break in the target's routine.

So now, I generally act very subserviently and just tell the truth, but don't elaborate: ex army working in uniform contract security. The police tend to go easy on you then. A lot of them are ex services anyway, and what's more, it's probably something to do with forward thinking on their part. A lot of police who leave the force tend to end up in the security industry.

As we approached the bank for the second time the BMW was nowhere to be seen, so Vic slid his 'tool' back out of sight.

Two of the bank's security men had come out to meet us. They were dressed in matching black two-piece uniforms with the usual shoulder epaulettes indicating the bank's uniform security branch.

'Thank Christ there's no red carpet, that would be a right giveaway,' Vic muttered as he pulled smoothly in behind Red One. Suhail had evidently phoned through to let them know we were coming. As that was happening I quickly made a mental note to talk to him reference unnecessary use of phone. Bad security procedure. Stop it.

Ken and I were now out of our vehicles. I gave my door a hearty slam and heard the central-locking system being shut again. I was focusing on escorting Suhail in to the building.

'Hiya. I'm Steve and that's Ken,' I said as I held out my hand. Ken was closing with Suhail and just looked across to make an eye-contact acknowledgement.

'Derrick Daley, ex Coldstream Guards,' the bigger guard said, taking my hand. He was tall, about 60, with a full head of brown hair. I noticed a faded black spider's-web tattoo covering the space between his thumb and fore-finger on his right hand. 'And this is Richard, ex Engineers,' he went on in a very formal manner, trying to establish an immediate pecking order. Richard looked ten years younger, with a protruding beer belly, but of the same genre.

The two security guards confirmed our names and ushered us in through two electronically operated doors, opened by another uniformed guard from behind a reception console more at home on the bridge of *HMS Invincible*. Once we were secure in the bank, that was the signal for the two vehicles to pull off and lie up somewhere out of the way, about five minutes out.

Suhail said we would be here for about two hours at the most. Neither Ken nor I were allowed into the meeting so we had to sit outside and play corridor men. It was OK; the bank security guys fed us with tea and biscuits. And because both of them were old military men, at least we had some common conversation.

Derrick offered me the option of parking the Range Rovers in the bank's underground car park, but I said they were needed somewhere else. It was a white lie, but I didn't want our mode of transport tied up in a building that I wasn't familiar with.

If we had been followed, then the odds of our pursuers blocking our path as we made our exit were not worth taking. If those people were desperate to get to Suhail, then hitting him coming out of the bank would be a good tactic. Get him while his head is full of money tunes.

I got Vic on the mobile and told him how long we were looking at hanging around for, and said to pass it on to Mike. Vic then told me where they were laying up. I finished the conversation, letting him know that both Ken and I were having the pants bored off us with the war stories from a couple of old soldiers.

The job was hard enough without getting an autobiographical account of what it was like during their time in the services. It was harmless conversation, but I felt a little uncomfortable that I might end up like that, spinning old yarns to my grandchildren. I made another note: *Retire from this business early.*

Seventy minutes later, and we were a bit wiser to the reasons for the need for drill, as described at length by Derrick. Apparently, it's something to do with instilling discipline in soldiers. Of course, that went straight over my head. Anyway, we were now back, heading into the West End.

There was a change of plan. Suhail had to go to an address at

Ennismore Gardens, just off Knightsbridge. Why? Clearly this had something to do with the bank meeting. I wasn't told, but obviously, I found this really worrying.

'I think it might be prudent if you could give me some notice of any change in locations,' I said to him later.

'As you wish,' was all he said, as if he wasn't concerned one way or the other. But what I really deduced from that comment was that he really hadn't got with the programme. So many of my clients consider any form of forward planning on my part to be premature — until it's too late. However, Suhail did seem to be a bit more relaxed after he'd come out of his bankers' meeting. I hoped that was a good sign.

Both Ken and I had tried to winkle useful information out of the two security guards, but they weren't forthcoming. Every time we made an advance in that direction they would skilfully bat it away. Not for any other reason than it wasn't for them to discuss the business of the bank with outsiders. (A refreshing and totally professional attitude, I thought. Something you don't often get from the uniform fraternity in the industry. Too many of them are only too quick to spill the beans about the institution or company that employs them. It's not malicious or anything like that, it's just a lack of education about the need-to-know basis.) Any more pushing in that direction might be understood as: 'What, don't you know what your boss does? Good security team you are!' So we left the intelligence-gathering routine alone.

The one bit of info I did manage to screw out of these two was this: it wasn't unusual for the bank to stay open after working hours. 'Not for the public of course; we don't get the public coming here. Businessmen, you understand.' But it *was* unusual for 'Mr Beman' to stay late.

'He is the bank's Russian expert,' the other guard explained.

No great secret to anyone, in fact. His name was on his office door, in both English and Russian. For me, though, it was the realisation of Russian involvement. Not total confirmation, but as near as damn it. It was certainly good enough for me.

10.

KNOWING THE LAW

DAY THREE, EARLY HOURS

Ennismore Gardens is a beautifully laid out Victorian square, typical of that part of London. It is surrounded by three- and four- storey townhouses overlooking the railinged garden of tall trees and mature shrubs. You would need a single win on the National Lottery to buy one of these places. The entire setting could have come from one of those popular 'rags-to-riches' period drama productions, it was that unchanged.

Whilst stagging on in our vehicles and burning the midnight oil, a police patrol vehicle 'clocked' both Range Rovers. They didn't come over the first time, just drove by. An hour or so later they came around again, by which time we'd parked up in another place. We hadn't actually gone anywhere, just changed position.

My earpiece crackled into life, and hissed in two slightly long but precise static transmissions. It was Ken, letting me know that the police were back in the location. They cruised past seemingly uninterested, after all it wasn't unusual for chauffeur-driven vehicles to be parked up in this neighbourhood all hours of the day. I made no direct eye contact but felt the look they gave us was one of, 'Shall we check them out or not?'

Later, when I told John, he knew exactly what they were playing at; it was a game a lot of patrols play. 'They sometimes make a bet with one another, that if the passenger looks over to them, they'll pull 'em, if he doesn't, then they'll let 'em go, or vice versa.' It was as simple as that. Pure boredom, a bit like us. He played the same mundane mind-game when he was in the Force. Still, it kept us on our guard.

Fatigue and stress were beginning to take their toll. I gave a quick call to see if John and co. were OK and then prompted Vic into a debate about the state of Welsh rugby. If anything, that was sure to keep my thoughts occupied. It worked, but by the time he was about to make his main point, we got the call to move. Then silence, back into switched-on mode.

Twenty minutes later we were safely squared away back in the hotel. There was a debrief with the team, which highlighted a couple of admin points, the main one to do with Mike and Vic's driving skills.

'Hey, Mike,' said Vic, 'do me a favour, boy, and don't pull away like the friggin' start of the British Grand Prix, will ya? It's a right twat trying to keep out the fuckin' motor bikes, isn't it!'

'I don't know, *is it?*' Mike was taking the piss out of Vic's accent — not a clever thing to do at any time. 'Try switching on and in a couple of days you'll get the fucking hang of it,' he added.

His comments didn't help, especially this time of the morning when tempers were bound to be on the tender side — usual drivers' stuff, handbags at ten paces. I could see that Vic had logged Mike's comments for future reference. But nothing more was said now.

I don't want to take sides, but Vic did have a valid point. The obligation was on the lead driver to drive for his back-up as well. This is paramount in order to keep the convoy together — a very important aspect of driving in convoy. If any of the vehicles are attacked, it's no good having the back-up vehicle (or for that matter, the lead vehicle carrying the Principal) isolated from the rest of the team, unable to come up in support because the lead driver has left his back-up stuck behind a number 16 bus.

I managed to get my head down at around three o'clock in the morning. I'd been solidly on the go for over 21 hours and was looking forward to my three-and-a-half hours' kip.

But I couldn't sleep! Vic was snoring his head off, so I just tossed and turned in a bed of sweat, going over in my head the game-plan for the next few days. Daylight came, the first full day on the job. A quick shower, then out to see the corridor men. They'd had an uneventful night and were on their starting blocks waiting to be relieved, but that would not happen for another couple of hours.

You might imagine that because the hotel had air-conditioning, it wouldn't get stuffy. Well, it wouldn't if you were a normal guest who spent time either in his or her room or in the bar — you'd spend hardly any time in the corridor. And all hotel air-conditioning systems reflect that, putting more emphasis on room air-conditioning than that of the corridor, and quite rightly — who lives in the corridors of hotels, apart from the corridor men on a BG team?

We had the corridor covered 24 hours of the day and consequently it was *stifling*, particularly as the fire doors were shut during the night as part of the hotel's safety plan, and could not be propped open to allow a draft to waft through. I made another note: *Buy an electric fan*. That would stop the guys whingeing, and keep 'em happy.

No plans had been made for Suhail's programme for the day. This was very frustrating: *I* couldn't plan either, I could only predict the run of play. The only sure thing was that the radio batteries were going to be changed and the drivers of the vehicles would be 'first-parading' them. That's as far forward as we could go. Otherwise, the team had to wait for Suhail to dictate the pace of the day's events. Very frustrating.

DAY THREE, MID MORNING

Quite strangely, Suhail appeared around ten thirty, knocking on my door, with one of the corridor men in tow. He wanted to have a quick word with me about his daughter's trip to school. I thought it a bit late in the day to start thinking about that. However, he'd made arrangements for his wife and daughter to see the school's head that afternoon to make arrangements for her to join the class, as from tomorrow.

'Steve, I want you to take a Mercedes to school and I think that it's better if your man Al stays with Suni and my wife,' he said. It was a bit of an unusual comment for him to make. But at least it showed me he was now thinking security and not just self, and I had to be thankful I was being given more than just a couple of minutes' notice of a pending move. Nonetheless, the mountain coming to Mohammed was out of character. Was he now beginning to switch on and realise the impending danger?

The team generally scoffed when they could. Luckily room service was pretty efficient in this hotel, and 20 minutes from placing the order, it was wheeled into the room. So after breakfast I told Al and John to carry out a map study, go out and recce as many different routes, in and out of the school's location, as possible, and then at some time during the day make the rest of the team aware of its location, and make sure they, too, drove over the routes. I wanted every team member to know where the school was, and where the bug-out routes were, and the ERV.

I worked out that it would be a 15-minute drive from where we were, 30 minutes max during the rush hour. School drop-off and pick-up times *are* the rush hour; that's how the rush hour is caused, everyone taking their kids 300 metres down the road to school. Funny that, isn't it? During school holidays you could do this particular journey in five minutes.

The day was panning out to be rather a slack one. It transpired there would be no movement by Suhail until later in the afternoon, when there was to be another trip back to the bank in the City. The wife was looking after the daughter's school business, but I left Al in charge of all that.

This gave me ample time to sort out the team's 'tools'. This was an area which I wanted to avoid, but I had to address it — highly illegal, but what to do? I felt another command decision coming on. I was left no choice: this operation required it. So, I sent a couple of the guys out on a mission to purchase four sets of complete rounders kit: the gloves, a couple of balls, and three bats per set — two short ones and one standard-size. Selfridges and Hamleys would be the most obvious places to shop at, they would have all the kit needed to get 'tooled' up. Last item on the shopping list was one black leather, hard-sided briefcase.

I then briefed the guys up to carry their personal training kit and the rounders gear in the vehicles *at all times*, so, if they ever got stopped by the police, they would have at least a sporting chance of getting away with the excuse that they were part of a rounders team. To cover us more, I phoned up a mate who runs a local West End bar, and who sides a couple of rounders teams once a week in the Hyde Park League. I asked him if he would cover us should the police want to push the point. He agreed and even offered to give us a couple of his team's T-shirts for good measure. The last thing I told them to do was to take the whole lot over to Regent's Park and have a bit of a practice session — get the gear soiled up a bit. After all it was Wednesday, which, in the Armed Forces, is 'sports afternoon'.

To the reader, this cover might seem a bit excessive, but I would call it the belts-and-braces approach. Never take anything for granted, and never take the easy way out. If you do, it's like dropping your guard at boxing. You may get away with it once or twice against a poor opponent, but you won't be so lucky with a boxer with class. You'll get floored. You have to assume that every one of your opponents will have 'class', even if you know different. At this level in this business, you could get yourself killed if you didn't. It isn't worth it.

Certainly you have to cover all eventualities which you believe threaten you and your Principal. If it means going that extra mile, do it. That's why the SAS are so very good at what they do. They cover for all eventualities, plan and work to the worst-case scenario, and assume the only easy day is yesterday. It's a good doctrine to adhere to, because more often than not, it works. I'm living proof of that.

Surprisingly, unlike other hotels I've worked in (described in my last book *No Fear*), this one didn't supply room fax machines. This added to my concerns that I didn't even have half-control over the security and the passage of information. It was bad enough not being able to listen in to Suhail's phone conversations, let alone not being able to sanitise our incoming fax messages.

During the day a steady stream of faxes was still being brought up from reception by the concierge, who carried them in a brown envelope, and, no doubt, had read its contents before sealing it. And of course, that's *after* the hotel's fax operator had a quick read of it too.

Every fax was checked and read by me before it arrived in Suhail's hand. At least I had total control over that. If I wasn't about, then the corridor man would tell me something had arrived, and depending on what Suhail said he was expecting, I would either get the corridor man to read it to me over the phone, or hold it until I could get to him. The corridor men were briefed to hide any documents out of eyesight of Suhail until I'd glanced over them.

These faxes and messages were mostly from banks. Thirty million dollars on one fax, a couple of hundred thousand pounds on another — telephone numbers. There were a few mentions of Letters of Credit, mostly written in banking language.

Whether it was all bullshit or not I didn't know, but they were quite convincing to me. Christ knows who the hotel staff thought they had living up on the fourth floor. There were references to banks and accounts in Russia, Turkey, Italy, and Geneva in Switzerland. Of course, this helped me build up more of an intelligence picture of what was going on. As long as I could keep getting access to these documents, and Suhail was still in contact with the banks — as evidently he was — then, if the Russians were in hot pursuit, at least I knew that Suhail would have some form of paperwork to throw in their faces and so perhaps keep them at bay.

Maybe he'd been talking to them ever since he'd landed in the country. Maybe he was heavily in negotiations with them. Despite seeing these faxes, really I had no idea. I'd tried earlier, on the first day, to pin him down and try and curtail, or at least monitor, his mobile calls, but he still wasn't having any of it. As far as he was concerned, he was going to be the one person privy to what was going on; he was the only person who was going to dictate the pace of this operation. He was being the paymaster general. The boss.

That was fine for him, but I didn't fancy being kept in the dark.

Still, what choice did I have? I couldn't *order* him to tell me what
was going on. So I had two choices: stay on the job like a blind
man, or walk. My financial constraints didn't allow me to walk, so
I stayed. Throwing one's teddy bear in the corner on day three
wasn't good practice on any job. I'd had my say, it had fallen on
deaf ears, and that was that.

11.

TECHNICAL COVER

DAY FOUR

For personal reasons Pete Litman was a day late in arriving but he eventually turned up bright and early the following morning, suited and booted and looking the part. A little under six foot, small-framed compared to the rest of us, probably weighing in at no more than 12 stone, he was nonetheless fit-looking. He was late 30s with a nondescript clean-shaven face. Straight black hair just covering his ears gave the impression that he needed to get styled soon. It was that scruffy cut which allowed him to blend confidently into the murky underworld of the streets of West Belfast. Mr Compact, Vic had called him. Like, you knew it was a car, but you couldn't remember the colour or make.

The team was now settling into a nice routine. Al was getting on as well as could be expected with the daughter, given the short length of time they'd been together. She appeared settled as she attended her first day at her new school and somewhat happy in her new environment and new-found friend. Al had the ability to make her giggle. It was a funny sight, seeing him walk down the corridor, with her by his side excitedly chattering away like kids do on their way to school, and carrying her little designer-made backpack.

All the team had managed to carry out a recce of the school's location. Vic and I had to do it at night. Small and unusual-looking compared to most schools, it was a large detached two-storey mid-Victorian house, set amongst the urban sprawl of the middle classes, tucked away off Belsize Park, just to the north of the nice part of Camden Town. An area typically favoured by TV executives and other wealthy media people. A neighbourhood where a convertible Saab or a BMW Tourer was an essential part of life.

Although it was only five minutes' walk to Belsize Park tube, many of the residents opted to drive to their offices in the West End. They favoured the safety and comfort of four wheels rather than the everyday grime and chore of the Northern Line — the most unreliable of all the Underground lines in London. During the early-morning rush hour, cars would be seen heading out of their urban hamlet, their parking spaces immediately taken by those who worked locally but couldn't afford to live there.

It was up to Al and John to make a proper tactical appreciation of the location and escape routes surrounding the school. It was decided that nothing would be said to the school's head, and it was hoped that Al, and whoever the driver was at the time, would be able to blend in with the daily events of the school's timetable. It helped that drop-offs and pick-ups by parents or chauffeur-driven cars were not an unusual event.

However, I decided that the back-up vehicle would 'stand off' at every pick-up, pretending to be detached from Al's car. At least this would give some sort of normality to the task. The only drawback to this tactic was that, over a period, the stand-off vehicle might be spotted arriving and leaving every day without a member of the 'little people' brigade in it. It would only be a matter of time before some sharp-eyed parent or teacher would spot the vehicle and probably inform the police that there was a possible paedophile 'snatch squad' waiting in the area.

This was a real worry, but it was a problem the guys would have to deal with if it arose. I took into consideration the principle that the police would carry out their enquiry as covertly as possible, and that the guys who got 'dicked' would tell the truth about why they were there. Well, not the *whole* truth, but merely that they were acting as a back-up vehicle for Al's. Hopefully it wouldn't come to that.

The wife had still not left the confines of the hotel — except to sort out the daughter's schooling — eating either in her suite or in one of the two hotel restaurants. She hadn't, for example, expressed any wish to go shopping. There was still a lot of tension between 'him and her' — they'd had very little dialogue since their arrival.

'Is there anything you would like, or would you like to go somewhere?' I once asked. Her reply was guarded but courteous. 'No, thank you. If I want to go somewhere I will give ample warning. I need nothing but for this business to go away.'

I took this as a pointer that she was not at all happy with the situation her husband had got her and her daughter into. I also sensed that she'd been in a similar predicament before.

In the meantime, I'd been out and about with Suhail: same bank, same midnight visit to Ennismore Gardens. On one of these visits Ken found out that the Ennismore connection was a banker from Singapore. He gleaned this information from the 'in-house' security guard, who couldn't help himself spilling the beans about all of his residents' life stories. Once again, it was an interesting piece of news, but one I couldn't confirm.

This roundabout way of gleaning vital intelligence information was far from unusual. It was one of the idiosyncrasies of BG work. On the one hand, the client wants you to protect them from everyday dangers, and on the other, they are very reluctant to tell you about their movements or contacts. Had my Principal been a bona fide politician (if there's ever such a thing), I would have known every detail of his daily schedule, but since it now seemed that Suhail was swimming in some *very* murky waters, he still treated us with an air of disdain. His interpretation of 'the-need-to-know' basis was just that. He needed to know, and we didn't. In holding this opinion, he couldn't have been more wrong.

Because of our high profile on the fourth floor — what with corridor men and BGs hanging about all over the place — I'd rigged up a bit of a portable camera system, to confine the level of their physical presence to a minimum and to save comments like, 'Oh, I wonder who's staying in that room,' from other guests. Although we were situated at the end of the corridor, I still thought it wise to have this 'belts-and-braces' approach.

I strategically positioned two remote miniature cameras either side of the main suite, set some 12 metres apart. They sent two separate images of any corridor movement on to a split-screen monitor, set just inside John and Mike's room. When Suhail or the daughter was out, one of the corridor men would conceal himself in the room and watch the monitor — pretty boring stuff, but that's the nature of the game.

To act as a secondary 'trigger', I'd placed two portable miniature infra-red alarm devices. One was on the ceiling of the corridor, and emitted an invisible beam covering the main doors to the corridor; it was set to sound a low, but audible series of 'pings', a bit like the noise an echo-sounder gives out inside a submarine. All the hotel staff had been told to use these doors as their point of access for the corridor.

The other alarm I rigged up to cover a set of fire exit doors, to which anyone could gain access, from the floor below or via a side door at ground level on the outside, without even entering the main foyer of the hotel. This entrance point was my main concern. This pair of doors was never used by the public and seldom used by the staff, but because of the nature of the hotel industry, a lot of agency staff are used. They might not have been briefed by their department's manager to use the designated doors, or they might have simply forgotten and use it as a short cut between duties.

Jamming these doors shut to prevent total access would have been the best bet. However, by law, access through them had to be available 24 hours of the day, because of fire regulations.

I tuned the alarm's 'sounder' to a very high pitch and the volume to maximum. Hotel security also covered all these particular doors as a matter of routine. In addition the external one at ground level was covered with a camera and a pressure-release-mechanism switch which instantly triggered an intermittent, ear-piercing siren when opened, at which point the relevant light would also flash up on the hotel's security-control console. As always, I tried to get along with any hotel security, and this time was no different. They were a good bunch of guys, ex police, and only too happy to fit into my security plan. Once again, there was no point in pissing off these blokes for no reason. They could only act as an asset to me and my team — any unusual incidents or suspicious characters entering the hotel, we would be the first to know about them through the hotel security. We worked well together.

Once I had put in place this technical security plan, all I had to do was tweak it every now and then to fit in with the movements of the family and team. The hotel management posed no problems for us, and we were all getting along rather nicely. As long as our bills were being paid and we didn't do any damage, then they were happy to play along with us.

Our floor staff were great; not much chance of their faces changing suddenly for temporary staff. Roberto, a thin and well-groomed Italian guy in his mid-20s, was floor manager of the fourth floor. He ran his team in a typical military fashion, and they appeared to like his style since none had missed any of their shifts for over seven months: 'A bit of hotel record,' Roberto had said.

His team included three cleaners (two for this particular part of the floor), and three floor waiters working in shifts. There was a feeling of friendly rivalry with the other floors and departments within the hotel. That's because the hotel ran a monthly 'brownie-points' scheme: best manager, best waiter, that sort of thing. Prizes ranged from bottles of champagne to a free weekend break for two in any one of the chain's hotels within the UK — and, of course, the carrot of moving up the hotel's pecking order of employment.

Roberto helped to keep unnecessary faces out of the corridor in his polite and very humble manner. Early on I recognised that he was a bit of a flyer within the hotel's chain; he knew it, and so did his staff. If he did well, then his staff would undoubtedly shine under his banner. I had seen Roberto's face on the previous 'Employee of the Month' poster whilst walking to and from the security office in the admin department of the hotel — he was a regular winner.

One should never get complacent in this job, though I'll be the first to admit that it's very hard not to. One spends a lot of the time living in the realms of luxury and driving around in big flash cars, eating the very best quality food and lounging around in comfy chairs. Fresh flowers and bowls of exotic fruit delivered every day to the room, their smell, colours and presentation, are just some of the treats which make life that little bit more pleasant. Small, sweet-smelling bars of designer soap wrapped in that paper which dissolves when immersed in water, and the whole array of accoutrements which occupy your bathroom ... yeah, it can definitely lead a lesser mortal into a false sense of security.

Suhail had been a bit more talkative but not in a cheerful 'Hello,' or 'Good morning,' sort of way. He came across in a more concerned and immediate manner, asking me if the team was happy with the set-up and if things were going OK for its members.

This was the first sign he had shown that suggested concern for the team's well-being. At first I took it to mean he was now in semi-relaxed mode, and that things were going OK on the bank front, so as a result he had a bit of time to be pleasant to the people who were looking after him and his family.

The faxes and messages arriving from downstairs had certainly slowed up, which also suggested to me that the deals were now being addressed head-to-head in his meetings, cutting down the need to correspond by fax. It was as if Suhail knew something — something which he should have passed on to me, but decided against it for some reason.

DAY FIVE

Having spent another uneventful part of the early hours of the morning parked up around Ennismore Gardens, I was glad to get my head down. I felt absolutely bollocked. After another quick debrief and a shower, I managed to sleep for a few hours. The brief I got from Suhail was 'No move before eleven this morning,' so I passed this on to the team, and told them to get their heads down too.

The other part of the operational team, Al's, was now working as a separate unit. This wasn't intentional, it was just the way the school run was panning out. Two trips a day taking anything up to over 45 minutes for one return journey tied up a lot of manpower for just a short task. Because of this situation, I had to make sure that I was briefed as to what they'd been up to, and in turn I kept them informed as to what *I'd* been doing.

This took time, and it was becoming apparent that it wasn't really a sensible idea to have set times to brief and debrief one another. The briefings took the form of a quick five-minute chat in one of the rooms; it was then off again, either to eat, take a nap, refuel the vehicles or change radios, or stand in for one of the corridor men whilst he took a break — there always seemed to be something to do.

I decided to go firm on keeping two separate BG teams, 'A' and 'B'. The Principal's team was team 'A'; still Ken as principal BG for Suhail and Mike acting as the Principal's driver, with Vic and I still as back-up.

Team 'B', the daughter's team, still included Al as the principal BG, with John as principal driver. The back-up vehicle now carried Tom as back-up BG and Pete as driver. This came from keeping in mind the continuity I'd opted for at the beginning of the operation.

I also had the option of using one or two of the corridor-cum-garage men, should I have to chop and change the BG team due to any unforeseen admin problems. It wouldn't be ideal, but it was at least an option. To that end I swapped around the corridor/garage men, so that those most suitable for being pulled off and swapped with a BG member were now corridor men. Once again I was adopting a belts-and-braces approach, trying to cover every eventuality.

I still had to brief up the corridor men on what both teams were up to, of course, but this was scaled down to only the information they needed to know. It wasn't a case of keeping anything from them or having a game of oneupmanship, it was the nature of the operation.

In short, I was looking after the corridor and garage men, bringing them in, making them part of the team — as indeed they were. On a lot of jobs I've worked on, however, I've known some BGs to shun the corridor men.

I've never forgotten that on one job I ran out of the Dorchester where only the BGs were given rooms, the corridor men had to do their 12 hours and go home to sleep. If you lived outside London, commuting was a right bastard. All four BGs helped out the corridor men if they wanted a break, or if they needed to eat — on some jobs you have to eat out on the fire escape or, worse, in the corridor where you stag on — but on this occasion we let the guys use our rooms and watch a bit of TV whilst they relaxed a bit.

Nonetheless, one BG on this job wouldn't give up his room; he wouldn't even relieve any of the corridor men for a piss. The only forward movement he made to accommodate them was after one of the massive scoffs he was always ordering from the room service menu (courtesy of the client), when he couldn't finish what he'd ordered. Still wrapped up in his dressing gown (courtesy of the Dorchester Hotel), he opened his door and wheeled a table of £100 worth of shellfish and steak into the corridor, and beckoned to the corridor man to come and 'pig out' on his gift, pretending he was doing him a favour.

I was standing in this particular corridor, so I saw all this. My first impressions were: Well, at least he's making the effort. Maybe the slagging by the rest of the team has rubbed off on him. And now here he is, making some kind of offering. Is the worm on the turn? Tomorrow's move might be to offer to stand in for one of the corridor men.

Not a friggin' chance! I looked closely at what he'd left on the table. It had been swept clean of anything vaguely edible. A couple of crusty rolls and the remnants of a lobster tail was all that was on offer. The corridor man, unsure of what to say, turned to me for support. The door had by now closed, so I knocked on it hard. The BG (I won't mention his name, but he knows who he is) opened it a little, expecting to see the corridor man. I kicked it wide open. 'What, what's the ...' he said.

'Who the fuck do you think you are?' I growled. I'd just about had enough of this jerk upsetting everyone on the team. I didn't want to cause a major scene in the corridor, especially since the Sheikh's people were constantly coming in and out of the 40 or so rooms he had booked. But something had to be said.

'You're a right twat. Why take the piss out of the corridor men? The job's hard enough as it is, without having a prick like you to deal with.'

'I didn't, I didn't,' he pleaded. 'I was just offering him some ...'

We both moved further into the room, which allowed the door to close on its own behind me.

'You're a big fat cunt, you know that? You're the only one who doesn't help with these guys. What's up, you too good for them? Think you're the big BG, do ya?'

He took a couple of steps back and started to gesture with his hands. 'Well, I *am* the BG, and they're on corridors. They have their job and I have mine. I was only having a bit of a laugh.'

'Never heard of working as a team?' I'd had enough of him. If I'd stayed any longer, I would have put one on him, and it just wasn't worth it. I'd said my piece. But as I left, I fired one across his bow.

'The rest of the team know that you're a big wanker, so it's not only me. Log that in your fucking brain. Oh, by the way, the colonel [the Sheikh's right-hand man] knows what you've ordered. He saw it being brought in.' I was lying, actually.

'No, he didn't,' he protested.

'Oh, fuckin' have it your way,' I said. I turned to leave. 'If I were you, I'd get hold of room service and get it off the bill. Pay for the fucker, you know what the Arabs are like about people taking the piss.'

I left, leaving him looking dumb, and wondering if I was bluffing or not. It didn't matter anyway because Andy, another member of the team, stitched him up a couple of days later. Andy told him he'd got a message from the colonel in charge to tell him that his Principal wasn't going out for his usual afternoon appointment. In fact, the Principal *was*, and spent a couple of minutes waiting for his BG. By the time this guy knew he'd been stitched up, it was too late — the Principal had called on another BG from the team, who just 'happened' to be taking a bit of fresh air outside the hotel. He was eventually booted off the team, never to be seen working on the circuit again.

That little episode has always stuck with me, the selfishness of some people, so I'm always conscious of the less glamorous side of this work and try to assist the corridor men the best I can.

So, amongst other jobs, I had to balance the needs of corridor men, too. I had constantly to make sure they were doing what they had been told to do. And, like the 'B' team, I had to get a brief off them as to what had been occurring during the day on their patch.

On top of all that, I had to sort out what admin problems there were. There are always admin problems, usually to do with the feeding arrangements or a clash of personalities. Most of the time I tell them to sort it out amongst themselves and if they can't do that, then tell me. The deal then is that if I get involved and make a command decision, that decision is what everyone agrees to abide by — no comebacks.

As always, my use of this style was meant to let the men — the corridor men in particular — deal with their own admin problems, and if they couldn't, they understood that I would make a decision which, more often than not, would not be agreeable to *either* party. To a degree it kept the bitchiness and personality problems this job was bound to uncover well away from me.

PART FOUR

12.

A RAPID BUG-OUT

It was late morning, and I was taking a tactical shower, when Vic came screaming in the room and barged into the toilet where I was having a quite five minutes preening myself.

'Steve, Steve, we've gotta scoot, they're on their way.'

'Who's on their —?'

'Suhail's just told me that his brother's been pulled out at gunpoint by some fuckin' Russians. In the middle of sweet suburbia. Can you fuckin' believe it!'

The shower shut off with a resounding clunk as water under pressure suddenly stopped. I started to wrestle with a fresh towel. I could now hear properly. I cleared the soap from my ears, still trying to get a grip on why Vic was so wound up. I could now see that he was in a bit of a panic — he'd disappeared back into the room and had started throwing his gear into a suitcase.

I followed him, and he filled me in on what Suhail had just told him.

'He's just had a call from his nephew, a bloke called Charles ...'

'Whose nephew?'

'Suhail's nephew has just called from his flat. His father — that's Suhail's brother — says he's just been pulled out of his house in front of his family at gunpoint. Is that clear enough for you, or do you want it a bit slower?'

I struggled with a pair of trousers. 'For frig's sake, that's all we need! What else?' I turned to face Vic, balancing precariously, one leg in and one leg out of my strides. 'You said Russians?' I was now tuning in to Vic's urgency.

'Well, yeah, that's it, fucking Russians, and they're heading over to us now.'

'How the fuck do they know where we are?'

As I said that, the penny dropped. It was blatantly obvious: Suhail's brother was one of the weak links in my game-plan. With all the extra admin shite I'd had to deal with, I'd totally forgotten about Suhail's brother and nephew and how they fitted into this bastard jigsaw puzzle of a job. I didn't even consider that they might be in London.

'Bollocks [the brother] isn't gonna risk getting his brains blown away, is he? He told them, of course!'

Under pressure Vic had a habit of classifying anyone or anything as 'bollocks'. It could be a bit ambiguous, but anyone listening got the gist of who or what he was referring to.

'Did he get any descriptions of these tossers?'

'No. He only said that there were four of 'em. Wife and kids were screaming their heads off. Must have made great viewing for the neighbours. Too much in a state of shock to think of fuck all, if you ask me.'

Fully dressed, I started grabbing large handfuls of kit and chucking it into suitcases.

'I'd better get a debrief out of Suhail. He may have forgotten something.'

'I don't think so,' Vic said, opening the door and swinging his suitcase out into the corridor. 'I personally grilled the twat; the only other thing he said was that when they got the address, they fucked off in a dark-coloured car as quickly as they appeared. His brother and the wife couldn't remember the make, or anything else.'

'Police?'

'Well, we can't rule that out, can we?'

'How long have we got?' I said as I felt my shirt sticking to the sweat rolling down my back. Tie or no tie? I pondered. Fuck it, I've got time to tie a tie. Can't wear a suit without a tie, it looks a bit naff.

'The hit was in Wood Green.'

'Shit, that's at least an hour away, even for Damon Hill with a police escort, the way the traffic is this time of day.' I looked at my watch. Twelve forty-five: I confirmed it as a good hour away.

'The problem is that Bollocks, Suhail I mean,' Vic corrected himself, 'said he got the call from his nephew about 20 minutes ago. I couldn't make out why he didn't tell us straightaway. What's more, he didn't tell me how long before Charles got the call from his old man the incident happened. I pushed him on that point, but he's flapping like a fuckin' budgie.'

'I see your point,' I said, realising the seriousness of the situation. It was good that Vic had taken the initiative. The ability to do so was an essential quality of any team member, that's why I'd picked them in the first place. There are times when you've got to make a calculated command decision — to sit back and do frig all is never the order of the day.

'I've already told John and Mike to pass it around to pack up and bug out asap.'

'Nice one. Who's in with Suhail and the wife?' I said.

'Tom. Pete and Al have gone down to sort out the vehicle, ready to pick up the daughter.' Vic closed another suitcase; he was packed and ready to move. 'Corridor man is packing away the radios and the cameras and stuff. I told him to leave the fire escape alarm until we leave.'

'Good.' I was working out a simple surveillance plan in my head, along with frantically grabbing shirts, socks and skiddies. Clearing out my wardrobe and stuffing the contents into a suit holder, cases and grips, like some old burglar.

'Take your kit down to the wagon with Suhail and Ken. I want this bug out to be as covert as possible. Don't tell any hotel staff, pass it on. And tell Pete I want him with me, send him up asap.' I was going to set up a little surveillance operation in the hotel's foyer to try and 'eyeball' the Russians — and indeed, any police, in hot pursuit, should they turn up too.

Vic nodded. He knew the score. I noticed he had a bit of a sweat on. Unusual for the big man.

'Oh, one last thing, get Tom for me, we'll do a last sweep of the rooms and then I'll see you at the ERV.'

'What about all Suhail's kit?'

'Leave it. We'll pick it up later when we check out.'

'I don't suppose they're in any frame of mind to pack,' Vic said. 'The last I saw of him, he was just sitting. Looked like he was praying or something.' Then he opened the door and was gone.

I calculated the shooter incident had taken place at about midday. Allowing for the time factor and for the human factor to slow down the passage of information, I worked out that we had less than 15 minutes — and that was on the outside — from receiving the message to bugging out of the hotel.

At two minutes to one, all vehicles left the Marriott heading for the team's main ERV, a prearranged position along South Carriage Drive, Hyde Park. I turned my mobile phone down. It was constantly ringing as both teams rang in to let me know where they were at every stage of the bug out, in fact it was giving me a bit of a headache. The 'B' team was on its way to the school pick-up, since I couldn't risk leaving the daughter there whilst unconfirmed reports of Russians and guns were hanging over us. Meanwhile, the corridor men arrived via black cab at the ERV just before the 'A' team arrived.

After the team had bugged out, I went down to the foyer and made eye contact with Pete. He turned away quite naturally. The place was quite busy. There was a couple of Americans, probably husband and wife, talking loudly to the receptionist about a sightseeing trip on an open-topped bus. One other male was waiting patiently behind them. Not much traffic in and out of the hotel, but a few people mingling around. Four seated on separate sofas and three waiting for a lift. A quick look around told me that we were early. I picked up a copy of *The Times* and pretended to read it. The way you pretend to read a newspaper is actually to read it, believe it or not. Pick an article that doesn't interest you and your mind won't wander.

My phone was set to ring Pete's, and his was set to ring mine. Should we see what we thought to be Russians entering the foyer, one of us would alert the other. The problem is, I thought whilst sitting there, how do you tell what a Russian looks like? Do they have that pale-looking vitamin-starved skin, or sport beards with Cossack hats? I hadn't a clue, but I was sure that when they did turn up, I would recognise them, just by their body language. Anyone who pulls a gun on an unarmed person, in broad daylight and in front of witnesses, ain't all there.

At ten past one neither Pete nor I had spotted any likely suspects, and at about a quarter past I got a call from Vic saying that they were moving from the ERV about a mile to the other side of Hyde Park, and were going to park up by the Serpentine (the large lake in the middle of Hyde Park) for an ice cream. That way they would attract less attention.

The only reason why South Carriage Drive was chosen for the ERV was that if things did go tits up, then we'd have the sanctuary of the Brigade of Guards to help us out — their barracks were 100 metres from the ERV. Vic was right, he'd waited long enough at the ERV, and it's easier to blend in at the car park by the Serpentine. That's where all the Arabs and Indians go for their daily exercise, and it's not unusual to see families out for a stroll with their bodyguards close in tow.

On more than one occasion I've gone training (running) around Hyde Park, deliberately to spot working BGs. Not for any perverse reason you understand, but purely to see how they operate. To look at their mannerisms, to work out if they seem switched-on or not, relaxed or tense. One can build up a very good overall picture of the attitude and professionalism of this business just by sitting back and observing. It helps me in my method of operating. What's more, I sometimes bump into old mates, and on a couple of occasions I've even bumped into past clients.

Al's pick-up went OK, and they managed to hook up with Vic and share an ice cream whilst I worked out where we were going to sleep that particular night. It would be tactical suicide to return to the Marriott, that option was blown — dead and buried. The only option available to us was to covertly return for the rest of our kit, pay the bill and pick up the contents of the safe deposit box. We co-ordinated this little operation through the hotel's manager.

So I was going through the list of options open to me. I recalled that I'd stayed at a similar hotel sometime the year before, the Regents Plaza at Maida Vale, a modern hotel. It had a selection of nice large suites, it was central, and the underground car park was just as good as the Marriott's. Indeed, if anything it would be more suited, because its lifts were strategically better placed for the car park. You could actually arrive at the car park without having to change lifts on the ground floor, unlike at the Marriott. I gave them a call.

At a quarter to two, and several bottles of mineral water later, I put a wrap on the surveillance. Pete and I casually left the foyer of the Marriott and headed off to the Regents Plaza. No sign of Boris and friends, which was a bit of a let-down. Had we been spun a line by Suhail's brother? And if so, why? I'd have to have a mini-interrogation session with him and Charles, before I could draw any conclusions from today's activities. But for the moment nothing had changed on the team. Ice creams all round, yes, but we were still all in the highest state of readiness — Bikini State Black as the Army calls it.

The Regents Plaza Hotel is set on its own where the Kilburn High Road meets a road called simply Maida Vale, which runs south, straight into the Edgware Road, then on into the West End. To its north is the staunchly Irish community of Kilburn, to its east the plush areas of St John's Wood and South Hampstead. Turn right out of the Regents Plaza entrance and you're in something like West Belfast and IRA country; turn left and you're on the borders of pure conservatism and millionaires' row. Not the best place for a mixed team of ex servicemen to operate in, and certainly not the place for Pete either. He might just walk into one of his many known 'players'. Still, it was ideal for Al and his daily school run, since he was a lot closer to the school. Time spent on the ground doing the school run would now be halved.

Once Suhail and family had settled in, the team's main priority was once more to establish a security cordon. That meant going through the same routine with the hotel management. I made the initial introductions and left Mike and John in charge of that whilst I took Vic with me to set about arranging a meet with Suhail's brother and nephew; I wanted a nice little chat with them. I asked Suhail if his brother or nephew had called the police. He said they hadn't.

'Right, Suhail. Now you've gotta start switching. This ain't a game anymore.' I'd taken him to one side. 'You're paying me and my team good money for our skills, you've gotta trust me.' That's a laugh, I thought. Trust? So far that's been a one-way street in his favour.

'Steve, I hear what you say. Where do we go from here, then?'

'The first thing is to get your brother on the phone so I can debrief him.'

'That will not be possible. I've spoken to him already —'

'What? Since the incident?' I quickly corrected myself. 'Since he almost got his brains blown out?' I thought *that* might instil a sense of urgency into Suhail's way of thinking.

'Yes.'

I instantly readjusted my thinking. The first thing I had to do was to take the friggin' phone off him.

'And?' I tried to prise whatever he was hesitating over out of him.

'He's taken himself and his family to stay at a friend's house, somewhere in south London. He's too scared to go back to his house. And he doesn't want to talk to me.'

'I'm not fucking surprised.' I never swear in front of, or at, clients, but I was changing the rules for this one. 'What's he got to do with your business anyway?'

'He's nothing, he's just my brother.' Suhail evidently wasn't going to expand on that point. I put it down as a lie and tried another approach.

'This Charles guy, your nephew?' I said, standing by not to believe his answer. 'What's the score with him? Is he just your nephew?'

'Yes, that's correct.' But he said it in a way that told me that was probably a lie, too. 'He is really scared and wants to stay with me and my family. He knows I've got security.'

I thought for a moment. On the one hand, it would be good to have a little chat with Charles, to find out what the fuck was going on; but on the other hand it would mean another loose cannon in with us. I went for the 'better have him in', rather than the 'having him on the outside' option. That way if he was a 'player', I could control things.

'Get him on the phone,' I said. 'Has he got a mobile?'

'Yes.'

'Well, get him on it, tell him not to use the land line.'

I handed him my mobile and let him dial the number. It rang. Suhail handed the phone back. A male answered.

'Charles?' I said.

'Yes.' The voice sounded tense, very guarded.

'A mutual friend of your uncle. He's standing next to me.' I passed the phone to Suhail. 'Just confirm who you are — in English — and pass the phone back.'

Charles sounded genuine. But he was a new 'player' coming in to the game, and I had rapidly to assess what he was all about on the strength of one phone conversation. And I didn't trust anyone any more. I've met a lot of very good actors in this game, whose abilities outshine anyone nominated for an Oscar. This could be a 'come on', I thought. It's possible Charles is working for the other side and he could turn out to be the wooden horse in my camp. Oh, what the hell! I made a command decision. I set about making a plan to bring him in.

I asked him where he lived and how long it would take him to meet me at Bond Street tube.

'Just off King's Cross. I've got a flat there.' He paused. 'Straight on the Victoria Line and change at Oxford Circus — 20 minutes.' He sounded anxious. But he knew his way around the tube. That would help.

'All right, see you by the Gilbert Street entrance, the small side street. You know it?'

'Yes, yes, of course. What time?'

I looked at my watch. Suhail hadn't expressed any desire to go banking this afternoon — the thought of death might have made him lose his appetite for money.

It was 16.30. 'Let's say five thirty.' I refrained from using the 24-hour clock. Didn't want to sound too military.

'Five thirty,' he repeated.

'Five thirty *this evening*.' I was confirming that the meet would be in an hour's time and not tomorrow morning. Some people panic, go into brain-dead mode and can't even remember a basic instruction, especially if they're not used to having their family threatened by gun-toting Russians.

'And, Charles?'

'Yes?'

'Don't tell a soul where you're going, got it?'

He paused. 'I've got a girlfriend and she's really shitting herself about what's happened.'

I brought my head away from the phone and made a gesture to Vic. 'He's got company,' I said, indicating the phone.

'That's all we need,' Vic said, thinking the worst. 'Russians, fuckin' outrageous?'

'No, his girlfriend.'

He nodded and went over to explain it all to John, who was by now setting up the radio equipment.

Charles carried on. 'I can't leave her here on her own. It wouldn't be right.'

'All right, bring her with you. But listen, don't panic, just go to the tube as normal, don't get a taxi or even a bus. Use the tube, understand?'

'Yes, and Shelley, I have to bring her with me, OK?'

'I just said it's OK, didn't I?'

'Yes, sorry, I'm scared, man. I mean, I'm *really* scared. I'm not used to this kind of shit.'

'OK, I understand.' I wanted to save the small talk. I wanted to get on with it.

Suhail had given me a description of him: 21, gelled short black hair, flat top, quite thin, about five seven. 'A trendy-looking chap,' were Suhail's words.

'Now listen again.' I was conscious of giving a scared man too much to think about — people sometimes do the complete opposite of what you ask them to do when they're shitting themselves. But I had to make sure he wasn't about to compromise me or any member of the team. I went for the stand-off approach.

'When you get outside the tube, carry a copy of the *Evening Standard* with you. Wait for a bit, like you're having a chat with

Shelley, deciding what to do. Got it so far?'

'Yes.' He sounded a bit more switched-on. Eager to obey.

'Then ...' I had to be matter-of-fact to say the next bit. I didn't want to send him back into panic mode. '... if you think you *haven't* been followed, give it a couple of minutes, pull out the pink business section of the paper and put it in the bin by the tube's entrance. Do it normally, don't look up and try and look for me; you won't see me, OK?'

'Yes.'

'Then I'll give you a call. Got it —'

'What happens if I think I *have* been followed?'

I felt like saying, 'I'll leave you there, twat!', but replied instead: 'I'll give you a call anyway and we'll take it from there. All right mate?'

'Yes. I've got it.'

'One last thing. Don't forget to take your mobile with you, but dump my mobile number off it, will ya? Do it now.'

I hung up. When working on an operation, I always set my mobile to default: to show my own number. That way, the guys knew it was me calling before they answered. I didn't have the time to turn default off before making this call, and if Charles got 'lifted' by the Russians, I didn't want them to scroll down the list of 'last numbers dialled', and getting to us that way.

For sure, I had to get to him before anyone else did. I didn't know if Suhail's brother had had second thoughts and called the police, who were now on their way to Charles's place, or whether Suhail was still not switched on to 'security mode' and had started dialling every contact he had in his notebook, panicking and telling them all sorts of shit. But really, I was sure that wasn't the case. I think he'd got the message by now. This game he played behind a large stash of money was worth frig all if he didn't have a life in which to spend it.

I deliberately gave Charles a fast ball. The less time for him to think, the less danger he could put himself or the team in. The twist being that in giving him a fast ball I had inadvertently given myself one, too. At the very best I was 20 minutes away from the RV. My plan was to use four of the team plus myself. I had to be sure he was 'clean' before he came up to meet his uncle. I also wanted to meet with him face to face to have a little chat, in order to gauge his attitude and mannerisms. I couldn't be too careful. There's nothing like inadvertently bringing spies into the camp to piss one's hard anti-surveillance work down the drain.

Before I left, I made Suhail aware that Charles and his girlfriend were coming up to see him immediately on their arrival — a small attempt to stir the shit and get one of them to spill the beans.

'Charles seems pretty pissed off with this entire affair. He's on his starting blocks to see you.'

'That's quite possible,' Suhail replied, not particularly worried. 'He's very inexperienced.'

By now we were just approaching the drop-off. Vic was driving, John was in the back. Earlier, as soon as I'd put the phone down on Charles, I'd sent Tom and Pete to sit in the KFC restaurant by Marble Arch, to wait for my call, just to get someone on the ground if my plan didn't go the way it was supposed to.

'This will do,' I said to Vic, pointing to the only obvious parking space. We had pulled off the Edgware Road and into Seymour Street.

'Right, John, do your stuff. Keep in contact.'

'No probs.' I watched him cross Seymour Street and disappear, heading towards the rear entrance of the Cumberland Hotel.

I looked at my watch: quarter past five, the traffic was very busy. I was pushing the RV with Charles. I turned to Vic. 'I'll see you when you're better dressed.'

'You got it.'

'I'll call you when I have him visual. Then I'll make my way to the Churchill Hotel and wait for you there.' With that I got out and hailed the next available black cab.

The next 20–25 minutes were crucial. Planning an 'Agent Contact' — which is how I planned the Charles pick-up — is hard at the best of times. Timings were everything. I had four guys on the ground, all of whom knew the area in which we were working very well, but that on its own wasn't enough to make the operation a success. Luck is also an important factor — it always is. It doesn't matter how many professional people you put on the ground, something will always fail to go according to plan.

Who knows, the tube in which Charles would be travelling

might break down for 15 minutes, on either the Victoria or Central Lines such things were an everyday pain in the arse. And out of mobile contact, there would be no way he could reach us. Then again he might have got snatched even before he reached the tube. It's all a question of luck and timing at the end of the day.

The black cab pulled up some 20 metres from the tube entrance along Gilbert Street. It was twenty-five past — good, right on time. Hordes of office and shop workers were pouring into Bond Street tube. Umbrellas pitched at different heights and angles, all shapes and sizes, were being snapped shut with surprising accuracy and ease as they hit the entrance. I looked at my watch again. Almost half past, it was peak rush hour and everyone was on their way home. It was very difficult to spot anyone for more than just a brief second. You would look at someone, and then in the blink of an eye, they were gone. This brought home to me just how difficult surveillance really is.

John had called me earlier to say that he was now in position in the foyer of the Cumberland Hotel. 'Found a nice safe spot. Just ordered a coffee and I'm putting my feet up,' he chuckled.

'Don't make yourself too comfortable.' I dropped the call.

I'm aware that most black cabbies like to chew the fat with their passengers, and this one was no different. Without sounding rude, I tried to carry the conversation on in veiled speech. Talking about the weather and nothing in general. I wanted him on my side, so a bit of dialogue did no harm. We might be waiting for Charles for more than five minutes, and that's a sort of unwritten law of time between driver and passenger. Once over that five-minute timeframe, the old cabbies start getting a bit anxious, even though the meter would still be running.

It was still raining, not hard, but enough for women (and some men) to think, Hair. The ideal climate for a cabbie to make up his daily wage from what might have ordinarily been a slack day.

'So, what do you do, then?' the cabbie asked, looking into the rear mirror, hoping to make eye contact with me.

'I'm, err, waiting for a friend.' I pretended to misinterpret his question and looked out of the window and up to an apartment block which lined one side of the small street. My mobile rang. The cabbie let me take my call.

It was Vic. He'd parked up and was in place, no problems so far. I knew he would have to drive around if he was told to move on by eagled-eyed traffic wardens. Knowing Vic, he wouldn't cause them grief. As I've said before, the idea is to blend into the background, playing the grey man. There were no prizes in this game for getting compromised.

'Any sign, then?' he asked.

Although the cabbie was looking straight ahead and fiddling with his cab's radio, he was trying like hell to listen into my conversation. What a game life is!

Again I replied in veiled speech. 'Looks like he's not in.' I bent forward again, looking up at the same apartment. 'I'll give it another five minutes.' At the same time I spotted an Asian guy, plus a white girl, about 18, clearly together. They came out of the tube entrance and had to move off to a flank because of the amount of people heading against their direction. Common courtesy goes right out of the window when the rat race is scampering away home.

'Yes, Yes, I know ...' I began speaking to Vic in a nonsense style. He immediately picked up on it.

'You can't speak, can you?'

'That's right, got it, got it.' I rumbled on, not wanting to give the game away to the cabbie.

'Can you see the target?' It was good Vic was thinking on the same wavelength as I was.

'Yes, Yes. It's OK.' I carried on in the same style.

'Is he with the girlfriend?'

'Yeah, yeah, no problems,' I muttered, my eyes never wandering from the target, wanting, *willing* Charles to give me the sign that it was OK. Then he did it. I gripped my phone tighter. I felt a massive warm feeling whip around my body and cut across the back of my shoulders. A nice, confident sensation.

'Hey, mate, you know that newspaper article, chuck it away, will ya? I don't need it now,' I said casually.

'I take it the target has done the obvious.'

'Yes.'

'Right then, I'll call up Pete and Tom and let them know the score.'

'Yes, OK,' I said.

Pete and Tom should have left the KFC by now, and would be in place either side of Oxford Street, just around the corner from me, hanging about waiting for my call, which was now to be made by Vic.

'Are you gonna send them straight up or what?' Vic wanted to know if I was going to tell Charles to stroll casually up Oxford Street in shopper's mode, or tell him to make his way to the RV asap.

'Yes, let's do the second one. If things go according to plan, you'll be meeting John in about ten minutes, so wait to hear from him.' I closed the phone and then quickly dialled up Charles on his mobile.

'Charles, it's Steve. You OK?' I could see him look around trying in some way to spot me. He obviously didn't know what I looked like — it was a natural response. He put an arm around his young girlfriend and pulled her closer. Strength in an embrace.

'Yes, where are you?' He sounded even more anxious than before.

'Listen. Do you know the Cumberland Hotel, Marble Arch?' I kept my voice down low, still conscious of the other set of ears.

'Yes, of course.'

'Make your way up there right now. Don't ponce around but don't exaggerate your movements either. A bit faster than normal, it's raining, right? Go through the main entrance on Great Cumberland Place as if you're a guest —'

'Yes, and then what?'

'Walk through the foyer casually and head straight through the complex; you'll eventually come out of the rear entrance. You'll be picked up on Quebec Street.'

'How will I recognise you?'

'You won't. If someone asks you if your dog's dead, say "Yes, it died today" and do what he says. Got it?'

'Yes.'

I hung up. I wasn't going to pick him up — that was John's task, once Pete and Tom had 'handed' the two targets over to him.

Spotting if there were any 'tails' on Charles — other than Pete and Tom — would be a lot easier if he walked normally, but it was raining, and nobody walks normally in the rain. The point was, I didn't want Charles to drag his girlfriend up Oxford Street at a rapid rate of knots, as he might well do if still in a panic. It was a real issue. There was no reason for me to think that he was nothing more than a complete bag of nerves. I mean, who wouldn't be, given the situation he'd found himself in?

As planned, I got the cab to drop me off outside the Churchill Hotel, a superb five-star-plus hotel overlooking Portman Square — and very close to the Cumberland. I knew it well, having had the pleasure of working in it many times before. I've always said that if I ever won the Lottery, I'd do a couple of nights in this place whilst planning the rest of my life, I liked it so much.

I walked through the large revolving glass doors and into a vast marble-clad foyer. Hotel staff wearing dark but distinctive uniforms were directing a large group of businessmen with identity passes clipped on to their lapels towards the area of the lifts. Other people in less formal attire were making use of the comfy chairs. No one noticed me, but I knew that I had been caught on at least two of the overt cameras sited in the foyer. Once past the lifts, I turned right, pausing only long enough to spot any 'tails' by the in-house gift shop. All clear, I headed out through the side exit, walked around the back of the hotel, and waited.

The rear of the Churchill was an ideal 'agent' pick-up location for London. The street it was on wasn't as wide as a normal one and had very little traffic passing through it, but was wide enough to put in a 'J' turn if the situation required. On one side was a line of low-level mews-type lock-ups with their entrances uninhibited by parked vehicles; the hotel was on the other. The area had two entry and exit points (escape routes), which was the minimum for this type of pick-up.

My phone rang — John. 'Targets safe, with you figures two. I'll link up with Tom and Pete. So far, so good.'

At that precise moment, I saw the Range Rover. 'Good. I've got them visual now.' The Range Rover had just turned into the mews. I walked casually towards it. Vic drove straight past me without any sign of recognition and made a right at the other end. I walked out of the mews across the road and over to the corner of Portman and Wigmore streets, making sure that no other vehicle had turned in behind Vic. As planned, he picked me up a little later, after he had gone around Portman Square.

'All clear?'

'All clear,' Vic replied.

I turned round to face two very nervous people — just kids, really. 'Charles, Shelley, I'm Steve.' I made my introduction.

'Didn't I see just see you walking behind the Hotel?' Charles said, surprised.

'Yes, you did. Just making sure you guys hadn't been followed.' I wiped my face dry of sweat and rain with a towel I pulled out of one of the grips of training kit. 'Can't be too careful.'

Vic cut into the steady stream of traffic heading up to Gloucester Place. We were taking the long way home. It would give me the chance to listen to the short life-story of Charles so far.

I was very conscious of how carefully I had to word my questions. I didn't want to come across as his interrogator — after all, I was still being employed by his uncle, it wouldn't have been right to go straight into the jugular first off; and obviously, anything I said to him would get straight back to uncle.

Vic was taking it easy. It was still raining and the windows of the vehicle were beginning to mist up from the nervous sweat coming off the bodies of two young people in a state of shock. The interview began.

'So, what's your uncle's background, then?'

'His professional skills are in banking ...' he stuttered nervously, as if giving away a big secret.

'I know that much at least.' I let him continue.

'He used to be the manager of a bank in Madras, India, and that's how he knows his way around the banking world. Basically he left banking and set up as an independent agent for a couple of large commercial world banks who fancied having operations in India.'

'How long ago was that, then?'

'Thirty years maybe. It's all he's ever done — banking.'

'Go on then, what next?' I ordered. I'd let him talk now.

'My uncle would act as their man on the ground, their eyes and ears. Being able to speak several languages — Arabic, French, German, Spanish and of course a few local to India — meant the banks saw him as one in a million. He's also well read — King's

College, Cambridge — and is gifted with an extremely quick mind, all this made him a suitable and believable character.'

'Seems like he's got it all, apart from his looks,' Vic interjected.

Charles apparently ignored Vic's remark and carried on talking. 'As his relationship with these banks grew, the main core of business was selling commercial mortgages. His commissions mounted up and thus he quite deservedly gained the respect of his two main paymasters.'

'A sort of glorified financial adviser?' I said.

'You could say, but I don't think they made as much on their deals as Uncle. Once he earned 1.4 million from one deal alone ...'

'Pounds or dollars?' Vic said, eyes still fixed on the road ahead.

'Does it matter? What matters is that it was an awful lot of money from one deal,' Charles answered. 'Most recently, he's been doing business in and around the old Soviet-bloc countries and getting to know the way they do business. Since the collapse of a couple of well-known money houses, the banking world has really tightened up its rules of operation, especially out of the UK. Uncle said, "Setting up the deals becomes more bureaucratic and long-winded." But there's always a way around any system, especially if that system is a means to make money. It's basically a case of who, and what, you know.'

Charles was speaking rather eloquently and I got the impression that he quite admired his uncle. He certainly didn't sound like the crazed man I'd spoken to, not so long ago.

'So, the change in the banking rules affected countries like the up-and-coming Russia — its "rich landowners" were seeking another tool with which to turn their assets into US dollars. Uncle saw this niche in the market and exploited it — this need of the landowners to find another route by which they could capitalise on their assets. It was an almost totally virginal market to break into. Uncle could have quite easily written his own rules — and he did.'

Charles spoke at length about the fact that the family had never been short of money. Sometimes Charles's father would help his brother in brokering some of the deals, but generally they hadn't spoken for over three months. In fact, Charles said that his father didn't even know what his brother was up to these days.

'The first I heard was when father called me this ...'

'When the Russians cometh,' Vic said. I gave a sideways glance to him. Vic always had a weird sense of humour.

'Are you still taking this job seriously or what?' I said.

Ignoring me and right on cue, Vic said, 'Charles, just cut the crap and get to the point, will ya? Your old man and quite possibly your whole fuckin' family almost got their fuckin' heads blown off this morning. Get with the fuckin' programme, and tell us some shit that might help us identify the fuckers who are after us.'

'I don't fucking know,' Charles almost wailed, close to tears. He pulled his girlfriend closer. 'If I did, don't you think I'd have told you? I don't want to die, do I!' Charles was now sobbing incoherently. I looked across at Vic, who still had his sight fixed firmly on the road.

The good guy/bad guy approach generally works, and after Charles regained his composure he carried on with his uncle's life story.

It transpired that all of Suhail's deals were guaranteed through UK and US banks. This showed prospective clients the validity of Suhail's connections. Of course, the clients didn't know that Suhail was acting on behalf of the bank — as far as the client was concerned, Suhail was on *their* side and so would get paid by them when he delivered the funds. The banks on the other hand employed Suhail — just like many of the high-street banks do in this country, with their mortgage consultants — on a commission basis; close a deal and get weighed in with commission.

Suhail saw this as a way to act as a sort of double agent — the bank's man *and* the client's man. Either way, he would collect from both sides. Mr Ten Per Cent. But nobody likes people who collect from both sides of the deal.

Many of these deals would involve Suhail setting himself up as a client's Mr Fix It. The clients would all hold influential positions within their respective governments or industries, and — having got a sniff of, say, some land prime for redeveloping — would get Suhail to raise the necessary finance through his relationships with external banks in order to buy the land. Not your usual high-street real-estate broker's deal. These transactions were worth millions — sometimes hundreds of millions — of dollars, and would be transferred through several banks at any one time.

Suhail would then convince the bank that the land was worth

the amount involved. The land would be bought and then sold almost immediately, *for a higher sum*, even before the correct legal documents had been received by all parties. It was as simple as that. (It would be easy to bribe local government officials in these Third World countries; a lot of the time they got paid peanuts and welcomed joining in with the true spirit of capitalism. They were very grateful.)

Charles had said a lot, maybe a lot more than his uncle would have liked him to do, but he was truly scared about the shooter business. On that point I let him know that all he was doing was confirming what I already knew but I had to hear it from him in person. Of course, in reality I hadn't had a *clue* about the background of his uncle's operation, until this cosy little chat.

Now there was the business of Charles's father being grabbed at gunpoint to discuss. From the way his father had described the weapon, it had to be a semi-automatic pistol, maybe a Russian-made 9-millimetre Makarov. Apparently the Russians had said, 'If you're lying, then we'll be back. We know where you live.'

'Who did you think these guys really were? Russians or the Turks? The real players, or just the heavies employed by the real players?' I asked. Charles looked dull and shrugged his shoulders.

Suddenly Vic swerved violently to avoid missing his turning. He was driving in an anti-surveillance manner and was on the look-out for any followers, though the chances of being followed now were pretty remote. Not even the SAS would have been able to keep up with us. Vic was employing a number of driving tactics to throw off any potential tails, and he was now sure we weren't being followed.

'I thought they were Russians,' Charles stated. 'But the way my father described them, I think, maybe, they might be Turkish. Whatever, my uncle had definitely pissed off both tribes.'

Charles's father had said that one of the men called another Rohit, which I knew from working over in Turkey was a Turkish first name, and furthermore, there's a large Turkish community in North London. So now I couldn't be too sure *who* was after us. From now on, all calls into Suhail would definitely be monitored by the team. I would have a permanent telephone receptionist. This would filter any admin calls away from him, to his wife; any calls which came in to do with the banks and the like, *I* would be 'listening in' to.

Doing that, I could get names, then start to put these names to faces and places; then, hopefully start to build up a proper intelligence picture. More importantly, if the Turks or the Russians eventually got hold of Suhail's mobile number or our whereabouts, we would be ready for that, too. And to save any confusion amongst the team, I went firm on calling the people after Suhail Russians, until otherwise confirmed.

By the time we arrived back at the hotel, I'd heard all I wanted to hear, but the long and short of it all was, until Suhail gave us the 'services no longer required' certificate, it would be a case of waiting for the Russians to show. Suhail only had to slip up once — a passing comment to a bank associate, a private phone call — and he would probably be history. So I decided that the best form of defence was attack.

13.

STREET SLAGS

DAY SEVEN

So now Charles and Shelley were staying with us at the Regents Plaza. As far as I could make out (and there were no reasons to suggest otherwise) Shelley was just what she seemed — a girlfriend who just happened to get caught up in something which had nothing to do with her. This meant company for Suhail's wife and daughter, but more importantly, it was the ideal opportunity to put forward my game-plan. To take the strain off the family and to try to get to the root of Suhail's problem, I would put it to him that we should have a meet with those who were after him. He told me he would see how the next two days worked out before giving me his decision on that. Meanwhile, he had more meetings with the bank, and in addition, two acquaintances were flying in to see him. I didn't know if these two people were also involved with the land deal or not, but I had to assume that — at the very least — he was going to take advice from them.

The first to arrive was a Mr Abdul Wahab, a small bald Lebanese man in his early 50s, with the annoying habit of coughing up phlegm every other minute. Mr Abdul Wahab was a businessman who appeared to be a personal friend of Suhail. He'd booked himself into The White House Hotel, a rather discreetly situated, unshowy (but highly regarded by its guests) hotel standing in Osnaburgh Terrace, just off the south-east corner of Regent's Park.

At first, I thought he was over here on his own accord, but from his first meeting with Suhail, it became clear he was now another person the team had to look after. There were many trips to and from from his hotel every day. He even attended the late meetings which were still happening at Ennismore Gardens.

The other man to arrive, a little later, was a Greek, a Mr Christos, slightly older-looking than Mr Abdul Wahab (possibly in his mid-60s) but of the same posture and size; only he had a full head of white hair in need of a trim. He booked into the Regents Plaza, so there was no need to ferry him around. He too appeared to be more Suhail's friend than just an acquaintance. Initially I assumed he was over here to help Suhail out with the Russian deal, but he wasn't. He let slip quite early on, during his first day, that he was over here to see what exactly Suhail had done with the ten million pounds entrusted to him by an Italian friend for the purchase of two country estates in the Home Counties.

As you can imagine, this was all news to me. But I wasn't particularly surprised, given the way this job was panning out. Over the next couple of days Mr Christos would frequently come up and spend time with the team, chewing the fat and trying to get to know us, that sort of thing, possibly trying to find out how loyal we were to Suhail. At the time, we all thought that he was just being friendly.

On one occasion he appeared to be quite irritated during a non-stop stand-up conversation with me in the corridor. '... and you haven't taken a trip out of London since working for him [Mr Suhail]?'

'No,' I said. I didn't want to get involved in a long drawn-out interrogation over something I knew nothing about. 'The furthest any of us have been is to the City. Maybe he's seeing solicitors and estate agents during these meetings, I really wouldn't know.' I tried to deflate the atmosphere, knowing that some of this money might well be financing my security operation.

'Maybe you should ask him?' I added, matter of fact, suspecting he had probably done that immediately on his arrival, but had been skilfully bullshitted by Suhail.

His reply was very diplomatic. 'Maybe I should. Maybe it's time to get to the bottom of all this.'

I wasn't the least bit worried about Mr Christos's problem. When people talk in telephone numbers regarding money, it tends to go in through one ear and out the other with me — and in my experience, such things ain't always what they appear to be, anyway. And that was especially the case on this job. Mr Christos's problem was a sideline into which neither I nor the team was going to be drawn.

It was a strange period all round. The day started off with 'B' Team on the school run whilst the 'A' Team went to pick up Mr Abdul Wahab and bring him to the Regents Plaza. Then there would be a trip into the City, and then back to the hotel. At six most evenings, Mr Abdul Wahab was taken back to The White House, only to be picked up a few hours later for the trip over to Kensington, where Mr Christos would join them, and then finally return back to the hotel in the early hours of the day.

This routine was to go on for the next day or so, and we hadn't been hit yet, which was a good thing, to say the least. Whether it had been down to Suhail's brother lying low and keeping his mouth shut, or the security cover I'd put in force, I would never find out. Certainly the system of filtering telephone calls was working well, and the team guys were all working with some uniformity.

During this time I got to know more about the Singapore banker at Ennismore Gardens. She turned out to be a woman married to a billionaire merchant banker who was always on the other side of the world. I got to know her as Patricia, through her frequent phone calls to Suhail. According to him, she was an agoraphobic, and had not left the confines of her house for over ten years — and that was the period of time Suhail had been doing business with her.

So it was a bit of a shock, and a huge wake-up call to me as to how much everyone involved with this deal had at risk, when, late one morning, she appeared in the foyer of the Regents Plaza: a very small and frail-looking woman in her later years, grey hair tied back in a bun neatly sitting squarely on the top of her head. She looked like a woman you might expect to see reading people's palms at a psychic fair and not someone who could quite easily finance the national Lottery for the next couple of months.

'What's a billionaire meant to look like, anyway?' Vic said when seeing her. He was right — what *is* a billionaire agoraphobic meant to look like?

'I don't know,' I replied. 'Would have thought that she would have had at least one BG with her.'

'There you go, mate. I've just got my next contract,' Vic joked.

'No problem, mate, I'll have a word and put a good word in for you. You look like her type.'

Another name picked up from the phone filter was a chap called John Golding, who worked out of a high-street bank near the Ritz Hotel. It was a place we had not yet visited, but were sure to do so in the not-too-distant future.

Being in a state of readiness to bug out at the drop of a hat for such a long period wasn't good for the team's effectiveness or morale. I'd seen it happen before, on less high-risk BG operations. The blokes get bored, bitchy and complacent. I'm not saying it was happening with the team just yet, but it was a point I had to bear in mind — it wouldn't be long before the shit started to creep in.

Because we had to work a 24-hour plan, all the team members were on stand-by at the same level of readiness, if they weren't tasked on a job. No one left the confines of the hotel unless it was a very local trip, allowed out only to get a newspaper or to stretch the legs for a couple of minutes at the most.

The only men who were allowed off were the corridor men. They worked their shifts around each other, and as long as the areas I had designated were covered by the right amount of men, then I had no objections if they went home after their shifts. They had limited knowledge of what the job was about, and part of my brief to them was the 'need-to-know' routine. They needed to know certain things but not everything, and anyone outside the team didn't need to know anything.

Even if they inadvertently let slip to one of their wives, girlfriends or mates something about the job — which I was pretty sure they wouldn't do — then what they knew wasn't of any great consequence. They knew of this small, ineffectual, Asian-looking man, living in a half-decent hotel with his wife and daughter, who had few visitors, and who usually only went out in the evening. Nothing particularly strange about that, just usual routine for many BG operations.

The only exception, of course, was the precise location of the operation, and I stressed to all of them, even the BGs, that this *had* to be kept a secret. I couldn't afford *any* member to get slack. Some of the guys had taken to using a café just across from the hotel. They were becoming regulars, and Al and Mike were sniffing around one of the waitresses. Thinking, Dick ruling brains, I had to tactically reiterate to them the delicate nature of the job. Blow the team's cover and we might as well put an advert out on national radio. If a leak came, then I didn't want it to come from my side.

'Fucking hell, Steve, don't get paranoid,' Al said.

'Yeah, lighten up. We're in sales, you know, office equipment and all that,' Mike added. 'Anyway, she's not interested in Al, it's me she fancies.'

'Bollocks is it!' Al jumped in with. 'It's *me* she wants to shag, not you, you fuckin' wart-head!'

'Office sales — right, like she's gonna believe *that* old bollocks,' I said.

'Well, whatever, I've always got my sales catalogue with me when we go for a scoff or brew.' Mike produced a thick colour brochure, a bit like one of those home-shopping catalogues.

'He borrowed it off one of the girls on reception. He's sniffing around that one too,' Al declared.

Their cover was good enough and I didn't push it any further. They knew the score, and were both professional enough not to cut around with dicks on their foreheads.

However, what Suhail was telling his family and friends in the confines of his own suite, and who Mr Christos and Mr Abdul Wahab phoned after their regular meetings — all that was totally out of my control. Hence the need for us to be on our toes all the time.

Keeping up a state of fitness was another problem. All the guys worked out regularly. A run, then into the gym, that was the usual routine. They could sustain up to a week off without doing anything physical, but by now the levels of stress were rising. A diet of club sandwiches, French fries and coffee — the staple diet of a lot of resident BG teams from our fast and accessible room service food — was becoming a pain in the arse.

Eating when you can, in anticipation of a fast ball, was par for the course. One of the family might just want to go somewhere, and the general pattern set since the job kicked off was that we didn't get any prior warning of a pending trip, apart from the evening trip to the City. This made it difficult to keep to a half-decent training routine.

The hotel had a gym, but it was temporarily closed for a refit. So the team had to make do with working out in the large suite we used as an operations and day room. It wasn't ideal, but doing sit ups and press ups was better than doing nothing. I don't want to give the impression that the team members were all psyched up practising their kick boxing and karate moves, waiting for that moment when they could bash someone up — that wasn't the case. The point is that all the guys on the job were total professionals, and this job required us to keep up a certain level of fitness in order to do the job — so that's what we achieved.

In some circles of society, people — nice liberals, say — may still have this very stereotyped image of the security industry, as made up of a bunch of thugs, ex soldiers and ex felons, but this wasn't the case with my team. It might be the case in some circumstances at the lower end of the industry, but not at the level I work at. A liberal's line of thinking might see no need to have such a security cordon around an individual, they would probably maintain 'That's why we have a police force,' and they might find the entire idea of bodyguards as something to be kept well within the confines of Hollywood studios. I accept the existence of that view, but of course definitely don't agree with it. I have a life, I live in the real world, not in their world of the Shopping-on-Saturdays and Sex-on-Sundays routine. Many of the guys on the 'circuit' are ex military, and have served their time in theatres of war all over the world, fighting for the sorts of rights these 'wet liberals' take for granted, such as the freedom of speech to judge others without really experiencing what life's all about.

Now I don't want to get on my soap-box and start sounding like some wet crusty with a degree in Social Studies walking around with a head full of statistics, but it's blatantly obvious to me that violence is now on the increase, big style, especially in the bigger cities such as Manchester and London — two cities that I know very well. I'm sure it's the same case in Birmingham and Liverpool (a bit of lateral thinking coming in there). So there's a growing need for people with my experience. It's an expanding market — the curtailing of violence.

Whether it's drink- or drugs-related or a product of the kill-kill-kill computer-game age of the 1980s and 1990s I'm not sure. Probably it's a bit of a cocktail of all of it, mixed with a tonic of a greed-is-good society — money and materialism = madness.

TWO DAYS LATER, DAY NINE

Madness, or to put it another way, an act of controlled aggression, that's what happened when John and I left to head off into the West End on a shopping trip for Suhail. He wanted a resup of toiletries and underwear, so we headed for Selfridges, since I knew I could get all his requirements in one hit. We took one of the Mercs and John parked it around the back of the store, where there's an unofficial waiting zone for chauffeurs and the like.

'I'll probably be no more than half an hour,' I said as I got out. 'I'll give you a call if I'm going to be longer.'

'Take as long as you like,' John replied. 'I'm going to enjoy this bit of time off.'

Traffic was bumper-to-bumper and the pavement was teeming with pedestrians, all shuffling about on missions of their own. It had just begun to rain again so I turned up the collar of my coat, joined the masses and hurriedly made my way to the store's side entrance. Before going in, I stopped off at a phone booth to call a friend. I didn't want to use the mobile; I wanted that line clear just in case I got a call from John or one of the team back at the hotel.

I saw a double booth, the first one was being used by an elderly lady struggling with a head scarf and handbag. I opened the door of the second, grabbed the receiver and started to dial. The booth was covered in these call-girl picture postcards, offering straight sex or more advanced sessions with girls like 'Busty Brunette Bondage Babe'. A picture made out to be the girl on offer, but in truth, it wouldn't be the girl in the picture — that had been lifted straight from a porno magazine. 'Caribbean Caprice, just 18 and new in town' said another. Every flat surface at eye level and above was covered with these postcards.

Someone picked the phone up at the other end of the line.

'Jamie, it's Steve.' I started to peel off some of the postcards and made a ball with the blue putty-like substance that was used to stick them on to the booth.

'How's it goin', Steve, still on for the weekend?'

'No mate, sorry, that's why I'm calling ...' Through the booth window, in which I had made an opening by pulling away the postcards, I could see two workmen across the road, sheltering out of the rain in a doorway, drinking a hot brew out of polystyrene cups. Suddenly, a face appeared looking straight into my eyes, a white face: a young lad, no more than 15 or 16, smaller than me. He then slapped the outside of the phone booth right where I was looking — and his palmed hand trapping air and hitting a strengthened polymer made a hell of a crack. It made me jump back, the move was totally aggressive and unprovoked. Jamie was still speaking.

'What the hell was *that*?' Jamie had plainly heard the crack.

'Hang on a minute, mate, I've got some clever twat outside.' I dropped the receiver and sprang out of the phone box. The lad hadn't anticipated my move; neither had the two builders who were now looking across at me, wondering what I was going to do, with slightly amused expressions.

'What's your problem, prick?' My verbal attack appeared to catch him off guard.

'Hey man, hey man ...' He replied, standing and shaking his hands in a loose manner like some dancer in a rap video.

Then three of his mates arrived and 'closed in', in a very intimidating manner. But they didn't cross the game line, the game line being, in my case, about two metres. All were dressed the same, baseball caps, baggy designer puffer jackets, jeans you could sail around the world in, and trainers with thick soles, soles which you could use to walk across a field of burning coals. The only thing out of context were their faces, two black and two white. I made a mental note: *no racial hang-ups in this gang.*

'Hey man, what's your problem, man, what's your problem?' He didn't advance.

His mates joined in a chorus of, 'Yeah man, yeah man, what's your problem?', still using the 'loose-hands' method to convey their aggressive stance.

I still had my right hand gripped around the phone booth's door. I had to make a command decision as to what I was going to do. On the one hand, I was fuming at the intimidation these young lads were putting on me: Fucking cheek, I thought. On the other, I was aware of the builders looking over, seeing what I was going to do. It was a sort of macho thing — something I thought I'd had kicked out of me in the SAS. But I was seething with anger and I wasn't in the SAS now. I had to sort it. It was my move. I made a stab at a negotiated settlement without losing face and fucking up my good suit.

'What's all this "man" bollocks, you pricks? I'm on the fuckin' phone. FUCK OFF,' I said, with some element of control.

They shut up jibing and I stood my ground. 'IF YOU WANT SOME, YOU CAN FUCKIN' HAVE SOME,' I screamed, as I slammed the booth door shut. The buffer wasn't as strong as it should have been, so when it made contact with the frame it made a loud bang and then sprang back open again, almost as fast as I had closed it. I thought it was going to shatter, I'd slammed it so hard.

'COME ON THEN, COME ON THEN, YOU FUCKERS, WANT SOME, DO YOU?' I was still screaming, but I was in control. I knew what I was doing. I was playing them at their own game — intimidation. Any onlookers would probably have thought that I was a 'suit' in the middle of having a mental breakdown. 'He's flipped, he's gone over the edge!'

Now I made my advance, prepared to take on all four. Their body language told me that they could easily have been either confident or dumb enough to stand their ground. They didn't, they backed off pretty fast. Then one of them said, 'He's fuckin' mad, man, he's fuckin' mad.'

'Yeah, you're fuckin' mad,' the one who started this whole escapade replied. 'You're fuckin' mad.' He pointed to his temple with his index finger, indicating that I had something loose upstairs.

'Yeah, fucking damn right I'm mad.'

Not once did I lose eye-contact with any of them. My eyes darted from one pair of eyes to another. I let them know that I meant business, and it was beginning to be all too much for them. Then all of a sudden this guy with the mouth pulled out a double-blade knife from inside his jacket.

'Come on then, come on then, you want some now, fucker,' he shouted at me, beckoning me to go towards the blade. I kept quiet and didn't move, and because of that he thought it safe to advance on me. Now, that was this prick's first mistake. I was aware that a major incident might take place. Onlookers made no attempt to intervene, and I was glad of that. The last thing I wanted was for some do-gooder to stick a nose in. I wanted to teach this wanker the art of good manners.

A couple of pedestrians just goose-necked, as though they were looking at a crash on the motorway. I remember thinking that this just happened to be just off the busiest shopping street in the whole of Europe, and here I was being attacked by a blade-wielding kid and his mates! It was fucking outrageous, they must have been on drugs or reliving a computer game in their heads. He was still shouting while being urged on by his mates. Now all my thoughts were concentrated on this creature in front of me. He held the blade out rigid, his arm straight. I ran the situation through my mind; a young kid, a four-inch blade, looking sharp. He meant business, he meant to use it and if he caught me right, he could quite easily kill me. Then I suddenly closed the distance — he didn't expect it and neither did his mates.

As he advanced I caught his stare and that confirmed too that his intentions still weren't honourable. He still expected me to run off, or at the very least back off. I got the feeling he'd done this party piece on more than one occasion, because he now looked quite confident. He made the lunge; he was fast, but he was now committed. A quick move to my left and forward found me almost eyeball to eyeball with him. Again I looked into his stare, and suddenly he knew that he had fucked up, because my right hand had come over *his* right and gripped his wrist.

In street fights, as in war, it's a very powerful thing, knowing that you, as defender, now have the upper hand. I could sense that my attacker knew this, too. I wasn't going to kill him if I could help it, but he didn't know that. I had to use reasonable force to disarm and incapacitate him, still fully aware that the other three might also be carrying knives. I was aware that they had now moved back.

In less than a second my grip had tightened tenfold, brought on by masses of adrenalin flowing around my body, and knowing that my attacker couldn't move an inch. I twisted his wrist with so much force that he let out a piercing scream like a stuck pig. I then drew my right knee hard up into his groin. I hoped to push his balls up into the back of his neck. He bent down double, which put him in the position I wanted. Still with the Vulcan death grip on his wrist, I stepped back and straightened out his arm. The blade now dropped to the ground. He had no choice but to stay bent double.

With the minimal amount of pressure I pushed his wrist hard back with both of my hands, until I heard it click. This told me it was broken. Lastly, holding him under control with my left hand, I brought my right down on the rear of his damaged arm and snapped his elbow like a match-stick. I let him fall to the ground in a screaming heap. That threat now contained, I moved towards the other three, but they weren't having any of it — they skulked away and disappeared into the hordes of Oxford Street, hopefully all more enlightened from their most recent experience — don't talk to strangers!

The entire incident couldn't have taken more than 30 seconds from beginning to end. But those 30 seconds could have changed any of our five lives for ever. But it didn't — well, not for me it didn't.

As I opened the door to carry on talking to Jamie, I heard someone applauding. I turned and looked.

'Nice one, mate, good on ya.' It was one of the builders. 'That'll teach the bastards,' he added. I put an arm up in acknowledgement, and calmly picked up the receiver and told Jamie I would call him back in five minutes.

Even though this little altercation came to nothing, I had built up a bowl of adrenalin inside my stomach. I began to shake a bit so I hot-footed it away from the crowds and into a back street in search of another phone booth. The last thing I wanted was for the four lads — well, three of them — to reorganise themselves, pluck up enough courage and come hunting for me — this time, maybe, with their knives. Who knew? I wasn't about to hang around and find out.

Gangs, we all used to be in one: been there, seen it, done it. Cowards. Strength in depth and a sackload of Dutch Courage. One on one, and they drop like falling plates on a rifle range.

Some minutes later I was in another phone booth, staring at another screen full of porno postcards. I was feeling a little bit more relaxed now. The brisk walk had settled me a bit. I composed myself and redialled Jamie's number.

'What the hell happened there?' Jamie's voice was more inquisitive than anxious.

'Oh, the usual shit one has to put up with in London.' I changed the subject. 'Sorry about Hereford this weekend, I'm tied up with a job.'

I'd planned to do a spot of salmon-fishing with Jamie, a long lazy weekend relaxing on the banks of the River Wye. It wasn't going to happen. It was a shame. Apart from working out, I had very few pastimes; the job wouldn't allow it. I'd given up rugby a couple of years before, and had taken to watching it from an armchair — I couldn't afford the injuries.

Fishing gives me an outlet I need. I can go out early morning and sit on the bank for hours, just looking at the tip of my rod, contemplating the meaning of life. I don't even have to catch anything. (It's nice when you do, of course!) The ability I have to sit there, come rain or shine, probably comes from years of sitting in ambushes, waiting and more waiting, almost willing the target to cross into the killing zone, and then letting rip. At that point you could move without fear of compromising the operation, to bring some life back into your numbed body.

Once an ambush is 'set', with all the cut-off groups and the killer group in place, then the only activity allowed, indeed tolerated, is that of slow, deliberate, millimetre movements of the body to release the pressure and stiffness which come from lying prone on the ground for hours on end. It's a discipline that has to be mastered by all infantry soldiers if they want to get on in the army.

Anyway, I was just about to hang up when again I noticed two other guys opening the door of the booth next to me. The guy who went inside was pulling off some of the porno postcards and replacing them with others from a little knapsack he had slung over his shoulder. He had replaced three in as many seconds, working at speed. He was about six two tall, mid-20s, skinny as a rake, had thick matted red hair with a few days' growth, and was dressed in a pretty scruffy-looking Val Doonican style jumper. Even though it was raining quite heavily now, his hair seemed to have soaked up what rain had fallen on him; either that or it was so matted with shite that the rain couldn't penetrate it.

His side-kick, the look-out, was much shorter but of the same strain and street fashion. He reminded me of a ferret.

I made quick eye contact with 'Ginger' then turned away, not wanting to cause trouble. Jamie had hung up at the other end but I was still holding my receiver. I knew what was coming next. It had happened to me before, just like it had happened to a lot of other Londoners who use public phone booths, no doubt.

I saw Ginger move towards my booth. Here we go again, I sensed. 'Fuck it!' I said to myself. The door of my booth was yanked open as if I wasn't even in there, and then an arm entered my space; it touched me, but couldn't make the grip stick, followed by a 'Come on, mate,' from Ginger, as if I shouldn't have been in there. It was a tone a policeman might use when making an arrest.

I'd been leaning on the door, so as he opened it I came out like a car-spring being released under compression. It all happened so fast. It startled him, so much that he jumped back about ten feet. His mate also took a few paces back.

No time for talking now. They'd made the first aggressive move, and now they had to pay the consequences of severely pissing me off. I didn't give a fuck by now. I'd just about had it with these slags for one day. So before he had time to readjust his position, I covered the ground between us in lightning speed and landed one square on his nose. I felt this feature give way as my right fist made the connection. The punch lifted him clean off his feet and sent him crashing down on his back. His head hit the ground with a definite crack. Porno postcards all over the place.

The threat Ginger posed to me was lessened as I noticed him lift his head off the ground. Noted: *Not dead — just dazed. Good.* He was out of the game for the time being. I turned my attention to the look-out, saw him weighing up the situation. It looked like he was up for it. His mind must have been saying, 'This isn't meant to happen. He's a "suit", for fuck's sake.' He was definitely thinking, Should I, shouldn't I? What would Ginger think?

I saw him make a move. 'Don't even go there, bollocks,' I shouted.

'What did you do that for?' he said, looking down at his mate. Then he made a lunge in my direction, more of a token effort than anything else. Fully aware that I was dressed in a suit and tie, that I was on a job which was paying the bill, and that this was my second altercation in almost as many minutes, I made no effort to meet him. Instead, I swerved to one side as he shot past me. His own body-weight and lack of fancy footwork led to him finding himself lying face down on the ground.

In the meantime Ginger had made it to his knees, but was still well out of it. 'Minimum force necessary' was the code of conduct the British Army always drums into its soldiers when dealing with potentially violent and life-threatening situations, and I've always tried to carry that over into my civilian life. But Ginger had really pissed me off, and so had the gang of four. I'd done his face, it was awash with really bright-red blood, well oxygenated. His heart must have been pumping at full rate.

My punch had not only split his nose but had also forced his bottom lip through a couple of teeth, and now he was trying to sort that personal problem out. Maybe I'd caught him on his mouth first off? But I didn't give a shit by now. So, as I made my escape, I planted one swift kick into his ribs, and did them too. He squealed in pain as he was half lifted off the ground by the force of my kick — the only audible sound that had come from his mouth since I'd hit him.

My senses were obviously up big time. A quick look around to see who was watching — no one that I could see, though maybe some office workers had seen what was going on from their windows. I didn't know, and I wasn't interested. My only concern was to leave the area as soon as possible. The police around this part of London are really sharp and on the ball, and are always there when you don't want them to be. Accidentally jump an amber light, and they're there. Get caught short, and they're there. Get burgled, and they can't even bother to take a statement.

They would see me as an easy nick, and one for their pub talk later. Of fixed abode, tax-payer, with family and financial commitments, yes: 'He ain't going to cause too much paper work or loose ends — a nice and clinical case of GBH.' Even though it was the couple of slags who'd started it. 'Slags, not worth getting the notebook out for. They have no money to pay fines, they have no fixed address; they are, in short, unaccountable. They clog up the "in" trays, a right pain in the arse. Too much hassle.' I could hear the police saying all of this.

I cut through the back of Oxford Street, shaking myself down as I went. I straightened my tie, brushed my hair and generally composed myself and started to act like any other 'suit' out of the office and on a mission to the coffee shop. I was purposely heading away from John.

Once I got inside the paved zone of St Christopher's Place (a bit of a trendy area, just off Oxford Street), littered with the empty tables and chairs of the many restaurants which make up the majority of the commercial outlets, I called up John and told him to meet me at a safe house, a café we use just off Marylebone High Street.

'What's the problem. You get it all?' he asked.

'No, I haven't even started yet. No problem,' I lied. 'I'll tell you about it when you get to the safe house.'

He sounded a bit pissed off, probably because he was parked up in an ideal space and was loath to give it up if I hadn't done the shopping.

It would take me several minutes to get to the RV, time enough to shake off any pursuing PC, and time enough to grab a can of Coke from a 'Greasy Joe's' that I knew was just around the next corner. It would take John twice as long as me to get to the RV; he would be driving against the one-way system. I had time to do one more thing. I phoned Jamie. Luckily I'd previously called him on his mobile and not at his home address. I found another telephone, third time lucky, and dialled his home number.

'Jamie, do me a favour? You might get a call from the police on your mobile. They might want to know who you were speaking to on it around about the time I first phoned you.'

'So, what's up?'

'Well, I bashed a couple of slags earlier, well one actually, and fucked off. It was their fault, frig all to do with me. Anyway, the police might trace the call I made to you from the phone booth I used. They probably won't; they should have better things to do than that, but just in case ...'

While I was talking I could hear Jamie laughing his head off. There he was, 200 miles away surrounded by acres of countryside, the best kept secret in England — Herefordshire — taking it easy, and here I was in a bag of bollocks in 'Stress City'. It wasn't fair.

'You want me to deny all knowledge, is that it?'

'Yeah, can you do that? I owe you one.'

'I'll do better than that, mate. I'll just turn the bugger off for a day or two.'

Just outside the safe house I flagged John down and told him to drive off to Whiteleys shopping precinct, just off the bottom of Queensway, in Bayswater. A less crowded, troubled and volatile environment to do my shopping in.

About four months later I was sitting outside one of the many Lebanese restaurants on the Edgware Road, enjoying an Arabic coffee and smoking a strawberry shisha (the Hubble-Bubble water pipe affair. It really does smell and taste of strawberry, whereas in warmer countries, it could well taste of something a lot stronger.) when, all of a sudden, I saw the ferret-like guy scurry out of one phone booth and wait impatiently outside another one, which was in use. I held a burning stare in his direction. We made eye contact; the penny suddenly dropped with him, and he high-tailed it across the Edgware Road and out of sight. What had happened to his mate Ginger I don't know, but at least it looked like ferret-face had learnt a lesson in common courtesy.

The whole episode was an example of how something can happen anywhere at any time. All sorts of things lurk around every corner in London, which are totally unconnected with 'the job', but which are everyday occurrences that many of us living and working in the big city have to endure. Only sometimes, these slags pick on the wrong person.

14.

WEAPON PICK-UP

Over the past few days I had been seriously toying with the idea of picking up the Walther. I figured that if this Russian was prepared to run around London with his piece with a good chance of getting caught, then it was a damn good bet that he would probably end up using it — if not on Suhail and his family, then on me or one of my team.

It didn't take long for me to make my decision. I would use this slack period to make the pick-up.

It was just by coincidence that the evening I'd chosen to get the Walther was the evening that I'd been asked by a TV company to take part in a documentary entitled *Who Killed WPC Fletcher?* about the policewoman murdered at the start of the Libyan Embassy siege some years earlier. The whole meat of the programme focused on new evidence which suggested that the shot that killed her didn't come from the direction of the embassy — as the Government had said in its post-incident report, thus pointing blame to someone inside; instead it put forward the idea that a lone assassin had purposely killed WPC Fletcher from another building. One possible reason for this apparent assassination was to bring the UK more on the side of the anti-Libyan, American point of view, and consequently, the ultimate bombing of Libya.

The producer wanted me to give my tactical and professional appreciation, as an SAS guy who had been on the ground at the time, based on the programme's latest information. It was quite eerie because I was interviewed outside the embassy, giving my point of view about the bullet trajectory and types of weapons which I thought might have been used in the shooting, and then, within a couple of hours, I was up on the roof of my office unwrapping the Walther 9-millimetre. From another part of the roof I located the package which contained the ammunition. I took both packages back down to the relative safety of my office. I stripped both the pistol and magazine, and gave the barrel a good pull through, wiped off all the excess oil that I'd covered it in, to stop the rust creeping in during years of lying idle, and generally gave it the once-over. I made sure that the magazine spring was working and was still strong enough to feed in rounds.

I stripped it and rebuilt it six or seven times, every time cocking it and then firing off its action, just to make sure it was in full working order. The Walther is a very basic and very reliable pistol, so I had no worries about it not performing when I pulled the trigger. The ammunition was my biggest concern. The base of the rounds had no real identity marks on them to suggest when and where they were produced, only the number 80. This wasn't enough to tell me if it came from a German or Argentine manufacturer.

If it was German, then I was sure it would fire off, but if it was Argy, then it might just go puff instead of bang when I squeezed the trigger. It was crucial that I test-fire a couple of rounds, so I quickly loaded four rounds, placed a copy of the Yellow Pages and two three-inch thick London Business directories on top of one another, and with the aid of an old army sleeping bag draped over the pistol to deaden the noise, fired four deliberate rounds in short succession at almost point-blank range into the directories. (Each time I checked to make sure none of the rounds had passed right through the directories.) On firing the final round I allowed the ejected case to fully eject from the weapon. This was to see just how far this pistol would eject empty cases — quite critical if I had to retrieve them.

All four rounds fired off with force and sounded OK. The years spent underground appeared not to have affected their killing power, and the ejected round travelled only a couple of feet, and so would be easy enough to collect if the situation allowed.

I'm always aware of leaving evidence behind — a spent case is very good evidence for the police to get their teeth into. Perhaps, in this instance, sufficient to trace this particular batch of ammunition, but maybe not giving enough clues as to who was the firer.

A revolver would be a better weapon for a one-off assassination. They don't eject their empty cases. But as far as accuracy and the ability to put rounds down on a target in one hit is concerned, a pistol is far better. A pistol can carry up to 20 rounds against the five- or six-shot revolver drum. Also, a pistol is a lot quicker to change magazines on during a firefight, and a firefight was what the Russians were going to get, even if only one round was fired in my direction.

Because I didn't want the rest of the team knowing I was carrying, I had to bastardise one of the two shoulder-holsters I had knocking around the office. I cut off one of the back straps and secured the small, nylon-made pouch into the left-hand side of my suit jacket. That way, when the weapon was being carried, it wouldn't move about and make it obvious that I had something hanging under my armpit. It took several goes to get the holster and pistol just how I wanted it.

By looking in a mirror I was able to see if the pistol's weight was disrupting the cut of my jacket. No, it looked OK, a slight bulge, no more than the average mobile phone would make. The only other adjustment I made was to unscrew the hand grips on both sides of the pistol in order to reduce its overall bulkiness.

One last thing was to clean every one of my fingerprints off both the pistol, magazine and bullets. I was working to the worst-case scenario, that if I was to get stopped, I could quite easily get out of that problem. But it wouldn't be the case if my fingerprints were on the hand grip. It wasn't my intention to get stopped carrying, but one can never be too sure.

The law might look upon me 'carrying' in a not particularly good light — intent, quite possibly. But what you have to remember about someone from my professional background, with the level of training I have in the use of firearms, and in explosives too, is that, if caught, I might just get made an example of, and have the book thrown at me. Of course, this doesn't make me above the law, but I just want to let it be known and to alleviate any fears that I'm not another budding Michael Ryan or the nutter from Dunblane, who between them murdered many innocent people in two very tragic and heart-rending firearm incidents.

I'm highly trained always to use minimum force and I consider myself as level-headed and as sane as any police armed-response team member. Yes, I do understand that carrying is illegal and very politically incorrect, but it's one of the tools of my profession, and that's all there there is to it. In some countries you can 'carry'; in this country, you can't. It's another risk and moral judgement that guys in my profession have to make every time they take a job on.

I don't do any cockstands about how a particular weapon looks, or have any in-depth opinions about how it works or what trigger pressure suits me. I just need it to work when I want it to. What I'm trying to say is that I'm no gun nerd. Furthermore, you've got to remember is that I've been around guns for over 20 years.

To me, the whole concept of the gun culture in this country is no big deal. Personally, it does nothing for me to spend a day down at the ranges turning rounds into empty cases; I can't think of anything more boring. However, I respect the people who find this pastime pleasurable. And, as regards the anti-gun lobby, I can see why they make a big deal about banning the gun. They do have a point.

What *is* a big deal to me is carrying when I think the situation justifies it. In the final analysis, I would rather be tried by twelve good men and women than be carried by six. If one lives by the sword, then one might expect to die by it.

15.

AN ARMED RESPONSE

DAY TWELVE, EARLY AFTERNOON

Forcing the 'meet' option out of Suhail was hard work. Every time I approached him on the subject he very skilfully batted it away, or was distracted by the telephone. It wasn't until Vic, who was at the corridor man's position on a battery change run, came screeching into our room like a rollover Lottery winner, that things changed. I was kicking back on the bed at the time having a bit of an afternoon nap, rather like a lizard. I wasn't sleeping, just sort of resting with one eye open.

'Steve, Steve, you'd better come quickly, Bollocks has just had a call from the Russians.' It was apparent that Vic had now gone firm on his adopted name for our client.

It took me about two seconds to register what Vic had shouted out and then I delivered my reaction.

'Oh, that's just fucking great, fucking ideal!' I muttered. 'If they've got the phone number, then it won't be long before they get *our* location.'

'I don't think so, it's on his mobile — no way can they find the location from that.' Vic reassured me somewhat.

Immediately I jumped off the bed, grabbed my mobile, the radio and the handful of loose change from the top of the room's dresser and followed Vic in hot pursuit. 'What did they say?' I said, hurriedly putting on my suit jacket.

'Dunno, I left Suhail talking to the caller and came straight down here to get you.'

'Let's hope he's still on.'

But by the time we got to his room, Suhail's telephone conversation was over.

'Vic told me, what did he say, what did he say?' I said urgently.

Suhail didn't look up and didn't say a word, just waved me into the room as if I was his lackey. He might just as well have put a finger up to his lips to indicate not to speak — it was that sort of atmosphere. After a few days of being genial, he had reverted to his usual arrogance. He was sitting back on one of three lounge sofas, so I sat on the one nearest without being asked. I felt myself adopting a completely different approach to my client. The job was turning into more of a babysitting task than a BG one. Vic was still standing guard by the door — not that he had to, the corridor man was still outside, but I guess Vic felt more comfortable standing.

Suhail was smoking a cigarette, and in between quick, short, nervous puffs, he would roll it between his thumb and index finger. I looked at him in a rather glaring manner while waiting for him to speak. Just because *he* wasn't bothered about his well-being, didn't mean that my team and I weren't.

'Look, boss.' I tried a friendlier approach. 'Look, I need to know what was said. Vic says it was the Russians. Is that so?'

'Yes.'

'Well?'

'They're going to give me a call back and then arrange a meeting.'

'You know who these people are?' I shifted uncomfortably and grabbed a handful of grapes from a fruit bowl.

'Of course. They represent the Russian contingent of the deal.'

'You say they *represent*, is this the main man we're talking about, or are they middle men, men who take orders rather than give them?'

'He is the main man. Mr Vaclav Bresnevich.' He gave a sigh, as though it was some big deal that he'd actually mentioned the name and got it off his chest. Then he went on: 'Our relationship was, how you say, a partnership of convenience.'

'What is he? Ex KGB, Mafia, Turkish or what?' I didn't have a clue about the name, but it ceratainly sounded Russian. I'd never heard it mentioned during the past few days, or anything remotely similar. Personally, I didn't give a flying fig, Mafia or no Mafia. But what I very much needed to know right now was what the hell was actually said, so I could take it from there.

Suhail continued as if thinking out aloud. 'Turkish, no. Mafia and old KGB, whatever, does it matter? Russia is in complete financial turmoil and everyone wants the dollar. Russia *needs* the dollar and yet it's those in the Russian hierarchy who are ripping off their mother country. Capitalism at its most grotesque.' He paused. 'Russia is awash with US dollars. Good old US dollars, they can't get enough of them.'

Nothing more or less than what *you've* been doing for most of your life, I mused, so it's a bit late to make moral judgements. Every government — and I mean *every* government — at some stage rips off its people for its own personal gain. Every level of government department, even in good old Blighty, probably has its little scams: a way of getting paid for fraudulent travel expenses, paid for of course out of the tax coffers. What's new? And what was wrong with old communists doing the same?

'With all respect, Mr Suhail, what the hell was said?'

I felt Vic look at me as if to say, 'You can't talk to him like that!' But I carried on. 'I need to know what's going on. How much do you owe this man, and can you pay him off? Think of your wife and daughter, for Christ's sake, if you don't care for your own safety!'

He looked round at me quickly, as if I'd snapped him out of a trance. 'Vaclav is calling back in two hours and wants to meet. He wants to be paid off.'

'Can that happen?' I said. It begged the question of 'How much?' But I didn't want to raise that one again.

Suhail carried on. 'I think so! I told him that I'm still in negotiations with the banks.'

'You're stalling him then, yes?'

'It's not quite as simple as that. He seems to think that I've been paid for my part of the deal, which of course is absolutely absurd.'

'But have you? No bullshit now — please.'

'Part payment only. It's all to do with the banks. They're not moving quickly enough for me or Mr Vaclav. He doesn't understand the intricacies of the way the Western banks work.'

Join the rest of us, I thought. 'Is he in London?'

'Yes he is. He is the gentleman who visited my brother.'

'Fucking nice one. How many of them are we talking about?'

'Maybe three or four men. But no doubt he can call on as many as he requires,' Suhail finished off, rather nervously.

I now had less than two hours to sort out that game-plan, pick a suitable RV which was going to lend itself to the team's tactical needs, recce it and then put in a sleeper. If we were dealing with old KGB or Mafia people or some source within the new Russian Security Bureau, then so be it. Talking is always the best approach, a negotiated settlement has to be better than two men squaring up to each other with clubs — the cave-man approach. But if it came to that, then we as a team had to perform.

It wasn't exactly coming up to payday, but I was concerned about being had over. If there was any money in the pot, then I wanted to get to it first, so the team could get wedged up. That was most important, because if the job went tits up, then at least the guys would have been paid up for the next couple of weeks, and it would give me the advantage of bugging out from the job without the fear of getting 'knocked'. I had no idea how much cash was still left in Suhail's kitty.

We'd gone through quite a bit over the past two weeks, what with the cars, hotels and expenses. At a quick guess, it must have been around about 50 grand, and it was going to be that again for the next wage bill, and then a further 20 to cover the next two weeks' living costs. Understandably, I made getting paid my first priority.

I convinced Suhail that the guys were really loyal but they would only stay that way if they got paid. He took that on board, as a good businessman should. So before I took him through the finer points of the evening's activities, I made him part with the team's wages, Unfortunately it was only a week's worth. Still, if that's the way he wanted to play it, then that's the way it was going to be.

A week up-front was better than a week in arrears, but this change of the agreed policy of paying *two* weeks in advance set the alarm bells ringing. It was telling me that Suhail was probably looking forward to bugging out again. Where to, well, that was a minor concern to me. Any man who treats his wife and kid the way he was treating his, isn't a good man to deal with; but I knew that anyway, through the sort of shite he was involved in.

Mr Golding — the man from the bank by The Ritz — was contacted and we made a pick-up of cash. I concluded that this was Suhail's other bank, that is, his *personal* account, because Mr Abdul Wahab came along with us. I was pretty much convinced that he and Suhail were joint signatories for this account. How much was drawn out I didn't know, but I got paid and that was all I was interested in. Perhaps it came from the account which held the ten million of the Italian's money. But as I said, all I was really interested in was getting paid the agreed amount for my troubles.

Before payday the team was getting a bit edgy. They didn't mind working on the job but they were all of the opinion that if payment wasn't forthcoming, then all of them would split. They gave me until the following day to square things away. Only Vic didn't mind the risk of not getting paid: he had the keys to a brand new 45-grand Range Rover he could get shot of any time. There were plenty of lock-ups south of the Thames that would give him cash for it — no names, no pack drills.

As it turned out, Suhail came through with the money, with a little help from Mr Christos, and with that 'small' matter of money out of the way, the team was back in happy mode and really looking forward to the evening's little operation I had planned.

Suhail wasn't impressed when he parted with the cash, under the watchful eye of Abdul Wahab. He must have been thinking that I and the team were going to work in arrears. I don't think so. I would *not* have been impressed if he hadn't squared me and the team away. I would have given him one day extra, and then I would have walked. However, I was still quids in from the advance on day one.

It never ceases to amaze me how these people can go into a bank and draw out huge sums of cash; my business is full of them. Fifty grand here, 20 grand there, 120 from somewhere else — amazing, especially if you're like me, having to be careful about the overdraft. My overdraft limit is what a dinner for four costs these guys. It's really obscene!

When I got back from the bank trip, I put a call in to Doc up at Heathrow. Now that I had a name and point of origin I wanted to run it past him. I called him up on his mobile, since his office land-line number was probably taped as a matter of course.

'Doc, it's Steve, can you talk?' I said, not knowing if he was on the 'ground' or in a meeting.

'Yeah, go ahead, what can I do for you?'

'I'm on a job —'

'That's nice for you.' Doc was being sarcastic. Nice, he was in a good mood.

'On a job, not on the job. It's a bit of a doddle, if you know what I mean?' I wanted to sound as veiled as possible without coming across too ambiguously. Doc knew, though, that if I was calling him up and talking in that manner, then it was a covert sign that I was going to ask him for a favour.

'Give me a couple of minutes and I'll call you back,' he said. I guessed he was going to call me back on a totally secure telephone.

'Hear from you shortly,' I replied.

'You on your mobile?'

'Yes.'

Five minutes later, after I'd told him my predicament, I had a headful of theme tunes. At first I thought Doc was taking the piss and just trying to wind me up, but he wasn't. He was totally serious. He told me that they'd been given information about the movements of a Russian hit squad which was making its way slowly across Europe. It was the usual intelligence type of information. There's always a hit squad moving around some part of Europe. He hadn't taken too much interest in it, just logged it as everyday news. After all, that was his job, nothing out of the unusual.

'The Firm [M16] had been on their case for weeks. They lost them for a while, but two of them showed up at Charles de Gaulle Airport about two weeks ago, so they were back on with the surveillance. They gave us no idea why they were tracing them, they don't normally, they just give us the usual descriptions and hope we might pick 'em up if they were to fly in,' Doc said. 'Pretty low-key stuff usually. We only get to know a player's involvement in crime if he or she comes through on the daily mug-shot sheets.'

I felt goose pimples rise on my shoulders and my heart starting to beat faster as Doc carried on with his very unofficial intelligence brief.

'Then, about ten days ago, a very good contact of mine from SB [Special Branch] pitched up here with a surveillance team and said that one of the Russians was coming through Heathrow. We let him through, of course, and the last I heard was that SB had managed to keep a tail on him until he hit the Knightsbridge traffic and then ending up losing him.' He confirmed what all surveillance operators know: 'The West End. A right twat of a place to carry out surveillance in.'

'What can you tell me about where you think he is now, and how heavy he might be?' I paused to anticipate what might be Doc's response. He might just fuck me off at the high port. But he didn't.

'Haven't a clue where they're now, and of course, if SB and M16 are involved then, it must be heavy shit.' Doc paused. 'They don't get involved with anything these days unless it's got some balls to it. Budgets and all that. Know what I mean? Have to go on the strongest of leads. Gone are the days of hunches, costs too much to see them through.'

'Yeah, I know what you mean.'

'Why the interest in a Russian, anyway? I thought you only concerned yourself with the Arabs. They haven't pissed any Russians off, have they?' he asked jokingly.

I went on to tell him a bit about the bigger picture I was involved in. Not enough to get him excited, we all have a living to earn. But I knew I could count on him to bring in the cavalry if I needed it. It would only take him a phone call to the right government department and I would have all the back-up I needed. For now, though, I sensed that he was in a bit of a rush, so I thanked him for his time and said I'd be in touch.

It was a little past four in the afternoon that we got the call we'd all been waiting for. Suhail did the speaking, so not as to confuse the issue or give away the fact that there were other parties listening in. I told him to play it straight and not to mention us at all, even if he were asked. I guessed there was no need to brief him up on what to say. He was a past master of the Art of Untruths.

The meeting, if Suhail could somehow persuade Vaclav to play along, was to take place in the London Regents Park Hilton, just opposite the Lord's Cricket Ground. I chose this location because it's situated on a very busy crossroads just north of Marylebone. The roads are wide and there are always a lot of people about. If the shite did hit the fan, my guess was that Mr Vaclav and party would not risk coming out guns a-blazing.

The entire area was well furnished with many escape routes, but that's a bit of a double-edged sword. On the one hand, it gave me a few options for lying up and bugging out if the need arose, but on the other, it gave the Russians the same options. However, I wasn't counting on them acting out this meet as professionally as we were. After all, their main concern was getting their money, and they hadn't shown any covert moves in their approach so far. I gambled on the fact that they were desperate. I hoped I was right.

After a bit of verbal jockeying for position, Vaclav did agree to meet at the Hilton. Two men from their side, two from ours. I let Suhail take along his nephew, that way it would appear to the Russians that Suhail wasn't coming across as strong-handed; and anyway, his nephew was feeling a bit braver, probably because he thought he was in safe hands. He was now quite enjoying the game. I was happy for him to go with his uncle — that way, I wouldn't have to compromise any of my team so early on.

On their side was Mr Vaclav plus an English-sounding chap, not Scottish or Welsh. From what I could get out of Suhail, he also sounded like a bit of a heavy villain, but I couldn't confirm or deny that, so I tried to put him at ease. 'This guy, he's probably a bit of hired muscle to act as Mr Intimidation,' I said, looking directly at him. I could see he wasn't all that convinced.

'Don't worry. Nothing's going to happen inside the hotel.' I tried to reassure him — and at the same time tried to reassure myself.

In fact, I had already anticipated that the meet would take place, and sent John off to the hotel to make himself comfortable but scarce. I told him to book in for one night, if necessary, and to get to know the lay-out of the place. If anyone should ask, as a matter of conversation, what he was doing, I told him to make up a plausible cover story. 'Say you're waiting for a business meeting.' My guess was that even though the Russians were agitated and pretty overt in their approach to this business, they might still be switched-on enough to cover the hotel with their men. They would probably use a minimum of four: one driver, one internal 'sleeper', and two for the meeting. So it was very important that I got a foot on the ground first, and started getting my own real-time intelligence of any suspects sent back to me via mobile phone.

The Hilton was only 15 minutes' drive, at the most, from the Regents Plaza. I wanted all team members who were going to be involved on the operation (everyone apart from Al and the corridor men, they would have to hold the fort) to carry out a quick recce of the area we were going to work in and around, and, if time allowed, of the inside of the Hilton as well.

I had two main reasons for this: firstly, to identify if there were any road works and traffic diversions in progress; and secondly, to find out if there were any other funnies happening in and around the area, such as a cricket match or another activity being hosted at Lord's.

All these factors would greatly affect the ability of the team to select their OPs (Observation Posts), restricted parking and extra police on the ground being the main problems. Luckily for us at the time, everything was looking normal. It was all clear!

The meeting was scheduled for six in the evening, and at about ten minutes to six, Suhail plus one pulled up in a black cab and entered the rather small foyer of this particular Hilton. It was rather less cluttered with furniture than one might have expected from such an up-market hotel. John made eyeball with them and relayed their movements back to me via his mobile. There was only one area where you could actually sit and conduct a meeting, and that was around the lounge and bar areas. A large modern, brightly coloured room, furnished with dozens of comfy chairs and tables, it had modern art on the walls and clear downlights giving it a gallery feel. An ideal place to mix in.

They picked an area in the middle of the bar as briefed, a place where, if voices were raised, it would attract the attention of those around. The idea was that if any threats were made, those making the threats would be overheard. I was in luck, John said that the bar was busy and filling up nicely. Even in such a busy hotel lounge as this, most conversations were conducted in little more than whispers, for fear of being overheard.

From the bar area you could also see the main entrance through a series of large windows which overlooked the hotel's drive-in drive-out courtyard. Suhail was to make a gesture to John when he saw the arrival of the Russians. John would then call me and send through descriptions, and the number of the black cab which I reckoned they would arrive in. I could then get their pick-up point from my contacts in the black cab business. Hopefully they would have been picked up where they were staying and not from some pub or club.

I was laid up in Red One just seconds away around the corner on Park Road, the main thoroughfare which runs north–south along the western side of Regent's Park. With me was Pete, who was detailed the driver. I purposely had him with me because if the meeting went OK, then he would be the ideal driver to follow Mr Vaclav — now our primary target — hopefully without too many dramas. Vic and Ken were struggling for space in the back.

'There's not a lot of room in the back of these fuckin' Range Rovers, is there?' Vic said. 'Remind me not to fuckin' buy one when this job's over.'

Around the corner, facing Lord's on St John's Wood Road, were Mike and Tom in one of the Mercs. Both vehicles would be floating about the place, trying not to attract any attention. Ten minutes is about enough to stay in any one place, particularly with the Range Rover being four up. Not too many vehicles drive around the West End with bums on all four seats; we might just stick out somewhat.

With seven men on the ground and the two exit points behind the Hilton on Lodge Road and Oak Tree Road securely covered, I had the operation pretty much wrapped up. The only option I didn't have was someone hanging about on a motor bike. With the traffic building quite heavily now, it would be a pretty skilful driver on four wheels who could follow the target without being spotted or losing it. But you can't have everything, so that's where I thought Pete came in. He was meant to be the one with the most recent experience amongst us.

At ten past six, John phoned through.

'Suhail has just given me the nod. Game on.'

'Great, what can you see then?'

John began his talk-through. 'A graphite grey Merc 600 S-class has just pulled up.' He paused. 'Only two up plus the driver. Both targets getting out and entering my location.' He paused again. 'The Merc is now one up and parking.'

'Get the registration.' I stated the obvious.

'Two secs,' he replied.

I understood that John was working undercover and was trying to send over the most accurate descriptions possible while at the same time acting as covertly as possible. It's a bit of a skill in itself — people outside the business don't realise just how difficult the art of surveillance actually is, especially if you are trying to report accurately the description and movements of a couple of targets that are on their guard against someone doing precisely that.

Once I was an operator during a large surveillance operation being conducted 'over the water' (Northern Ireland). Even though we had well over 20 of us on the ground, with all obvious routes covered, we still managed to lose the target, and all she did was to hail a cab. So it ain't as easy as the TV makes it out to be.

John sent the registration, and then I patiently waited for him to send the targets' descriptions.

John relayed: 'One white male, big fat bastard, six foot plus, late 30s, shaven head, black bomber jacket and jeans. Probably the muscle.'

As I was receiving it, I was repeating it so Ken could write it down.

'Second target. Whitish. Fat bastard in a dark suit. Mid to late 40s. Foreign looking. Short, thick-looking, greasy black hair with same colour moustache, possibly the Russian or the Turk.' Again he paused and then carried on. 'Shaking hands with our people.' John rounded off his report with, 'A right pair of Herberts.' Then he hung up.

'That's it,' I said to the rest. 'Meeting in progress.'

'So it's hurry up and wait then, is it?' Vic replied.

I passed the details on to the other vehicle and told them to keep an eye open for possible 'dickers'.

I'd envisaged the meeting would only take 30 minutes at the most, but in the meantime we had to sit it out. Both vehicles would change their positions in about ten minutes.

Silence entered the vehicle as all four of us contemplated the next half hour or so. It was Ken who broke the silence.

'Hey, Steve, did that Mr Christos have a word with you?' he probed.

'About what?' I pre-empted his next question. 'The ten million Suhail has for a couple of house purchases, Mafia money no doubt, or about the operation to snatch the Turkish General?' I replied a bit lazily. I'd been in this game too long to let anyone get to me with great-sounding ideas without throwing a bit of capital on the table first.

'No, not about that stuff, about snatching a load of diamonds,' he said.

I got the feeling that Pete was a bit startled by what he'd just heard. This was obviously not the topic of conversation he was used to across the water.

'Well, go on then, tell me. Tell me what Christos has said to you and then I'll tell you what he offered me.' I sounded a bit like a kid coming out with the 'My dad's bigger than your dad' routine. Ken went on to tell his story.

Apparently, old Christos had got hold of Ken and a couple of the guys on the team and wanted to know if they were up for a job overseas when this one finished. The gist of the story was that he was looking for a team of Special Forces guys to go over to West Africa and hang about off the shore of the Ivory Coast and then intercept an Israeli-registered vessel, supposedly carrying a shed-load of diamonds bound for Israel.

We would all have a cover story, and Christos, being a Greek, would supply our boat and all the necessary weapons and equipment. In short, he wanted us to hijack a ship, storm aboard and steal its cargo.

After Ken had run his story by me, he asked me what I thought of the idea.

'Fuckin' outrageous. That's what I think. It's worth having a look at, but it's still a bit fuckin' outrageous,' I said.

I then went on to tell him what Christos had approached me and Vic about. Telling these stories helped pass the time and gave us all a bit of laugh, but I reckoned my story was particularly special. The main point of what Christos wanted me and a hand-picked team to carry out was the abduction of the officer who'd been in charge of the assault on Cyprus, and in particular the assault on the capital, Nicosia, during the Turkish invasion of Cyprus in 1974. The Turkish officer in question was apparently still alive, living out the rest of his life in peaceful retirement on a general's pension somewhere east of Istanbul.

Christos's intentions behind the two plans were totally different. The diamonds, that was purely for financial gain, but the 'snatch'-squad operation for the Turk that was totally political. The game-plan was this: once we kidnapped the general, we would then hand him over to the Greek Government who would then hold him as a bargaining chip against the Turkish Government.

Christos believed that the Turkish Government was still holding — even after 25 years — Greek prisoners of war captured during the invasion of Cyprus. I kind of went along with him. As a soldier, I could see that the thought of one side holding on to the other side's prisoners after the shooting had stopped might provide some moral justification for the abduction. And believe it or not, this was not as farfetched as it initially seemed. After all, many snatch-squad operations have been successfully carried out over the years. You only have to look at the Israelis' past successes.

However, nothing really came of these two potential money-earners. They were both viable operations and Christos was more than serious about proceeding. I gave him a figure, the sum of money he should consider if he wanted to take any of his ideas that one stage further. He said he would give it some serious thought. Whatever else it did, it passed the time away. It's not on every job that you get the opportunity to discuss modern pirate techniques in the Atlantic Ocean around the Equator, and running a snatch squad across the Aegean Sea. Well, not from the same source, anyway.

I looked at my watch. It was coming up to the 15-minute point. I got Vic to walk the route along to Lodge Road and then into the hotel to see what he could make of the driver in the Mercedes. On the vehicle change-around we would pick him up at the junction of St John's Wood and Oak Tree roads.

Vic's walk proved fruitless. He made out the Mercedes early enough because it was pointing towards the hotel entrance, so he had to act like a resident walking in through the foyer. He didn't want to give the game away by looking over in its direction.

At twenty-five past six we were parked up on the forecourt of the petrol station just a bit further down from our initial position. It was reaching the time when I thought the meeting would close. John hadn't phoned in to tell me that the meeting was going tits up, and this could only be a good sign. What wasn't a good sign was a continuing build-up of police patrol cars and 'meat wagons' hanging about Park Road. I'd counted six in the past ten minutes, and from across the garage forecourt I could make out armed police disembarking from vehicles and slowing down the traffic on either side of the street.

'For fuck's sake, can you see what's happening across the road? Fucking armed police,' Pete said. All of us looked over, only to see lines of police, mostly on the far side of the road; there were a few on our side, but too far down the road to be an immediate threat.

'The mosque. Of course, the mosque's just over there.' I pointed down and across the road on the Regent's Park side. It was a place I'd visited before on more than one occasion with clients, but had never been inside it. Only Muslims are allowed to enter. We were no more than 100 metres away from it.

'I bet there's been a incident,' Pete said. 'A bomb or something like that.'

'Fuck, you might just be right there,' I said.

'There's gotta be about 20 or so armed police now,' Vic reminded us.

The police were spaced about ten metres apart in a line that seemed to stretched the entire length on the far side of the pavement, from our position down towards the mosque. It looked like a police version of Trooping of the Colours, with horses, really quite extraordinary. I'd never seen so many policemen and women with guns before. The last time I saw that many was one weekend the London firearms unit came up to Hereford to have a go in the Regiment's Killing House, a building where you can fire live rounds to practise a 'room clearance' scenario during an anti-terrorist exercise.

There was a lot of activity going on around the mosque entrance. Traffic had slowed down almost to a standstill. Not that the police were stopping it — drivers on both lanes were goose-necking at the spectacle of so many armed police clad in body armour and helmets.

'Fuck me,' I said. 'It's like a remake of the Iranian Embassy siege!'

'Fucking outrageous,' Vic said.

'It will be if they pull us over. Look at all this fuckin' baseball kit,' Ken said. 'If we get pulled over now, it might just be end ex for us all, let's try and sort this shit out.'

It felt as if my back was having the shit kicked out of it as Vic and Ken did their best to hide the tools under the two front seats.

'Yeah, you're not wrong either,' I said, knowing that I was going to have to do a lot of fast talking if we got pulled over and searched.

Suddenly my phone rang; it was John.

'Steve, you're on. Meeting's over. I think it went OK. No punches pulled, at least. Looks like they're heading for the entrance and to the Merc. I won't be able to see in what direction they're gonna go, but you've got that covered, haven't you?'

'No problems,' I said. 'If they come out and turn left, *we* will pick 'em up; and if they turn right, then that's down to Mike and Tom; either way, one of us will follow the other. You make your way back to the Regents Plaza.' I was just about to ring off when I checked myself. 'No, don't go straight back, try and befriend a cabbie to follow Suhail. I don't trust that twat.'

'No problems,' John said, and hung up.

A quick message to Mike put him on guard, too. The brief was that if the target vehicle came out on my route, the Range Rover was lead, then the Mercedes would try and fit into surveillance pattern and take over if the traffic pushed us too close to the target vehicle, which invariably happens no matter how carefully you drive. That was the plan.

Vic was the first to spot the target vehicle nosing its way out of Lodge Road. I'd just taken my eyes off the turning for a couple of seconds to see what it was the police were up to. There was definitely something big building up behind us. For a brief second I recalled what Doc had said to me and I suddenly had this nightmare appear in front of my eyes, with the thought that this police show was all for our benefit. Suddenly I was brought back to sharp reality.

'There it is, there it is!' Vic screamed. The target vehicle had appeared very quickly and now had skilfully sneaked its way into the line of oncoming traffic.

'Shit, we're facing the wrong way!' I said.

Pete was a bit slow to react; I was surprised. All of a sudden the target vehicle was level with us, and then past us. Pete took off and did an immediate 'U' turn right in front of both lanes of traffic. The screeching of rubber was heard all around.

'JESUS CHRIST! FOR FUCK'S SAKE, PETE, WHAT THE FUCK ARE YOU ON?' Ken screamed. Pete had pulled out without even looking, right in front of a black cab, and Christ knows how he didn't hit us. It was a fucking miracle. Pete's action wasn't missed by the armed men in uniform either. We were now straddled halfway across Park Road blocking both lanes of traffic. Then I saw what I thought all the fuss was about. Coming out of the mosque, and turning towards the same direction as the target vehicle, I spotted a black bullet-proof Daimler, similar to the type our Queen regularly travels in. It was in the middle of a procession of other limousines and it was quite obviously carrying someone of great importance, or someone of a nervous disposition.

With an irate cabbie swearing his head off at us, the target vehicle disappearing towards the West End, and half-a-dozen armed police dressed in body armour with their MP5 machine pistols expertly trained up at us, we had nowhere to go. I now began to realise why the police were acting a bit pear-shaped. The way Pete had pulled away and done his 'U' turn must have looked to them as though we were a fucking hit team after whoever was riding in the Daimler.

Pete was halfway through his manoeuvre; the cabbie could not and would not reverse, and the rest of the traffic was bumper to bumper. So there was no other way to go apart from straightening the Range Rover up and heading towards one of the 'on-foot' armed police who was now beckoning at Pete to steer towards him, in a 'Take it easy, because any false move and I'll let you have it,' sort of way.

I was feeling pretty pissed off. Here we were in the middle of London, with one of Her Majesty's finest covert operators, who had just fucked the job up for us. I was fucking fuming, not only for me but also for Ken and Vic, who were still frantically trying to lose the baseball bats. The short ones were kicked under the front seats but the two larger weren't going anywhere, they had be covered over with training kit, without making it too obvious what the guys were doing.

Quickly I got hold of Mike and told him that we were getting pulled over by the police and there wasn't much chance of him catching up with the target vehicle either, but he could try if he wanted. I had more important things to address right now.

'I tell you what, if we get lifted you're in the shite as well, know what I mean,' I said to Pete. I was referring to his being a serving member of the Det. In some ways, my statement was intended to force his hand, so that he would bullshit his way through the next five minutes or so.

He said nothing. I could sense that he was pretty embarrassed about having screwed the job up, and the fact that we might just get nicked if he didn't think of something fast. He stayed silent trying to manoeuvre the Range Rover to exactly where the policeman was pointing. I was now starting to worry about what to do with the 9-millimetre which seemed to stick out of my jacket as never before. My heart began to pump a bit faster than it had been doing. Although the air conditioning was on low, I was beginning to feel the beads of nervous sweat run down the side of my face.

'Pete, you'd better get out that fucking ID card of yours and start to bullshit your way out of this one,' Vic subtly suggested.

The oncoming traffic was halted as the Range Rover was allowed to pull up in front of the police, still with weapons trained. It must have been a spectacle for the onlookers.

The mosque had now kicked out, and the pavement was awash

with hundreds of Muslim men heading off home after their evening prayer. It was like being in downtown Dhahran. Many of them were casually dressed, a few in collar and tie, but many more clad in dish-dashes, the traditional attire worn in the Middle East.

Some groups were chatting together as they headed towards us, and I could see more groups crossing to the other side of the road swarming around the traffic and police. This didn't ease my feeling about the situation.

It would only take one or two of them to see us being 'pulled' by the police, and think that we might be some extreme Western 'hit' team after whoever was being chauffeured in the Daimler, and that could set off the spark to ignite an already extremely tense situation. Having been caught in riots before, from Northern Ireland through to Africa, I wasn't particularly relishing the next five minutes.

It was another added distraction to take on board. I told the guys not to make eye contact with any of them. The guys knew the score but I felt that I had to say something, even if it was just to calm things down a little.

We were now parked up where the police wanted us, and were totally surrounded. I could see another policeman heading towards the driver's door.

'This is fuckin' outrageous, isn't it?' said Vic.

'You know what's coming next, don't you?' Ken said. 'We're all gonna get strip-searched and then fuckin' nicked. Anyone know the rules of baseball? I need some kind of cover story!'

'Three strikes and you're out apparently,' I tried to match Ken's humour. But it didn't come out the way I expected. It came out flat. I wished I'd never said it.

There were armed police around the vehicle by now, so close that I didn't dare look anywhere other than straight ahead. The original policeman ordered Pete to get out of the vehicle. 'Fuck it,' I said. I was now thinking that even if I wanted to ditch the pistol, there was no way I could do it. I'd have to sweat it out.

'Get that fucking ID ready,' I reminded Pete. 'That's our get-out-of-jail card. Use it, and turn the wagon off, but leave the keys in it.' I don't know what I was thinking of, a quick getaway? Maybe it had something to do with the built-in human instinct of survival we all have but which only appears when our freedom is at risk.

Pete got out and was now holding something out in front of him and aloft — it was his ID card. Then he was pulled to one side for an impromptu interrogation.

'Thank Christ for that,' Vic muttered.

'What do you mean by that then?' I said.

'Well, if Pete hadn't had his ID card out straight away he would be face down in the gutter now, followed by the rest of us,' Vic commented.

The only time I moved my stare away from Pete was when Ken spotted Mike and Tom driving past. I turned to my right. The windows were beginning to mist up from nervous breath. I slowly moved over to switch the ignition to auxiliary and put the blower on, totally aware that armed eyes were trained on every movement being made inside the Range Rover. Getting 'slotted' by a trigger-happy copper because he or she thought I was going to make a break for it wasn't how I wanted to leave this world.

The traffic was moving at a snail's pace and every driver north- and south-bound seemed to be rubber-necking at us. I caught Tom's face on his drive past. It was showing signs of total amusement; he had a big grin right across it probably saying 'Fuck you guys'. At least someone could see the funny side of this incident.

I looked back again to see how Pete was getting on. He was standing by the wall which bordered this part of the park, being covered by two armed police. I've had all sorts of weapons pulled on me over the years, and contrary to popular belief, you don't get used to it. I could see by the look on Pete's face that he wasn't too happy about the situation either.

Another policeman was on his radio, undoubtedly sending through a 'P' Check on our wagon. The policeman on the radio finished his transmission and began to question his suspect again. The policeman's body language told me that he was still not convinced about what Pete was saying to him. It was then that I realised just how tense and awkward the police surrounding us looked. They looked more afraid of us than we did of them.

It looked such an unnatural position for all of them to be in, with their weapons in the shoulder and ready at the aim. You can easily tell if someone who's 'carrying' a weapon is in control or not, by the way they hold themselves. Guys in the Regiment are past masters at handling all sorts of weapons, and when we carry them, in the aim or not, we look like we mean business. They become an extension of one's body — natural-looking.

By contrast, the police looked really out of place holding their MP5s, rather like the young kid in a Western holding up his dad's shotgun which is ten sizes too big for him and trying to scare off a couple of trespassers. Was it something in their training which made them all react like that, stiff and unbending as steel? A policeman's lot is, primarily, to save life and property and to uphold the law.

A soldier's lot is basically to kill first. I guess that's the long and short of it. I'm not having a go at the police, some of my police friends actually agree with me, but all I'm doing is giving a personal — and I hope, informed — perspective on the two forces.

It wasn't long before Pete was released. I saw him casually brush himself down, put his hand up to thank the questioning police officer, and make his way back to the vehicle.

The trip back to the Marriott was full of nervous laughter interspersed with remorseful comments from Pete. Ken didn't help matters by taking the piss out of Pete's tactical driving.

Pete told us the story how he'd flashed his ID card and spun a tale about us acting as the outer mobile cordon for 'the job': 'the job' being Pete's key bullshit phrase.

'You mean you're with the Saudi party?' the policeman said.

'Yeah, that's right, and sorry about the shite piece of driving.' he replied.

'There are Islamic Fundamentalists all over the place. We've had a hell of a job trying to control them down by the mosque entrance.'

'Yeah, that's what threw me, and what with this hired vehicle as well ...' Pete replied apologetically.

'That's what I thought. You guys suffering from cut-backs too, eh?' replied the copper before he let him go.

Pete felt it advisable to agree with what the policeman was saying. 'I just treated it like a routine "P" check across the water,' he said. 'A piece of piss.'

It was a big bluff, but then again, if you know the system you're up against, it's quite easy to drop a couple of key phrases to bullshit your way through. I too felt like I had been close to the edge, but I'd somehow enjoyed the nervous tension while sitting and sweating my socks off, wondering what my next move was going to be if I was asked to get out of the vehicle.

It was a great comfort to me to know that there was always the option of doing a runner. There were a hell of a lot of Muslims about the place and it would have taken a pretty quick-thinking and quick-talking policeman to order me to stop. I know the rules: they can't shoot and don't shoot without giving a warning first. I would have been off like the wind, dumping the pistol at the earliest possible opportunity, and then, if caught, I would have made myself available for questioning carrying a bag full of excuses. If I'd been shot, then it would have been a lucky day for the policeman — I was carrying — and an unlucky one for me.

As I've said, if one lives by the sword, one must be prepared to die by the sword.

PART FIVE

16.

M15 — THE SET-UP

DAY TWELVE, LATE EVENING

Things might have turned out differently if we had kept the target vehicle under surveillance, but as it worked out we had to count our blessings that we didn't get nicked. I was still spitting feathers over Pete's driving skills and told him so again. I thought at one stage he was going to walk off the job, but he stayed. I didn't particularly want him to walk but then again I wasn't about to plead with him to stay.

I told him, 'We always all have two choices in life.' He had fucked up and he had to deal with that himself. I also said, 'Everyone's allowed one fuck-up,' and that's how I left the incident.

Suhail's meeting had appeared to go without incident. John had managed to get a very detailed description of Vaclav and his sidekick, who turned out to be just a bit of hired help. Suhail had

managed to spin Vaclav a bit of a story about money transfers from
the bank. It seemed he had successfully stalled for time. But had
he? I concluded two possible things about Vaclav: one, he wasn't
past the talking stage and it was more important for him to secure
payment than to reap revenge; or two, he just happened to be in a
good mood that day, which would have led Suhail and my team
into a false sense of security. I tended to go firm on the second
conclusion.

Another meeting had been arranged for two days' time, only
on this occasion it was to be on Vaclav's terms, his choice of time
and location — a restaurant in West London. There Suhail would
hand over sufficient official paperwork to convince the Russians
that the deal was still on and things were all going according to
plan. What plan Suhail was actually carrying around in his head, I
really didn't have much of a clue about.

Only John confirmed to me that the meeting went OK. 'It
appeared to be conducted quite amicably,' he said. 'No apparent
voices raised, both of 'em looked and spoke as if they were old
friends.'

'Yeah, that's suspect for starters,' I said.

'Well suspect, but what's new?' he concluded. I had to agree
with him. But things could have been worse — at least Suhail had
come straight back to the hotel. We had John's cab to thank for
that bit of information.

It was Mike who suggested that we use another of his contacts
to help out with the restaurant meeting. I wasn't too sure about
that, since he'd given me Pete. I put this option on hold for the
time being.

Weeks earlier, Mike and I had run this little surveillance job just
outside Manchester. It had come through a guy called Richard T,
a contact of Mike's in the CCTV business. Two years before, a
particular manufacturer of metal castings had a multi-million-
pound MOD contract for producing things like the metal cases
for the Army radio system through to tank components, and they
now required a major re-vamp and re-installation of their security
equipment.

Richard won the contract from this company to supply and
install the security equipment, stuff like CCTVs that were all

linked up to a bank of monitors in a control room, plus infra-red lighting and the odd covert camera, for the boss's eyes only. Basically, the complete security package for the factory. The contract also included the installation of a state-of-the-art swipe-card system for every section of the factory and the offices.

Mike went on to say that he'd helped Richard with the installation. The boss of the company was so delighted with the new system that a trickle of repeat business started coming Richard's way. In addition, part of the deal was to supply a servicing contract for the equipment, so that saw Richard and Mike going up North every six months, just to check that everything was running smoothly, and of course to pick up on other business which came by way of recommendation.

Anyway, Mike and Richard had struck up a good working relationship with the MD (managing director) of this company, so it was no surprise when, one day Richard said to Mike that he'd been approached by the MD concerning an internal management problem, and could he help?

Now, Richard was only concerned with cameras, monitors and security fencing, low-key stuff like that. What his client required was more on the technical front, so what happened was that Richard subbed this contract out to Mike, who was more than capable of carrying out the job the client wanted.

The internal problem concerned two directors of the company. The MD feared that these two had been cooking the books. Because the company made many metal castings for tanks, it used huge amount of steel. It transpired that over a period of three or four years, these two suspect directors had been buying in steel from Germany at a reduced rate and selling it on to their company at slightly over-inflated prices.

With tens of thousands of tons of steel purchased every year, this skimming off the top equated to a nice little nest egg for the two directors. A basic scam, working on the old demolition formula I used when making up plastic explosives: 'P' for plenty and not 'G' for greedy.

No one would have suspected anything and these two might have been able to run the scam for years, especially as the professional skill of one of the two directors was accountancy. He could lose ten, sometimes fifteen dollars a ton by skimming off the top of orders. It was really quite professionally carried out. But, the weak link in all crimes of this nature is greed — the MD overheard the two directors arguing about money. He couldn't quite make it all out, but he knew there was a problem connected in some way with the company's business.

'The MD wanted all sorts of James Bond stuff to be installed,' Mike had said to me.

'What did you tell him?'

'I said that yes, I can bug this, and I can bug that, follow them here and follow them there. Basically, anything to do with surveillance. [Which of course Mike could do with the help from his people in the Firm.] I told the MD that it was no problem to do what he was asking for, but it was expensive, and if he wanted bugging outside of the offices, then that was illegal, but it could be done, too.'

So that's what happened. Mike set the job up and used a moonlighting team from M15 for the first couple of weeks to do the technical placement of equipment — bugs and cameras. I couldn't believe it when Mike said that he was using these guys.

'They were up for it. They even used all their own kit. I didn't have to supply anything,' Mike said. 'Even used the Firm's vehicles and petrol to come up on the job.'

'Fucking outrageous,' I said. 'What makes you so sure that they weren't moonlighting but actually working for the Government?' It was the obvious way for M15 to get into the closed shop of this side of the industry — using the operators' old service mates to gain entry and then extract the information needed.

'That's pretty easy,' Mike said. 'My old mate's from the Marines, he wouldn't stitch me up. He joined the Firm years back, and I've always kept in touch with him. He runs his own department now, still within the Firm, and anyway, there's no way any of the parties could have met to set this all up. There were too many permutations, it would have had to have been a million-to-one shot. All I did was just phone him to see if he wanted to earn some extra, and he was up for it. Luckily he and his team were on leave. He's done a bit for me in the past, probably looking out for himself when he leaves the mob. Who knows, maybe the pay's not that great in M15 or M16.'

The technical placement and part surveillance went in OK.

Mike and his team ran the job for 12 days, then the moonlighting M15 team's leave was up and they had to go back to London. That's when Mike called me up and I carried on the surveillance. The big problem for me was that, when I took over from the M15 team, they hadn't made available to me any areas of their previous LUPs (Lying Up Positions). This wasn't SOPs. Any surveillance team worth its salt should have made some effort to pass on relevant information to the incoming team to plan from, allowing it to read up on past incidents. At the very least, the information should be identified on a map, showing positions and stuff like that where they had put in OPs or LUPs. I asked Mike for this information but he said that they didn't do it. 'Probably forgot,' he said.

'Probably didn't give too much of a toss,' I replied.

That sort of pissed me off because I was going on the ground blind. I had to stay away from any obvious OP or LUP positions they might have used and, consequently, might have been compromised, during the M15 period. This left me very few options over the next week when carrying out the surveillance. It made the job twice as hard, as I had to keep moving around all the time, changing vehicles and changing disguises; and of course by doing this, I was creating unnecessary movement — I was twice as likely to be compromised. The job finished after I had spent a week on the ground, when the lawyers acting on behalf of the company thought we had dug up enough detailed evidence of the directors' movements and conversations to start legal proceedings.

So, as you can imagine, I was feeling a bit stand-offish as regards going down the same road with M15 moonlighters and using them in the restaurant meet. Though I didn't have enough technical kit of my own to carry out the surveillance, I was loath to use Mike's contacts just yet. So I asked Mike to hold his call; I was going to try and sort something out from my contacts. The last thing I did that night was about half an hour's phoning around, but I was pissing in the wind. All my contacts were either using their kit or I couldn't get hold of them. It was precious time wasted.

DAY THIRTEEN

As soon as I woke up some hours later, I went straight into thinking mode. Knowing that the restaurant was the choice of Mr Vaclav, I had to presume that this was local ground to him, and that he, too, might have a sleeper in place to listen into the conversation, or worse, to intimidate or kidnap Suhail and Charles. By now, Charles appeared to be more deeply involved in Suhail's business than I had first thought. I still couldn't work out if he was working for his uncle, the Russians or indeed himself, but I believed I had a usable dialogue with him, through which to glean information.

In the light of this, I had to think quickly. I made a decision that if I wanted to protect Suhail the best I could, then I had no other option than to take Mike up on his offer.

I briefed Mike about my recent conversation with Doc, and although I didn't have any hard evidence to put Mr Vaclav in the frame as the guy the SB had lost, I couldn't put him out of the equation either — after all, how many gun-toting Russians are there running around London right now?

'You reckon the Firm will be up for this one?' I said. 'I can't say that I'm overimpressed with Pete's abilities ...'

'You're not going to hold him to one mistake, are you?' Mike said in a way that showed he thought I was having a go at *him* for recommending Pete in the first place.

'No, it's not that, but I can't help feeling that there's something bigger happening. Something which I'm not aware of just yet.'

'You mean something like Big Brother?'

'Yeah, something like that, I suppose. I mean, that was a pretty basic mistake made by Pete at the most crucial part of the operation.'

'I know what you mean, it does come across a bit iffy. Don't read too much in to it, though.' Mike was silent for a second. 'I'll get rid of him if you want.'

'No. No need to do that,' I said. 'Just make sure your guys don't get wind of the bigger picture. To them this is just a bit of babysitting with a free scoff thrown in. For us, it's our living.'

By now I was trying to work out what Pete's angle was. His mistake wasn't even the sort of mistake you make on day one

week one of the defensive-driving course. It was too obvious.
The only explanation I could come up with was that he had been
complacent in his approach to the whole operation. It was hardly
the attitude I'd expected from him. But there is, of course, the
constant danger of accepting other people's recommendations,
and employing people whose main income derives from another
source.

Nonetheless, my options were limited. I wasn't at all happy
about the situation, but short of calling other operators — if
available — given the timeframe, there wasn't much I could do. I
shut it out of my thoughts and carried on with sorting out the
restaurant business.

DAY FOURTEEN

Mike now confirmed that the M15 team was still up for it, and
that his contact would be over to see us later in the day. The
location was to be an Italian restaurant, the Trattoria (possible
Mafia connections? I didn't know), a nice trendy place, just off the
Fulham Palace Road. The type of place where you end up paying
30 quid a head for a 50 pence bowl of pasta and sauce, and
another 15 quid for a bottle of supermarket special — *buon
appetito!*

Suhail wasn't aware that I'd arranged for a couple of my people
to sit in on the dinner. He and his nephew were only briefed on
the cover I'd put in place outside the restaurant, and that was just
to make them feel more at ease. The last thing I wanted was for
any of them to keep looking over their shoulders at the other
diners, in anticipation of seeing one of us pretending to tuck into
a plate of cannelloni and ready to spring into action should the
need arise.

'Don't worry about a thing.' I was using the same tactics and
approach as I had done for the Hilton meet.

'But what happens if he starts to get violent again? Look what
he did to my brother!' Suhail pleaded.

'He was OK in the Hilton, wasn't he?' I replied.

He nodded in agreement.

'And anyway, I'll have men waiting outside, ready to crash in if
there's any trouble. Here, take this alarm.' I pulled out one of

those matchbox-size anti-mugger alarms, designed to be carried in ladies' handbags.

'What's this?' he said suspiciously.

'It's a high-intensity alarm. Just pull this.' I showed him the activating rod you pull out to set it off. I gave it a tug and then all of a sudden Suhail jumped back in amazement as if to say, 'How can such a small object make such a loud and piercing noise?'

'See? Piece of piss.' I held it up to his ear. 'Loud, isn't it?' I said. I put the rod back in its place. The alarm was silenced.

'Put it in your pocket, and at the first signs of trouble, pull the pin out as if you're gonna throw a hand grenade.'

A recce of the Trattoria was carried out to see just exactly what the set-up was. Would we need to make prior table bookings? No. That was good, because we could probably then dictate the best place to sit, and check out the best seating arrangements for the two sleepers to operate from. Was the place large or small? It was small. Its layout was basic: about 15 metres by 12, with a small bar, and kitchens to the rear. How many tables? Ten. Toilets? Halfway on the right-hand side down a wrought-iron spiral staircase, no entry and escape route in either the ladies or the gents. Employees? Entry and exit points? The check-list went on. Answers were duly found to all these questions.

There would be no time to run any hard information on the restaurant through to Doc. In fact, it was just as well time didn't allow it. His network might throw up something on his computer screen which might connect the team with the SB target. That would really set the cat amongst the pigeons.

It wasn't too much of a surprise when I realised that I knew Mike's M15 contact. Previously, Mike had only mentioned this guy in passing, and I never really wanted to know who he was, sort of a need-to-know basis again — I didn't need to know. But I had to met with him this time, to brief him up on what I wanted him and his team to do.

Dinger T turned out to be an old contact of mine from Northern Ireland. I'd met him for the first time back in 1979, during the two-bomb Warrenpoint massacre. Dinger had been attached to part of the Royal Marine Boat Troop whose task it was to patrol the waters around Newry and Warrenpoint. And when my platoon caught the second bomb, it was Dinger and his troop which made up part of the QRF (Quick Reaction Force) sent to the incident.

After that tour of Northern Ireland, I met Dinger again, a couple of years later, down in the Falklands. That was the last time I'd seen him until Mike brought him into the foyer of the Regents Plaza. He was quite a small man, standing no more than five six, small framed and quite unassuming. His thinning brown hair gave him the appearance of having quite a high forehead, and he was about 30 pounds heavier than when I'd last seen him. I didn't think anyone now would have thought he used to be part one of the country's finest fighting units, nor would anyone have guessed that he was now a topnotch field operator working in M15. Now that was a good disguise!

After ten minutes spent catching up on the intervening years, we set about going through the evening's operation. We agreed a price (cash) and for that I would get him, and one female operator, acting as lovers to sit in the restaurant, one solo diner, and all the technical kit to record the meeting's conversation, plus one van and a back-up driver.

'No hands on,' Dinger stressed. 'That's your business. Can't afford to get into anything too dramatic.' He meant, if the situation requires a physical approach, don't expect any reaction from me or my operators, other than natural ones. Compromising their cover wasn't on the agenda. That was a fair one. We would be covering outside, and if it sounded like it was going to kick off, then we would only be matter of a few seconds away. So there would be no need for him or his team to get involved.

I let him carry on. 'If it's all right by you, I'll do my own recce on the location as soon as we're finished up here. I'll have an operator inside as soon as possible to check out the comms and all the bugging shite we're gonna use.'

'You think there might be a problem with some of your kit?' I said.

'No, it's not that, it's all state-of-the-art kit. Stuff you can't even get under the counter at the moment. Well, not legally anyway.' Dinger looked up at me and grinned. 'But as you know, anything electronic can be a right pisser if it don't work when you want it to. The operator will carry out the equipment check on his own, about an hour before your man arrives.'

'How's he gonna do that?' Mike queried. 'He can't just walk about the place with a handful of bugs, he'll easily get sussed.'

'He's a good operator, he'll find a way; that's his job, you daft fucker. That's what you taxpayers pay for,' Dinger joked. 'And anyway, he'll also get a free scoff out of it. He'll be a solo customer. The point is, he'll be gone by the time your show kicks off.'

I let Dinger go on with the rest of his plan uninterrupted.

'Your man is due to arrive about seven, is that right?' Dinger said, looking up at me.

'Yeah, that's right, but we don't know what time the party he's meeting will arrive,' I answered.

Dinger had no idea what this meet was about. He said he didn't *want* to know. I respected that. And the less Dinger knew about the job, the more natural he would act, I was sure of that.

'The party of two guests should arrive about the same time as ours,' Mike informed him. 'He's pretty punctual, he was only a few minutes late for the previous meeting.'

This was important. Dinger wanted to get to the restaurant earlier and get the most tactically-sited table available, because there was no way we could plan where Suhail was going to sit if the Russian turned up before him and chose a table out of the way, and away from the listening devices.

'OK, if that's the case, I'll plan to sit down with Ally, my girlfriend for the night, at about quarter to seven, and hopefully that should cover it. If it doesn't, then I'll sort something out. Don't worry, the restaurant doesn't sound that big, and if it's not busy, then I think we'll be OK.'

'So, assuming it all goes to plan and they leave, probably take only an hour to scoff, where do you want to meet for a debrief?' I said.

'Do it back here at the Regents Plaza if you want. I'll debrief my team, stand them down and come over on my own and fill you in on what's what.'

It was a basic plan, which the best usually are. Three phases: phase one, the insertion; phase two, the occupation; phase three, the extraction.

'Oh, just one last thing,' Dinger added. 'What's your man look like?'

'Good point,' I said. 'I'll get him down here in a minute to pick up something from reception so you can eyeball him. You got a minute?'

'Yeah, I'm here for the duration, I'm on your time now.'

'Basically he's a short fat Asian-looking guy, in his late 50s, with a large black mole on his left cheek. You really can't miss him. I'll walk him past you.'

17.

TRUE COLOURS

It was a little before six twenty-five when I got to the location.
Vic was with me in one Mercedes and Mike and Ken were in the
other. The Fulham Palace Road was busy at this time of night so
it wasn't too difficult to blend into the surroundings and keep an
eye on the Trattoria. Dinger's inside man, Jerry, had just come out
of the location and called me up on his mobile. He let me know
that communications were good between him and Dinger, and
that it wasn't busy; only six people eating.

Dinger was sitting off the location, in a van just around the
corner, and he and Jerry would just change places with each other
at their own prearranged time. This operation was very much
under their control, and they dictated the pace. My job was to act
as a sort of outer cordon, to observe if any of Vaclav's men or SB
were hanging about the area, and in the worse-case scenario, to

act as the QRF.

At dead on six forty-five I saw Dinger and his date enter the restaurant. I casually reached for my covert radio switch. 'All stations, friends on time,' I relayed.

Two lots of two static hisses came back through my earpiece. This told me that Mike and Ken had heard and understood my message. The fact that two *separate* lots of hisses came back told me that Ken was more than likely out of his vehicle — probably taking a piss or something.

Dinger was dressed in a grey suit while she wore a three-quarter-length navy-blue skirt and jacket, a typical plain-Jane girl in her late 20s or early 30s — like Dinger, the type of person you could pass in the street and not even notice — two totally Grey People.

Then, at a little after seven, a black cab pulled up on the other side of the road from the Trattoria, and Vaclav plus one, a man, both dressed in sharply cut suits, got out and crossed the road. He wasn't the same guy who had attended the first meeting, but younger, in his 30s and looked slightly feeble, with hunched shoulders. He was carrying a black briefcase and had to place it on the ground between his legs in order to pay the cabbie. Vaclav, hands in pocket, looked suspiciously over at the Trattoria.

'Looks like a bag man,' Vic said, referring to the younger of the two.

'Yeah, very much the servant. I wonder where the muscle is?' I said, trying not to appear to be taking too much notice of what two men who had just got out of a black cab on a busy evening just off the Fulham Palace Road were up to.

'I wonder if he's tooled up or not?' I said. I then reassuringly tucked my left elbow into my side, confirming that the unnatural bulge was still under my armpit. It was a comforting feeling. Would I use it if I had to? I guess the answer would be yes, if someone shot first and endangered my life or the lives of those around me — and that, of course, included the public. Not in some vigilante effort but just through natural reactions. I was then brought back to reality.

'Come to think of it, where the fuck's Bollocks?' Vic said disdainfully.

A few seconds later another black cab pulled up, this time right outside the Trattoria. Suhail and Charles. The two couples met up and only the main men shook hands whilst the two 'bag men' eyed each other up and nodded in a sort of acknowledgement. Then they approached the restaurant and disappeared inside.

'Now we wait,' I said.

At ten past eight Dinger and girlfriend left. They didn't try to make us out, they just turned and headed off in the direction of Fulham Palace Road. It was feasible that, because Vaclav had chosen the location, he might have had friendly employees in the Trattoria or an OP opposite in one of the flats.

Dinger leaving was the sign that it was quite possible Suhail and co. were also on the way out. A few minutes later Vic and I pulled off and let the other Mercedes take over the OP. And just after that, I got a call from Ken, this time on the phone. 'Suhail and Vaclav are now leaving the restaurant. They look friendly enough. Shaking hands and laughing.'

'Well, that don't seem too bad, does it, Ken?'

'Fuck knows. I wonder what Dinger's got to say?'

'We'll have to wait and see. Keep me updated.' I closed the phone.

Vic took us back to the Regents Plaza, whilst Mike tailed Vaclav. It was thought that Suhail would travel straight back to the hotel as well. But the 15-minute drive took him over two hours. He *said* he'd stopped by Charles's flat in King's Cross to pick up some kit and had come right back, but I got the feeling he was lying. On the other hand, I also sensed that his meeting had gone better than he'd expected. But I had very little time to talk to him because three things happened almost at once.

Firstly, Mr Christos and Abdul Wahab (who'd made his way to the Regents Plaza under his own steam) immediately cornered Suhail and set about cross-examining him in the suite.

The second thing was that Ken phoned through to say that they'd lost Vaclav's cab.

'We had him, and then almost immediately lost him under the Hammersmith Flyover,' he said rather apologetically. 'Luckily we saw in what direction he was heading, and managed to pick him up again heading off down the Great West Road. And that's where we lost him again. The fucking traffic's a right fucker, isn't it?'

It was good that they'd kept up with the cab for that long. It was a risky task with over an 80 per cent chance of failure, but I'd thought that I had to try it just the same.

Thirdly, Dinger was running a bit late, and when he finally pitched up I understood the reason. He was very guarded in his initial response as to why he had been held up, but I was already reading between the lines. He had no tapes on him, and it was then he told me that he wasn't at liberty to tell me anything: 'Official Secrets and all that,' he said. 'Sorry, you know the score.'

Because of the intelligence he'd gained during the meet, Dinger in his wisdom had decided that the content of the meeting was important to his employer, so that overruled his obligation to the team.

'Listen, mate,' he said. 'You know I've had my hands tied on this now. I shouldn't even be talking to you.'

'What the fuck are you on about?' I said. Mike stayed quiet and was looking a bit sheepish. 'It was *me* who put *you* on this fucking job. Or have you forgotten that?' I could feel myself getting more agitated, and what I wanted to do was stick one squarely on his chin.

'Yeah, I understand that, I didn't know what it was all about until I started hearing about all this shit that your man and the Russians are involved in.' Dinger was trying to back-pedal — just a bit. 'I was under the impression that it was just a basic static-surveillance job.'

'You didn't know fuck all about anything, because I didn't tell you and you didn't fuckin' ask. You were quite happy to take the money.' I was fuming. 'Look, Dinger, cut the crap will you? What the fuck is going on?'

At this point, Dinger explained. 'After listening in for about five minutes, I realised that this Russian was the same Russian wanted by SB, I remember seeing a memo —'

'Yeah, I know that too,' I said casually.

'How come?' Dinger asked.

'That doesn't matter.' I grinned. 'But what you've done is just confirmed to me what I thought about using you lot,' I muttered. I tried to keep composed. I was now beginning to regret ever having arranged this meeting, especially in such an open place like this foyer. It would have been better to have had it in my room, where I could control this Government prick — old acquaintance or not.

'Well, I can't say any more than what I've said already. The picture's a lot bigger than you think. It involves bank fraud and a billion pounds. It's gone right to the top. Number Ten.'

'Bollocks,' I said under my breath. I took a bit of a sigh and said calmly, 'I know all that.' Of course I didn't, I didn't have a clue, I was bluffing. 'What's your point?'

'That's just it. I have no point,' he said firmly.

'What's that meant to mean? You telling us to butt out or what?' I was purposely showing signs of going ballistic. It was a show for Dinger, but I could see he wasn't going to be intimidated.

'That's up to you guys. But what I will give you is this. A guy called Abdul Wahab is involved too, we don't know him yet, but he's in London now; apparently he is flying out sometime to transfer 30 million dollars from a dodgy insurance policy deal, set up by Suhail, and your man plus this Vaclav character is going to pick half of it up in cash. It's heavy stuff, you don't really want to be involved in that shit, do you?'

Dinger's question didn't require an answer. I could see he was through saying anything else. He went dead.

'Shit! What planet are you on? You haven't told me anything I didn't already know. You've just confirmed that Vaclav is a Russian hit-team man, and I reckon he's probably the leader, and a guy called Abdul Wahab is also involved in this big fuck-off fraud,' I retorted.

'You know this Abdul Wahab? Is he here?' Dinger sprang back into life.

'No, I don't. I was just after a reaction from you,' I lied.

Dinger didn't look too sure about that.

Mike butted in and asked what were the chances of the job running for another week, because he needed the money. Dinger glared at him as if he was looking at a man with two heads. I got the feeling that Mike wasn't taking anything too seriously now.

Mike turned to Dinger. 'Well, it's all right for you mate, you get a nice wedge at the end of each month, you don't have to worry where the next job's coming from.'

'You're right, Mike. Spot on,' I said. 'And we've just given him one more to rake his expenses up on.' As I spoke, I became aware of the Walther which was still tucked in quite naturally under my left armpit. I gave a little grin, knowing that M15 could decide to raid this job any time from now on. I would seriously have to address the problem of dumping it asap.

Dinger wasn't too keen to hang around with us any more. He said that he would try and get word to us if the Firm was going to 'lift' Suhail, and implied that their main target was more likely to be Vaclav, rather than Suhail. If I was to believe that, then he probably thought me a bit soft in the head. In all probability, they would lift them all, or none.

My guess was that Dinger was lying, and the Firm would now be doing everything to distract us in order to get us out of the way so they could move in, in full, and then put in place a total surveillance operation. In truth, I was now beginning to feel more than a little unconcerned about this job. My view was that we had had a good run for our money and now the end was near.

I was still pissed off about Dinger taking this job to his boss. But I suppose at the end of the day he had his conscience to think about. If the roles had been reversed, then I think if I'd still been serving, and had this Queen and Country mentality, I would have done the same. After all, life is all about earning brownie points for one's superiors, isn't it?

That was the last I saw of Dinger. Needless to say, he got paid from both ends that day — which, of course, as anyone in business will tell you, is the easiest way of getting one's balls cut off.

DAY FIFTEEN

I had a really uncomfortable sleep; I tossed and turned all night. It was like I was suffering from a bout of malaria, and come the morning I was feeling far from 100 per cent. I put it down to a higher than normal stress-level brought on by the outcome of the previous 24 hours.

There was no reason to remind the guys to be on their guard, because they always were. But since I had briefed them up on the M15 situation, they now saw it as a bit of a game, to be the first one to spot a tail. Al plus Tom had the first shot: they were still on the school run; then John had the second chance — I detailed him to drive Mr Abdul Wahab on a fast ball up to Heathrow Airport on his own. Abdul Wahab was flying back to Lebanon that morning. If Doc's men picked him up, well I couldn't give a toss. He wasn't my client and hosting him wasn't included in Suhail's brief.

Things were now begining to make some sense, and given the latest circumstances, Pete was reluctant to play outside. I could understand his point, he was scared of getting pinged by his own people.

I still had to keep playing the game as usual. Suhail said that he had to go to a meeting in a hotel just off Russell Square, around the corner from the British Museum. So the meetings continued. We'd never taken him there before but I wasn't too concerned now. I decided to treat the task as low-key, after all the job appeared to be going tits up.

We left in two vehicles: Vic with me, and Mike with Ken and Suhail. When we got to the hotel I walked in with Ken and Suhail. It was very much downmarket, probably less than two stars, what I call a transit hotel: stay for two days and leave sort of thing. The sort of place that would attract student types or travelling sales people.

I spotted Charles and two guys with their backs to us standing around the reception desk. It was fairly obvious they were waiting for us. The two guys were dressed in black bomber jackets and jeans, both carrying a larger than normal Motorola two-way radio, with the volume turned up higher than it needed to be. Probably for the benefit of us and other guests, to indicate that they were security and were very important people. A don't-fuck-with-us attitude. Definitely nightclub material.

Ken looked at me and whispered, 'What the fuck's going on?'

'Fuck knows. I guess we're going to find out though,' I answered.

Charles saw us and came over, all smiles and white teeth closely followed by his muscle. Suhail stayed silent.

'Charles, what's going on?' I asked sharply. I got the feeling that Charles in his wisdom thought that he could now run his uncle's security. Why? Possibly because he was over-ambitious, obviously under-experienced and just plain stupid and greedy.

He was standing in between the two security guys. One was

short and stocky, the other tall, bald and fat — a bit like a larger version of Buster Bloodvessel. They stayed silent, but I could feel Ken trying to exchange a daggered look with me.

'Look, I thought it best if my uncle stayed here for a bit. You know, just until things quieten down. I've got good security.' Charles motioned to his two bouncers.

'Yeah, fucking right,' Ken said in a sarcastic sort of way. 'I can see that.'

Suhail made his way to a seat towards the lounge area. It was all too much for him. Ken followed. There was a slight movement by Baldy to go with Ken, but Ken gave a him look to say, 'Don't even think about it.'

For the next few minutes we had a bit of a stand-up verbal battle in the foyer of this hotel. Voices weren't being raised, but you could feel the tension oozing out of everyone concerned. I now understood I'd definitely been double-crossed by Charles.

It transpired that in his wisdom (and probably for his own ego and self-gratification in his nightclub-guest pecking order), he had asked the bouncers of his local West End club if they fancied a bit of BG work. Of course they jumped at the chance, the trouble being that they weren't BGs, they were bouncers.

Ken knew all about this strain of beast. He could spot an idiot in their line of work at 20 paces.

I pulled him to one side, recognising that his temper was at boiling point. 'What do you think?' I whispered.

'Look at them, they're all bursting with self-importance. Fucking numpties. Fuck 'em off, Steve,' he said. 'They're fuckin' trash.'

Now, I wasn't about to have a stand-up battle with these guys. We'd walked into an ambush and the best way out of it was to back-track very carefully. I pulled Charles to one side but made sure we were still in earshot of both the bouncers and Suhail.

'What the hell are you playing at?' I said.

'Nothing to worry about, Steve,' he replied, in a pleading sort of tone. 'These are my security people ...' he said it in a quite matter-of-fact way. 'I need them.'

'They're fucking idiots,' I said scornfully. 'What the hell do you think you lot look like? This is a hotel, for Christ's sake. These fuckers belong in a nightclub.' He was now looking like a ten-year-old being told off by his father. I changed the subject. 'How many upstairs?'

'Six,' he said.

'Six! Who's paying for them then?'

'I am.'

I raised an eyebrow. How the hell was he affording that? This set-up had to be costing him a grand a day. It was now apparent that I actually knew very little about this wealthy but very complicated family.

I motioned him to sit down with me and whispered into his ear, 'We've got this job, and we're gonna see it through.' I pulled back and looked across the foyer at Suhail. He took one quick glance over in my direction and then dropped his head downwards.

The last time I'd seen a smirk like that was the previous winter. I got duped for 67 pence by this guy who stopped me one night, walking through Soho. He was carrying a petrol can; he looked pukka enough, and when he asked, 'Have you got 67 pence?' because he'd run out of petrol, I didn't think anything of it and gave him a pound.

Then a bit further on, but on the other side of the road was a different guy with the same problem, petrol can and all. I'd been scammed! So I went back, found the first guy, and told him what I thought of him. His reply was to give a supercilious grin, as if to say, 'What are you gonna do about it then?' He had the petrol can at the ready. Then I stuck the nut on him; he stumbled back into a shop doorway, totally stunned. I gripped his throat so hard with my left hand that I thought he might just pass out there and then, and with my right, dipped into his pocket, grabbed a handful of loose change, took my pound and threw the rest back in his face.

I carried on with Charles. 'I bet you've been planning this for some time now, haven't you?' I paused. 'That's why you were late coming back last night, wasn't it?'

'No, it wasn't, no,' he pleaded. But through his eyes I could see it all. He was definitely lying.

'It's all to do with the meeting last night, isn't it?' I said it as a statement rather than a question. 'Well, I know exactly what went on.' (Now here I lied — Dinger never let me hear the recordings.) 'I had a couple of sleepers in with you last night. They were sitting right next to you.'

'Yeah, sure,' Charles replied, very cocky.

'That bloke and his girlfriend. They heard everything. Abdul Wahab leaving and the 30 million,' I said.

Charles's face dropped. He stayed silent. I could see he was thinking that he'd fucked up by bringing in his own team. They were no match for my team. I was pretty certain that they were not for his protection, they were to keep Suhail under wraps until the money had been transferred and then he would take his chances in double-crossing his uncle and Vaclav under the security umbrella of half-a-dozen or so nightclub bouncers. No match for Vaclav's men, or the Firm either.

I got up. 'See you then,' I said. I gave Ken the nod. He took the hint and we walked out, not making eye-contact and not saying a single word. It was a pretty eerie feeling walking away from the job as we did. After all, we were professionals. But this job was now a big bag of bollocks.

My plan was to go back to the hotel and wait. We had the upper hand: we had the vehicles, the hotel was paid up for another two days, and we had been paid up too. The wife and daughter never came into my equation. They were unfortunate pawns in Suhail's web of deceit, and it wasn't my intention to use them in any way. They were free to do whatever they wanted. But as I walked out of that hotel, I knew that this wasn't going to be the last time I would see Suhail, and I suspected he would be of the same opinion once Charles had debriefed him on the Dinger situation.

18.

THE FINAL HOURS

DAY FIFTEEN, MIDDAY

Once back at the Regents Plaza I went and saw Mrs Suhail to tell her what I thought about this apparent subplot which was now emerging, and to offer any assistance to her and her daughter. I and all the team were genuinely concerned as to their security, having spent the past several days living in their faces and looking after their well-being. Like the rest of the team, I had built up an unexpected affinity to them both.

I knew that Al had got on really well with the daughter. He had been asked to take part in the school's Open Day in a couple of weeks' time. Suni had entered him in the parents' egg-and-spoon race. It was a source of amusement amongst the team, and when we found out about it, he had the piss taken out of him daily. Al's response was to say nothing but give the 'finger' in reply.

That morning Mrs Suhail had also received a phone call. 'My husband has told me to pack up,' she said. Her body language told me that she didn't want to expand on the conversation. 'We're moving hotels tomorrow, that's all I know.'

She didn't expand on the reasons why and I didn't push her on it. I realised that she didn't have a clue as to what was really going on. She was the wife and Suhail was the husband, and in their culture it wasn't a requirement of the female to have an opinion, let alone a voice.

By now I had had a tit-full of the entire affair. I was quids in with payment, so I decided to withdraw mine and my team's services, as and when I thought appropriate. I had no professional hang-ups about that.

I decided to search out Mr Christos to see if he could throw any light on what was happening, and found out that he had checked out that morning. If I'd known that then, it would have put me on my guard straightaway. He'd confided in the team many times, and it would have been unlike him to check out without at least saying goodbye to us first. On the other hand, this *was* typical client behaviour!

Suhail arrived back at the Regents Plaza about mid-afternoon, on his own. There was no security and we were given no warning of his arrival. He'd caught a black cab! Was he coming round to my way of thinking? Had he had another change of plan? Frankly I didn't give two shits any more.

The team had been in total rumour-control mode since I'd arrived back from the hotel near Russell Square with the latest twist. I gave Suhail five minutes to get his shit together before I used the corridor man's swipe card to enter his suite. I didn't knock — I was past all this bullshit of client/BG confidentiality. I wanted to know where the team stood.

As I entered the suite I saw him on the mobile. The conversation was loud and sounded like it was full of back-tracking bullshit. He was pacing around the room talking, pleading heavily into the mobile. He was so deep in concentration he didn't see me come in, or if he did, he didn't show it. I saw his wife in the master bedroom, sitting on the bed, covering her face with her hands.

I couldn't understand the language he was speaking, but it sounded Turkish. When he finished, he turned to me and said that we had to leave immediately.

'That was Rohit, Vaclav's right-hand man.'

'I know who he is. He was at the restaurant. Rohit is a Turkish name, and you were speaking in Turkish. So what the fuck's going on?'

'He says I'm double-crossing him and they are coming over here right now to kill me.'

'Well, how the fuck did that happen?' I shouted. 'How the fuck did they finally suss out where we are?'

He was looking shocked, and his face went a sort of light-red colour. Strange for that to happen to a man with brown skin. He started to burble on, almost in tears. He was violently shaking, out of control and he kept strutting up and down, mumbling about Charles stitching him up with the other security team, and about Vaclav coming over to kill him.

I asked him again, 'How does he know you're here?'

'How do I know? How do I know? Probably that bastard nephew of mine,' he wailed. 'We must leave *now!* He will kill me — truly. These men are animals.'

'I'll speak to you in the Range Rover,' I retorted curtly.

I wasn't sure what to believe — certainly I'd given up expecting the simple truth from him. 'What about Suni?' After a second I carried on without letting him reply. 'I'll get Al to pick her up straightaway.' It was quite clear Suhail was thinking of himself first rather than his daughter and wife. He was loathsome, but I couldn't hang about making moral judgements on the man. I'd suspected he was an arsehole on day one week one, and my opinion had just been confirmed.

I'd just popped in to find out when I could stand the guys down — we'd already planned the end-of-job piss-up — and now he wanted our help. I told him to grab whatever he needed, and then I passed the word around the team that it was 'game on' once more.

The news that the Russians were back on the hunt sent a buzz of excitement around the team. I was now really glad that I hadn't been too hasty in getting rid of the Walther.

I told Al and Tom to take the wife and go and pick up the

daughter. That was my first priority.

As regards the operation as a whole, now M15 were sniffing around, I certainly couldn't rely on them to act as 'the cavalry' should the shit hit the fan. They always work to their own agenda, and I could guess that it didn't include my safety or that of my team, even though we were all UK citizens. At the end of the day, we would all be expendable if the political situation so dictated.

'Where the hell do I take them once I've picked them up?' Al asked, slightly impatiently.

The only place which sprang to mind was the hotel near Russell Square. Charles was a bastard all right, but I was sure — as much as I could be sure of anything — that he wouldn't stoop to harming Suni. I'd noted that he had got on well with Suni during the time he and his girlfriend had spent with us. This was far from perfect, but it was the only option I could come up with in the time.

'The hotel where I was this morning, Russell Square, you know it?' I said. 'Just drop them off, make sure they go in. No wait, better get Tom to walk them in and sit them down in the lounge, and then get away from the place as quickly as possible,' I said. 'Give me a call when you've dropped them off and I'll give you the RV.'

'Yeah, of course, no problems, see you there then, or whenever,' Al said.

In five minutes Al telephoned me to confirm that he was now on his way. Then, a few seconds later, as the rest of the team and I were scurrying down the corridor carrying only the barest of kit, the hotel alarm bells suddenly went off. Initially I thought nothing of it, but when we got to the elevators we found that they'd been closed off. The thought of a real fire in the hotel didn't enter my head. It wasn't until one of the corridor men, Dave, came running up to me saying that there was a bomb warning in the hotel, that I found out the truth.

The corridor men weren't coming with us. I'd told them this was 'end ex' (an army expression meaning end of exercise, but in our case, end of the operation) for them: they could swan about our suite for as long as they wanted to, or until asked to leave the hotel, so Dave was taking advantage of that. Personally, I didn't give a shit if he stayed there for another week, that was down to him.

Over the ear-splitting noise of the fire alarm Dave screamed, 'I was just looking out of the window and admiring the view when I saw a police car stop the traffic coming from the West End. I didn't think anything of it, then I saw this ARU vehicle [a police Armed Response Unit] pull up, and half the Met pile out of the back of it.' He sounded really excited, like this was his first piece of real action.

I thought that if he stayed around here for much longer watching policemen with guns from afar, he might well have one stuck in his face by a pissed-off Russian.

He went on talking as we bundled ourselves down the fire-escape stairs. 'Then this one copper gets out a loud hailer and starts telling everyone to clear the area. Fucking amazing.'

By the time we'd got down into the garage, there was a member of the hotel's security staff talking to one of my static guys.

'You can't leave the hotel, mate,' the guy from the hotel said. 'The police have sealed the exit of the garage. They reckon there's a bomb in the hotel or somewhere behind Greville Road. The bomb squad are searching the hotel now.'

'You're fuckin' joking,' I replied. 'If there's a bomb in this hotel, don't you think the first thing the police are going to do is evacuate *this* place?'

'You've got a point,' he conceded. 'But the police have told us to stay put.'

'We'll see about *that*,' I said. I got hold of Pete and told him to do the business with his ID card again. He didn't say anything but the look he gave me suggested that this was going to be the last time. By now I was pretty much convinced that he and Dinger had somehow colluded with each other, so that should this job go completely pear-shaped, and their superiors started asking, 'Why were you on the job in the first place?' they would have covered their backs very well indeed.

But I really didn't give a flying fuck about that; as long as Pete got us out of the hotel, that was all I was worried about. There was, I suppose, only one good point about being kept in the hotel. If we couldn't leave, then Vaclav, Rohit and their team couldn't get in. Nonetheless, my way of thinking was that it was better to be out rather than in, and away from this location as soon as possible. And, for all any of us knew, this latest incident could well have been an MI5 set-up. They might have already received intelligence that Vaclav and friends were in the locality, and this was their way of tightening the net on them — and possibly on my team as well.

Meanwhile, Pete's patter had worked once again.

'What did you tell them this time?' I asked, intrigued.

'Well, I said who I was, and that my team needed to get out of here right away, and if they needed confirmation of who I was, to get on to their boss and tell him someone from the Firm wants a chat.'

'And he went for that?' I said curiously.

'No, not at first. It wasn't until I had a word with the big chief that he sent the password, and then: open sesame.' He pointed to the security gates and sounded quite pleased with himself.

I nodded in astonishment and sarcastically said, 'Job fucked then!'

The electronic security barrier was raised and two Range Rovers and one Mercedes slipped out behind the Regents Plaza, cutting through the back streets and on through Belsize Park. This was not before we had an uneasy wait while the policeman in charge got on his radio and cleared our request through his superiors. But had we *really* slipped the net, or was this part of the plan by the security services to entrap us? I didn't know.

In spite of what he'd just said, I knew Pete had spilled the beans on the job in order to get us out, and also to cover his own arse, because you can't keep going around London with your ID card, pulling rank at every bit of trouble that comes your way. It just doesn't work like that in real life. Sometimes, you have to look after number one, and Pete was only doing just that. I did blame him though — fuck his big pension and a possible extension of service. His actions could have cost us our lives.

That was probably why we had been allowed to leave the Regents Plaza so easily. So, about a couple of minutes after our escape, I changed the game on the hoof. I decided to split the convoy, because from past experience I knew that if anyone was tailing us, it would be doubly hard to tail two groups. The other reason was that I now realised that I'd let Al drive off to pick up

Suni, the key bargaining chip in this entire affair, without a back-up vehicle.

'She's the soft target in this whole business,' I said out aloud.

'Who is?' Vic said as he concentrated on keeping close up the lead vehicles rear.

'The daughter, of course. Vaclav and his boys just might try and snatch her.' I quickly punched the number up on my mobile. 'I'll get hold of Al and let him know we're heading his way.'

Then I got hold of Ken and told him the change of plan, and instructed him to find a safe RV for us to meet up later and to keep Suhail sweet.

It took Vic only several minutes to cross-grain through the backstreets and arrive just short of the street where the school was located. The neighbourhood was a classy tranquil backwater, a series of well-established streets lined with trees. These grew through well-kept grass verges, and many of their roots had attacked the pavement, lifting some of the slabs a couple of inches. They hadn't been repaired, probably because the residents wanted everything to look natural and 'in keeping'.

The streets, just wide enough for two cars to squeeze through without scraping the vehicles parked up on either side, twisted and turned their way through an estate of large detached properties. You wouldn't expect to see an area like this so close to the heart of a city like London. We could well have been in the sleepy suburbs of Surrey, had it not been for the fact that 500 metres in any direction would have brought us out into the constant flow, rumble and grime of the capital's horrendous traffic problem.

Vic carefully made a left, like a typical flat-cap-wearing resident who respected the local speed restrictions. This street went dead straight for about 100 metres or so, before it rose slightly, turned, and then disappeared out of view. Just before the rise, there was a staggered junction, and from an earlier recce I knew that the left turn looped around and led back out of the estate, whilst the right was a relatively short 'T' shaped cul-de-sac.

The trees on either side of the street signified the boundaries of each house, and because the houses were higher than the street, their gardens were held back by a series of stone-built six-foot-high walls, broken only by wrought-iron gates which marked their driveways.

Since it wasn't quite school kicking-out time, there were relatively few vehicles parked up on either side of the street. Vic took it steady. I could quite easily see Tom's Merc parked some 20 metres up on our left. He was sitting in the driver's seat and facing the way we were heading. Two long deliberate clicks hissed out of my radio, indicating that Tom had sighted us. It also confirmed that he hadn't spotted anything out of the usual.

A few minutes earlier, to save time, as soon as I got within a couple of hundred metres of the school, I'd phoned Al to let him know we were with him and to go and collect Suni. This would save us all time on the ground. We didn't want to be hanging around the area for too long, working on the principle that the quicker we could make the pick-up, the quicker we could secure everyone into a safe house.

Vic did the usual drive past as I covertly scanned each vehicle and driveway for anything out of the ordinary. Tom knew we were about but didn't make any acknowledgement. In the immediate area by the school, six cars lined the left-hand side whilst only four were parked up on the right. All were unoccupied.

'All clear,' I said. 'Let's go round again.'

As Vic made the loop to go back around I sent Tom the signal that we too hadn't seen anything untoward.

Within less than two minutes we were just coming up to turn left to make our second pass, when all of a sudden Vic spotted a short wheel-base Daihatsu FourTrak come racing up behind us and try and cut in between us and the pavement. Vic was already into the left turn.

'Fuck it, Steve, I think we've got company,' he said with some emotion.

Almost immediately I caught the sight of a green Fourtrak, two up, on my left, trying to cut inside and across the pavement. At the same time I saw Al and Mrs Suhail walking hand-in-hand with Suni. They were just a couple of metres short of the Merc, totally unaware of the danger.

'GO, GO, GO!' I screamed over the radio. 'AL, CONTACT TO YOUR REAR, MOVE IT. GREEN FOURTRAK,' was all I managed to blurt out.

'Roger out,' Al replied, as calm as if he was out on a Sunday stroll. He briefly looked back and then quickly ushered Suni and her mother into the back of the Merc.

There was a screech of tyres — I felt the Range Rover mount the curb and narrowly miss a tree. Vic cursed as he tried to close the gap between us and the threat. His manoeuvre caught the Fourtrak driver well off guard as he steered left instead of right. I saw the Fourtrak career towards and then smash into a fence which marked the garden of the house on the corner.

A moment later I looked up and saw the Merc speed off and disappear over the hill.

'Send sit rep, send sit rep.' It was Al, wanting to know what was going on.

'Get the fuck out of here, we've been hit, we've been hit,' I screamed back at the voice as Vic threw a right which put us back on the tarmac. Somehow, the Fourtrak had managed to straighten itself up and was now back up behind us. Vic then narrowly missed a lamppost as he skilfully positioned the Range Rover first on the left and then on the right. He was trying to keep the threat from overtaking, because it was pretty obvious this wasn't a classic example of 'road rage' — these men, whoever they were, wanted to pass us, because they were after the Merc and Suni.

Vic let out a string of obscenities as he wrestled with the steering of the Range Rover, still yanking it left and right. I looked behind and saw determination and terror in the eyes of the pursuing driver and passenger.

'Don't let him pass, don't let him pass,' I yelled back at Vic. I could see beads of sweat running down his face, the veins on his temple were all pumped up. His face had been totally distorted by a massive surge of strain and pressure brought on by the situation. He looked like some grotesque monster from a Spiderman comic.

'He's gonna ram us. Hold on,' Vic shouted as he slammed on the brakes. The Range Rover skidded and rocked to a halt. Almost immediately, Vic hit the accelerator again, and we sped off.

'Jesus Christ,' I bellowed.

I looked back again. The Fourtrak had briefly stopped. Then it lurched forward and sped towards us. But the driver's tactics were not the right ones to employ. Now Vic had already slammed the brakes back on again. I wasn't ready for it, and I was propelled forward. The inertia mechanism from my seat belt cut in, and for a brief second I felt the belt dig sharply into my left shoulder and take the full force of 210 pounds of bodyweight plus whatever the vehicle weighed. I made a grab at my weapon, my right hand was inside my jacket and holding on to its grips, ready to draw it out if necessary.

'Hang on, Steve, let's hope they're not wearing seat belts,' Vic shouted as he grappled with the gear selector, and almost as quickly as we'd been going forward, we were in reverse. I heard the whine of metal on metal and smelt burnt transmission fluid as Vic put the Range Rover's gearbox under extreme pressure. He had now sent the Range Rover into reverse at speed — foot flat down on the pedal. I braced myself for the impact, hand still wrapped around the Walther. In another second we made contact. The impact sucked the air out of my lungs and I was hurled forward.

Again held rigid by my seat belt, I felt the rear of the vehicle lift up. I looked back and saw the impact had shattered our rear window; it had also pushed the bull bars on the front of the Fourtrak into a mangled mass. Its windscreen was smashed and its bonnet had buckled up.

'That should fuckin' do it,' roared Vic as he tried to get to grips with forward drive. The Range Rover whined and jolted. He frantically tried to put it in drive. We weren't moving.

'Come on, come on, let's get the fuck out of here,' I kept shouting. For some reason the rear wheels were locked. They were spinning so much that burnt-rubber smoke came spewing in through the smashed rear window.

'Come on, baby.' Vic was *willing* the Range Rover to engage its forward gears. I looked all around — no traffic, no onlookers — then looked back at the Fourtrak; steam was billowing out of its engine compartment. The impact had been so severe that it had probably pushed the radiator and its steering gear so far back as to render it useless. It wasn't going anywhere — Vic had done a serious demolition job on it. Suddenly, through its crazed windscreen, I saw the passenger break through the glass with something solid in his hand.

'Jesus *fuck*, he's armed, he's got a gun,' I shouted. Instinctively I crouched behind my seat but the safety belt restricted full movement. I withdrew the Walther, cocked it, flipped the safety catch off and prepared to take aim. The gunman was only a couple of metres behind when I saw the muzzle flash as he fired off a round. I didn't hear or feel anything apart from the roar of the Range Rover's engine and the ever-increasing rocking of its chassis, as Vic struggled to make our escape. Strangely, through all this, I was concious of my mobile ringing. I ignored it!

In a real-time situation like this you never really have time to take everything in, you only act instinctively, and it's only after the event, when you're safe, or the firing has died down, that you have time to reflect on what has gone on before, and only then can you recall the sequence of events.

Another flash and a puff of smoke. The firer had squeezed off another round. Within three seconds of the first round being fired at us, I was in the aim and put down two rounds in rapid succession. I had to fire left-handed down through the middle of the Range Rover. I saw both rounds impact the Fourtrak. The first went low, to the right and through the windscreen; the second hit even lower and cut into the buckled bonnet.

'Fuck, Steve, I didn't know you were carrying!'

I ignored Vic's remark and fired off another double tap into the Fourtrak. 'Get it into four-wheel drive, for fuck's sake,' I roared out as a round ricocheted off the back of the tailgate and embedded itself in the back seat. Another pinged off something inside and smashed through the nearside rear window.

'Come on, Vic, let's move,' I grunted, not taking my sight off my point of aim. I fired two more rounds, one at the target and one deliberately into the engine. After those two shots I wasn't aware of any more incoming rounds. Had I wounded or even slotted him? Did he have a stoppage? Was he getting his head down and into cover? I couldn't tell. The next thing I knew, I was pushed back into my seat as Vic found forward drive. I managed to get two more rounds off before the increased momentum of the Range Rover made it unsafe to keep firing.

As we sped off, I was thinking of a number of things I had to do, and they all had to be done as soon as possible. Vic kept quiet. He knew what *he* had to do, and that was to get us far away from the scene of the contact, as quickly and as covertly as possible.

Initially we travelled straight at breakneck speed, doubling our distance with every passing second.

I kept looking behind to convince myself that we'd taken out the threat. 'I think we're losing them,' I said confidently. 'They don't seemed to be moving.'

'Let's hope so,' Vic replied as he continued to keep total control of his vehicle.

We followed the route of the Merc for about 100 metres before suddenly dropping our speed and making a right like nothing had happened. As we made this turn I saw a man on my side of the pavement walking his dog. He had his back to us and as we drove past, I looked into the near-side mirror — he didn't look up, he hadn't even noticed us. As far as he was concerned, we were just an everyday occurrence.

Some time later we pulled up in the car park of Sainsbury's at Camden Town — not before I sent a sit rep (situation report) through to Al, however. I told him I didn't want to discuss the incident. I would brief him and the rest of the guys later. I didn't want 'rumour control' sweeping through the team just yet. My main concern was that Suni was in a safe environment, and that the team now knew that we were now playing the game with big boys' rules, so they should keep a low profile and not take anything for granted. The whys and wherefores of the contact would be discussed later.

'You guys all right? No blood?' Al asked, very concerned.

I looked across at Vic who was half listening in to the conversation and half looking for the police or the Fourtrak. 'We're both OK. Don't worry. The vehicle's a bit battered, though.'

'Got any idea who it was? Dinger and his gang?' Al tried to push it.

He had a point there. I hadn't thought of that possibility. No, they wouldn't, it was too slapdash for an MI5 hit.

'Get real, Al. I fuckin' hope not. Look, the only thing I can tell you is that, whoever they were — Russians, Turks or whoever — they meant business. I'll brief you later, OK,' I replied. 'And don't mention fuck all about this to Pete, tell him diddly squat.' I couldn't afford for Pete to get even a sniff of the fact that something had gone down, and for him then to make a discreet phone call. That would really put us in the shit with the 'authorities'. Also, I didn't want to be drawn in to anything until I'd had time to cool down. I quickly changed the subject. 'How did your drop-off go?'

'Wifey and daughter are safe and sound in the hotel near Russell Square.'

'That's good. Any problems with Charles?'

'No, it all went sweet as a nut.' He was sounding really happy now that he'd finally got rid of his babysitter's image.

'There was one thing ...'

'Yeah, what's that?' I almost expected him to say that he had bashed up one of the bouncers or something like that.

He carried on. 'John wants a word.' I heard him pass over the mobile.

'Steve, guess who I saw at the hotel?'

'Go on then, try me.' I was thinking it might have been an MI5 cell or something like that. That was all I needed right now.

'Roberts. He was sitting in the bar having a drink. He didn't see me,' he said, in a tone that implied it might have mattered if Roberts *had* seen him.

Another subplot. I didn't have time to assimilate all this extra information, and to be blunt, I didn't give a flying toss either. I finished the conversation off. 'I'll send an RV in about 30 minutes. Pass it on.' I dropped the call.

Vic had parked up away from the security cameras and went about assessing the vehicle damage. Surprisingly, apart from a couple of broken windows, a pushed-in bumper and a dented tailgate with a couple of rounds through it, nothing else was damaged on the outside. We set about cleaning up the mess. I managed to find all eight empty cases and put them in my pocket. Vic didn't say anything about the weapon. I could feel he was pissed off that I hadn't told him I was carrying, but secretly I knew he was glad I'd used it. But now I had a serious dilemma: when should I get rid of it? I hoped to God I wouldn't have to use it again. The only way I could be sure of that was to ditch it at the earliest possible opportunity.

The two groups laid low until Vic and I had time to dust

ourselves down and thought it safe to rear our heads. I made the RV just inside the inner circle of Regent's Park, where we all arrived without incident. I purposely put Suhail into Vic's Range Rover, out of earshot. And with a bit of 'cross decking' with bodies, a game-plan was agreed.

All but Vic, Suhail and I would stay with one Range Rover whilst Mike would follow behind us in a black cab. The rest of the team — Al, Tom, Ken, John and Pete — would arrange to take the vehicles back, then we would all meet up together in a safe bar just off Shepherds Market in Mayfair. I had a private word with Al about keeping an eye on Pete. If he started to act funny, Al was to give me a call immediately; then I would change the safe bar. I could deal with Pete later. The last thing I wanted was to walk into an ambush full of spooks. If what I'd planned went well, it would take less than two hours to execute.

The three vehicles left, leaving me, Vic, Suhail and Mike. I pulled Mike to one side and spoke quietly. 'Mike, just to confirm, you know what to do, uh?'

'Yeah. I get into a cab and follow you. And when I see the obvious happening, I make my way to the obvious.'

'Good, let's get this show on the road.'

There had been a lot of good ideas flying around about what to do with Suhail. One was to kidnap him and hold him to ransom until Abdul Wahab came through with some money — after all, that's probably what Charles and Roberts had had in mind. Another was to sell him to Vaclav. These were a couple of the options we considered, and if it wasn't for the fact that M15, SB and God knows what other security agencies were now looking for him, then we might have stood a chance. Pete would have had to go, though — we couldn't have a team player batting for the other side.

But actually I decided on a third course of action. Finally Mike managed to hail a cab, and we sped off.

The afternoon traffic was moving at a bearable rate as Vic pulled off Park Lane and cut across Hyde Park Corner and through into South Carriage Drive. Mike was still behind us, and even before I had a good look, I saw a police vehicle parked up on the left some 100 metres away. And that's when I made my move.

'Right, Vic, you ready for this?'

'Yes, mate, let's do it.'

Immediately I could tell that Vic was working out what I had in mind, but he couldn't have felt my heart pumping and the adrenalin rushing around my body. I was still carrying and had just been involved in a major shoot-out. The entire situation we'd found ourselves in was totally insane, but I don't think I would have changed that feeling I had inside me for the world. Unfortunately, with me it's like a drug. Once you've had a taste of a massive adrenalin rush where your life or whole future is on the line, it's very difficult to resist it when it comes along. I would have great trouble living life without it.

'Just pull alongside him — I'll have my hand out, making out we're lost — and then pull up in front.'

'Yeah, that'll give him a shock. Think he's getting hit or something.'

I caught the eye of the police driver. The car was two up. I had to be careful, it was an ARV. It was too late to do anything else, but ideally I was looking for a basic patrol vehicle. However, we were committed now and any movement other than stopping might have given way to a chase, which wasn't the object of this particular operation. I caught sight of Mike and his cab whizzing by, then slowly got out of the Range Rover waving a large *A to Z of London* in one hand, at the same time keeping an eye on the two policemen.

The passenger made a move to get out. I quickly opened Suhail's nearside door.

'This is where we part, Mr Suhail. I wish I could say it's been a pleasure,' I said, helping him out.

'You've been a fucking menace. Fuck off, bollocks,' Vic shouted for good measure.

I made my way quickly back into our vehicle before anything else could happen. Vic was already on his starting blocks, his foot full on the accelerator, then we were gone. As I looked back I saw that we weren't being followed. The police looked like they were checking out why this Asian-looking man had suddenly been dumped in front of them, disturbing their tea-break.

Vic parked up in the car park by the Serpentine. He would put a call into the rental people and tell them that his vehicle had broken down. The added 'ventilation' would be an extra we wouldn't charge for — but did we care? No, not really. I didn't want the bomb squad being called out for no reason at all. Mike was in place waiting. Vic and I walked casually over to the cab, keeping an eye out for any police in hot pursuit. We were both sweating like a couple of bastards by the time the cabbie pulled out of the car park and turned in the opposite direction of the threat.

'I could murder a beer, I'm friggin' *gagging*. That little stunt was outrageous,' Vic said.

'Been busy then, lads?' the cabbie interjected before any of us had the chance to reply. Unfortunately I had accidentally made mirror eye contact with him as I'd got in the cab.

'Yeah, you could say something like that,' I replied, wiping the sweat away from my forehead.

What the hell, I thought, the sun was shining, the birds were singing, and life wasn't that bad after all. I looked back in the mirror. I caught sight of his tinted gold-rimmed glasses. That was all I needed to do, to give him his cue. 'What do you guys do then ...?' he enquired.

'Well, you could say we're teachers,' I said. Both Vic and Mike stared at me a bit dumbfounded.

'My oldest lad's a teacher in Canada,' the cabbie said. 'Teachers in what?'

'We try and teach Principals, principles.'

EPILOGUE

On every job — this one being no exception — I try to keep up a level of professionalism and humour which hopefully spreads throughout the team. I certainly think I achieved that on this one. The men on this team were probably the best I've ever worked with. We came from a variety of different backgrounds, yet everyone, surprisingly, got on really well. There were no drama queens, no Batman-utility-belt merchants, and only a hint of backstabbing. And, of course, the odd Judas.

What happened to Suhail? Once the police knew who he was, they arrested him on several charges of fraud. He was subsequently released on bail pending a court appearance. He hasn't been seen since. But, through the grapevine, I heard that he disappeared owing thousands to another security company which he covertly employed when he was released. I *also* heard, though, that MI5 had infiltrated this security team — so your guess is as good as mine as to what happened next. The great shame is that his wife and daughter were probably still being dragged around like extra baggage.

Vaclav and his people have not been heard of again, either. If it was they who'd tried to take me and Vic out, or another group or agency, there was no mention of it in any of the following day's newspapers. Maybe there were witnesses, maybe nobody saw a thing — after all, the entire contact was no more than a minute long from shooting to scooting. Maybe it was covered up as a police training exercise, or maybe it was *totally* covered up in the interests of keeping surveillance on Vaclav, to lead those whose need it was to know to a bigger prize. Only the 30-year rule will probably uncover the reasons why.

The team? Well, after meeting up at the safe bar, we had a Chinese Parliament. It was unanimously decided that no contact with the Regents Plaza should be made for kit retrieval. We would just have to put that down to experience. After all, we were quids in.

Shortly after the job folded I managed to get a contract from a Kuwait contact who wanted a personal possession retrieved, which just happened to be close to the border of Iraq. This kept me out of trouble for a few months. I would have liked to have stayed with the team, but I had to take the next job on offer, and unfortunately it was only a one-man job.

Vic pulled a very well-paid UK BG contract from a rival security company, and he invited Ken, Mike and the rest of the guys to join him. Pete was the only one who obviously couldn't make it. He had to go back across the water.

And the Walther? I was still concerned that maybe Dinger had put, or was trying to put, a surveillance team on us. I opted to stay in London but well away from the office. That night I stayed at a mate's house south of the river. Very early the next morning and when it was still dark, I took a train to Charing Cross. It would be days before I stopped employing anti-surveillance techniques. Across the station I hopped on the underground, the Bakerloo Line, got off at Oxford Circus and headed east along Oxford Street. At Tottenham Court Road, I caught the Northern Line south to Embankment. During this I stopped only once, at a bank's cash dispenser on Oxford Street.

I got to the bottom of Villiers Street having completed my

decoy loop. I walked on to the pedestrian footpath which runs across Hungerford Bridge. I was sure I hadn't been followed, and as I got to roughly the middle, I stopped and picked my spot. I couldn't see or hear if there were any vessels below, the noise of the trains immediately behind me bringing in the first batch of commuters put paid to that — I'd have to be lucky with that one.

There were several people on the bridge, but because it's so long they were too far off to see what I might be up to. So, in view of the Royal Festival Hall, as I'd done days earlier with the Brownings, I sprinkled the River Thames with bits of an old German-made pistol taken off a dead Argy soldier. An apt resting-place for the well-travelled pistol. I wondered how many people it had killed.

Moonlighting was never something I really had time to do when I was serving, so I was surprised that a man in Pete Litman's position would want to get involved in doing a bit on the side — especially if you consider what unit he came from. One also has to question the viability of some of the moves that I saw by M15 operators, and why they would risk putting their careers on the line, too. It's not as if they were small players in the Firm, noncombatants. These were the guys who did the business.

Now, I'm no angel, and I've had my fair share of grief in my time. And, like them, I too have served in the Armed Services of this country, so I think I can speak with some authority. My point is that I was unaware that now, as a civilian, I could hire the services of M15 — albeit 'on the side'. It's quite amazing to think that these so-called secret Government agencies employ operatives with such disregard for their own position, and for the rules of the system that employs them. After all, given some of the equipment both M15 and its sister agency M16 can get their hands on, the question arises: What *other* Government cells are working on the sly? I think it goes well over the top of the Government's new policy of 'opening up' the Security Services.

In the short term, until the working practices of the security services are tightened up, I don't hold much hope for the rest of the population. Who needs to worry about that ever-increasing argument about the use of city-centre CCTVs and people's rights to privacy? The Big Brother syndrome is the least of our worries, if certain members of our security services can be bought for private hire. What next, a moonlighting squad of SAS to covertly infiltrate your corporate competitor's offices? I hope not. That'll do me and a lot of ex Special Forces personnel out of a job.